FOOD LOVERS'
GUIDE TO®
VIRGINIA

Help Us Keep This Guide Up to Date

We would love to hear from you concerning your experiences with this guide and how you feel it could be improved and kept up to date. Please send your comments and suggestions to:

editorial@GlobePequot.com

Thanks for your input, and happy travels!

FOOD LOVERS' SERIES

FOOD LOVERS'
GUIDE TO®
VIRGINIA

The Best Restaurants, Markets
& Local Culinary Offerings

1st Edition

Lorraine Eaton and Jim Haag

Guilford, Connecticut

Copyright © 2014 by Morris Book Publishing, LLC

Food Lovers' Guide to® is a registered trademark of Morris Book Publishing, LLC

Editor: Tracee Williams
Project editor: Lynn Zelem
Layout artist: Mary Ballachino
Text design: Sheryl Kober
Illustrations by Jill Butler with additional art by Carleen Moira Powell and MaryAnn Dubé
Maps: Alena Pearce © Morris Book Publishing, LLC

ISSN 2332-0834

ISBN 978-0-7627-8122-5

Printed in the United States of America
10 9 8 7 6 5 4 3 2 1

All the information in this guidebook is subject to change. We recommend that you call ahead to obtain current information before traveling.

Contents

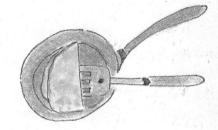

Appendices, 259

Index, 275

About the Authors

Lorraine Eaton is the food writer and blogger—aka staff epicure—for *The Virginian-Pilot,* the state's largest daily newspaper. She was raised in the South by New Yorkers in a home that never knew a grease-splattered stove. Her taste for Virginia food began down the street at her best friend's house, where shredded pork doused in vinegar and hot sauce was a staple—as luck would have it, her best friend's grand-daddy owned a barbecue company. A childhood filled with crab feasts, pig pickings, and oyster roasts provided the perfect foundation for her work today, exploring Virginia's rich foodways. Her award-winning work has appeared in the *Washington Post, Leite's Culinaria,* and is included in *Best Food Writing 2012,* an anthology of America's best stories and essays on the topic. Her cookbook, *Tidewater Table,* was published in 2013.

Jim Haag is a Midwest-born bacon lover who had the good sense to relocate to the pork country of Virginia. He's at home picking blue crabs with his fingers, delicately devouring the finest Southern fare and experimenting in the kitchen. He's an adventurous cook who had never tasted lemon chess pie until he vowed to win a ribbon with one at the State Fair of Virginia. With his eighth attempt, he brought home the blue. By day, he's the features editor at *The Virginian-Pilot,* where he finds himself fortunate to be Lorraine Eaton's editor. Together, they enjoy the culinary playground of the commonwealth, and he edited Eaton's *Tidewater Table* cookbook.

Acknowledgments

"The Virginia Gluttony Tour." That's what we jokingly—or maybe not—began to call the foraging that led to this book, months of sampling just about every cupcake, burger, cheese shop, barbecue stand, restaurant, and bar in our path. And it wouldn't have been possible without the skills and dedication of the chefs, watermen, farmers, pitmasters, producers, and others responsible for all the goodness we consumed. And it wouldn't have been as enjoyable without the sharp palates and patience of our partners—Lorraine's guy, Joe Trofe, who made many a reconnaissance mission to the central part of the state, and Jim's wife, Carol Lichti, who was always eager for another trip, another stop, another bite. Thanks, too, to our epicurean friends who steered us to the best eats across this vast state we call home. While canvassing the commonwealth, we know you'll find as much fun and flavor as we did!

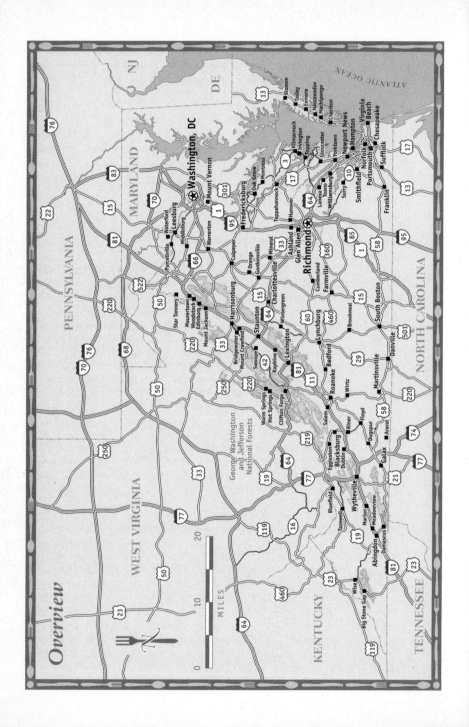

Overview

Introduction: Virginia— Pork, Peanuts, Presidents & A Gracious Plenty More

It happened twice.

The first time: at a gas station outside the state capital of Richmond. The roadster's fuel tank registered empty. Us, not so much. And with an ambitious itinerary of eating ahead, we had no intention of a pre-breakfast nibble. Yet, parked pump-side with the windows rolled up, we could smell goodness wafting from inside the station. Every exiting customer cradled a small box in both hands. An investigation was plainly in order.

Turns out, Wise Choice at the Citgo in rural Rockville serves up the state's finest fried pork chop sandwich and some of the finest fried chicken, too. So good, in fact, that we sucked the last bit of tender meat and crispy skin from a thigh before leaving the lot.

The second time, we had secured a slice of coconut cake to go from Cul's Courthouse Grille, a circa 1872 country store turned restaurant in Tidewater. While there, we witnessed banter between the owner and a couple from the West Coast, who begged (without success) for the restaurant's recipe. While driving away, we peeked into the box at the fluffy, white confection. At a stoplight, we ravaged the glove box for the emergency cutlery we keep on hand. One bite of the cake, and we collapsed into complete surrender.

Forgive our lapse in manners, but you'll have that in Virginia, home to America's first foodways and so many presidents (eight—Washington, Jefferson, Madison, Monroe, Harrison, Tyler, Taylor, and Wilson) that people say the soil and sea yield not only serious eats but also serious smarts.

It's a state that tempts epicures with five-star dining, roadside lean-on-the-side-of-the-trailer barbecue sandwiches, and everything in between.

When the first English settlers arrived here more than 400 years ago, they witnessed Native Americans slurping roasted oysters, a time-honored tradition in the Tidewater low country. Later, in the Colonial capital of Williamsburg, skilled slave cooks prepared elaborate suppers for the gentry, meals of ham and biscuits and seafood that historians replicate today in the restored historic district. Farther west, flatlands yield to the rolling hills of Central Virginia, a chessboard of peanut, corn, and winter wheat fields. Still farther west, toward the soaring Blue Ridge and Allegheny Mountains, beef and dairy cattle and even bison graze on rolling pastures, and cherry, apple, and peach orchards thrive.

Honestly, it's a wonder we're not all as fat as ticks.

We do, however, recommend a measure of restraint while traveling through the commonwealth. Here are our rules for the road:

- Resist taking a meal at a chain restaurant. We've been diligent in our search and have made sure that not more than a few miles pass between bites of inspired fare.
- Travel Virginia's official scenic byways whenever possible—they're stunning, calming stretches and home to many fine eating establishments. For a free map, contact the state Office of Public Affairs at (804) 786-2801 or VAmaps@VirginiaDOT.org.

- Eat your 'cue. You can't swing a stick in Virginia without hitting a barbecue joint, and the flavors change from east to west, just like residents' accents. We recommend several pork barbecues, but a trustworthy rule of thumb is that if you spot a smoker in the parking lot—either a cinderblock house with screened walls or a sort of smoking fuel tank with legs—that's the sign of a serious pitmaster.
- Do drink the sweet tea, calories be damned. We make it perfect.
- Set aside some space in your luggage or car. It would be a shame to return home without a country ham, award-winning Virginia wine (choose from more than 250 wineries), some cheeses and hard ciders, a sack of peanuts, some heirloom apples, artisan chocolates—well, you get the idea.
- Finally, come hungry. We have a gracious plenty ways to please. And stuff some cutlery into the glove box. Just in case.

How to Use This Book

With apologies to our state tourism department, we've can't resist saying this: Virginia Is for Food Lovers. In the east, the beaches offer surf and seafood. The Appalachians lure lovers of mountains and orchards to the west. In between are metro areas that teem with traffic tie-ups and tantalizing tastes, and quaint towns with old-time ways and mom-and-pop goodness. We've divided the state into nine regions to help you make your way through our geographic—and gastronomic—playground.

We begin on the commonwealth's ocean coast. The chapter on the Eastern Shore takes you to an isolated strip of land that is the southern tip of a peninsula that includes parts of Delaware and Maryland. Tidewater describes the portions of the mainland where the low country drains into the Chesapeake Bay and Atlantic Ocean. There, you'll find the commonwealth's three largest cities—Virginia Beach, Norfolk, and Chesapeake.

The Colonial capital of Williamsburg and the modern-day capital of Richmond each gets its own chapter, as does Charlottesville, the home of the University of Virginia. The Upper Piedmont covers an area bounded roughly by the mountains on the west, Maryland to the north, and Interstate 64, which runs through Richmond and Charlottesville to the south.

Central Virginia is that southern expanse between Tidewater and the mountains. The chapter covering the Mountains and Shenandoah Valley highlights the Appalachians and Alleghenies and the area in between. The final chapter visits the state's westernmost tip, the Southwest Blue Ridge Highlands.

The densely populated suburbs around the nation's capital, which those in the state refer to as "Northern Virginia," are covered in this series' *Food Lovers' Guide to® Washington, D.C.*

In this book, we've tried to strike a balance between well-known, must-visit places and off-the-beaten-path gems. The chapters divide our finds into these categories:

Foodie Faves

These eateries range from hole-in-the-wall joints to the state's best restaurants, places where the food is good and the backstory is often better. Welcome to the South, y'all.

Landmarks

These places have been around a while, and with good reason. For years, they've been putting out food we can't get enough of. Along the way, they've become part of our culinary culture.

Specialty Stores, Markets & Producers

Here you'll find our favorite indie food boutiques, seafood markets, and coffeehouses, as well as bakeries, ice cream shops, and kitchen stores.

Wineries, Breweries & Distilleries

A listing of the some of the best places to quench a thirst with wines and brews that have been created in our own backyard.

Farmers' Markets

A listing of our favorite places to buy locally grown fruits and veggies, as well as homemade jams, pies, and other goodies. These places are dependent on the season and the weather, so check before a visit to make sure they'll be open.

Pricing Code

Our favorite Virginia eateries range from fried chicken-liver dinners at a gas station to upscale restaurants with a sommelier on staff, so prices vary widely. We used the following system based on the average price of a single entree, but keep in mind that's it's only an estimate. Beverages, appetizers, and desserts are not included.

$	Less than $10
$$	$10 to $20
$$$	$20 to $25
$$$$	$25 and up

Culinary Connections in the Commonwealth

C-ville Weekly, c-ville.com. This alternative publication keeps readers abreast of the foodie world in the college town of Charlottesville.

Distinction, distinction.com. This upscale quarterly magazine in the Tidewater area covers all things gracious and good, including restaurant hot spots and buzzed-about chefs.

Eating Richmond, eatingrichmond.com. This website aggregates the best food blogs from the Richmond area, offering restaurant reviews, recipes, and more.

From Ballparks to BBQ, fromballparks tobbq.com. This blog, by David Aldridge, details his favorite things about the food world in his hometown of Roanoke—and beyond.

Mas to Millers, mastomillers.com. A married couple in Charlottesville, known only as Erin and Jed, started this blog to expound on culinary offerings in their hometown and have expanded to include views from other food lovers.

Richmond Magazine, richmondmagazine.com. This periodical follows food in the state capital and hands out annual culinary awards.

Richmond Times Dispatch, timesdispatch.com. Food news and restaurant reviews are found in the pages and website of this daily newspaper.

Style Weekly, styleweekly.com. This alternative weekly in Richmond watches the pulse and palate of the culinary scene in the state capital and surrounding suburbs. Its annual State of the Plate awards honor the best places to get a bite.

The Virginian-Pilot, **pilotonline.com, hamptonroads.com.** The weekly Flavor and Gracious Living sections of the state's largest newspaper cover the food and drink scene—from restaurant reviews to the local farmers' markets—in Chesapeake, Norfolk, Portsmouth, Suffolk, Virginia Beach, and the surrounding area. (*Full disclosure:* The coauthors of this book work there—Lorraine is the staff epicure and Jim is her editor.)

Virginia Living, **virginialiving.com.** This monthly magazine keeps readers informed on state food trends and hot spots they shouldn't miss.

Virginia Wine Lover, **virginiawinelovermag.com.** This semi-annual lifestyle magazine features information about Virginia wines, wineries, and travel.

Washington Post, **washingtonpost.com.** This daily newspaper in the nation's capital offers reviews restaurants of Northern Virginia hangouts and details food goings-on in parts of the commonwealth.

Food & Drink Events

February

Taste of Hampton Roads, on Facebook. Fifty bucks might seem like a steep admission for a food fest, but most every Hampton Roads restaurant of note brings its A-game to compete—and offer up generous samples—for this annual Foodbank fundraiser.

Virginia Wine Expo, virginiawineexpo.com. Virginia is studded with wineries and more than 70 participate in this Richmond event, paired with fine food purveyors.

March

Chocolate Lovers Festival, chocolatefestival.net. Two days of chocolate bliss set in charming Old Town Fairfax, adjacent to the nation's capital. Cakes, candies, brownies, fudge, ice cream, and more!

Highland Maple Festival, highlandcounty.org/ maplefestival.html. Come to Virginia's "Little Switzerland" high in the Allegheny Mountains for the "opening of the trees" and see how real maple syrup is made. Arts and crafts, tours, and entertainment, too.

April

Gnarly Hops & Barley Fest, gnarlyhops.com. Set in Culpeper, a central Virginia town that's a food lover's find, this newbie festival attracts craft beer and microbrewers from across the state, and a few from beyond.

Rockin Brews & BBQs, on Facebook. Smith Mountain Lake is a southwest Virginia playground, and this festival kicks off the spring season with brews and 'cues from near and far, paired with some mighty fine tunes.

Ruritan Club Shad Planking, shadplanking.com. Even if you don't care a whit about Virginia politics, don't miss this tradition that began in 1929 and continues to take place the third Wednesday in April, when the shad are running in the James River, the politicians come to stump, and the Ruritans cook whole shad on cedar planks, a dying culinary art if there ever was one.

She-Crab Soup Classic, beachstreetusa.com/festivals/east-coast-she-crab-soup-classic. Coastal restaurants are fiercely proud of their recipes, and the competition at this soup-only festival on the Virginia Beach oceanfront is palpable. Sample soups from scores of restaurants and vote for your favorite.

Shenandoah Apple Blossom Festival & Wine Fest, the bloom.com. A family-friendly smorgasbord of events—from parades to band competitions to dinners—celebrating the flowering of the orchards in Winchester, the heart of Virginia's apple-growing country.

May

White Top Mountain Ramp Festival, graysoncountyva .com/festivals. Travel up winding mountain roads to the highest peak in Virginia to celebrate the spring harvest of ramps, those coveted garlicky-oniony plants. A family-friendly, volunteer fire department fund-raiser complete with bluegrass music, barbecue chicken dinner, and ramp eating contest.

Gordonsville Famous Fried Chicken Festival, townof gordonsville .org/index.aspx?NID=309. Years ago, when trains blew through this central Virginia town, African-Americans met them carrying platters of fried chicken on their heads and served it through the windows, earning Gordonsville the title of "chicken leg center of the universe." That makes it the perfect spot for a fried chicken competition. Pies, too.

Shenandoah Valley Beer & Wine Festival, valleyfestbeer andwine.com. Massanutten, a ski resort in the winter months, kicks off the summer with this festival featuring regional wines, craft beers and micro-brews, music, and more.

Wine Festival at Monticello, monticello.org/site/visit/events/wine-festival-monticello. Thomas Jefferson was passionate about wine and his restored Charlottesville home and vineyard are the site of this Virginia wine festival, complete with tours of the house, vineyard, and cellar. This event sells out, so plan early.

June

Virginia Pork Festival, vaporkfestival.com. Pork burgers? Check. Barbecued loin chops? Check. Chitterlings? Check. BBQ? Duh. Everything pork comes hot off the grills at this enormous barbecue and party in Emporia in the heart of Virginia pork country.

July

Hanover Tomato Festival, co.hanover.va.us/parksrec/tomatofest. Hanover tomatoes are famous in these parts and this Mechanicsville festival honors the fruit with a day filled with tomato sandwiches, tomato pie, fried green tomatoes, tomato salsa and contests for the prettiest and ugliest 'mater. Plenty for sale, too.

Virginia State Peach Festival, patrickchamber.com/peach festival.cfm. Here in Patrick County, the "peach tree bottom" of Virginia at the foot of the Blue Ridge Mountains, peach season is celebrated with all manner of peach-centric foods—think butters, pies, shaved ice—plus music and swimming in the county's public pool.

September

Apple Gala & Cider Festival, greatcountryfarms.com. The fall apple harvest is celebrated on this farm in Loudon County with a weekend of apple picking, cider pressing, hard ciders, regular ciders, cider-making demos on the family's antique press, wagon rides, a corn maze and more.

October

Suffolk Peanut Fest, suffolkfest.org. Local businesses in this town, home of Mr. Peanut, shut down each fall so that everyone can flock to the peanut fest, where the humble legume is feted with tractor pulls, amusement park rides, fireworks, the famous Peanut Butter Sculpture Contest, and where the peanut queen once wore a gown of goobers. Yes, really.

Taste of Brunswick Festival, tasteofbrunswickfestival.com. Stewmasters. Brunswick County has 'em by the dozen, proud, pedigreed people who have honed their top-secret Brunswick stew recipes for decades and sometimes generations. Taste the best of the best at this Alberta gala.

Urbanna Oyster Festival, urbannaoysterfestival.com. Travel to Virginia's Northern Neck to eat plump oysters cooked every which way—or just slurp 'em raw—while watching the main attraction: the state oyster shucking championship, a contest that has yielded many a national champ.

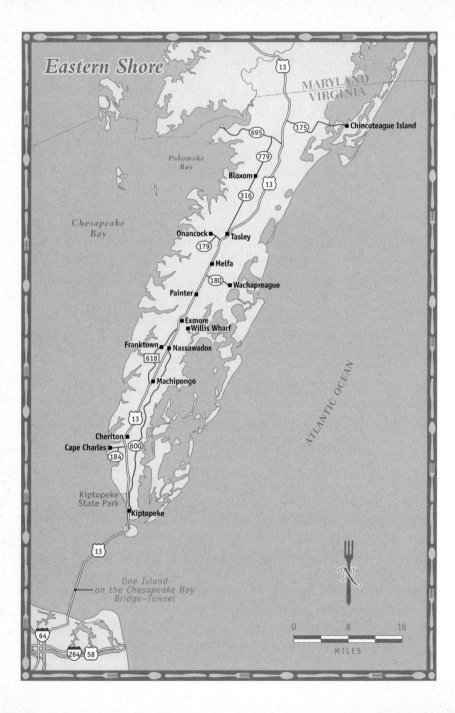

Eastern Shore

Whether coming to Virginia's Eastern Shore by land or by sea, it's best you come hungry. An empty cooler wouldn't be a bad idea either. US Route 13, the four-lane byway that forms the spine of the 70-mile-long peninsula, is dotted with markets offering native oysters, country-cured hams, fried chicken, and fresh produce—think tomatoes, collard greens, and legendary Hayman white sweet potatoes. Back when sweet spuds were king of the shore's crops, baseball great Joe DiMaggio crowned the sweet potato queen. The vibe here is relaxed; the region has remained largely rural since first being explored by English settlers in 1607. Hundreds of miles of Chesapeake Bay and Atlantic Ocean shoreline remain undeveloped, and most of the barrier islands are under the protection of the Nature Conservancy. Watermen harvest an astonishing variety of seafood from these waters—clams, conch, blue crabs, black drum, red drum, flounder, oysters, spot, ray, and more. Some restaurants along the way cook it up old-school style—such as the meaty fried drum ribs served at the Exmore Diner each spring. Others, such as Mallard's on the Wharf in Onancock, fry fat local oysters and serve them with a side of wasabi aioli. As we said, it's best you come hungry.

Big's Place, 35044 Lankford Hwy., Painter, VA 23420; (757) 442-5535; on Facebook; Seafood/Traditional Southern; $$. About halfway up the shore on the west side of the highway, Big's Place definitely does not beckon. It's a pale yellow building with peeling paint, a peaked roof and a low-slung front porch. But like cherry cordials and kin, it's what's on the inside that matters. Big's—a restaurant run by Eastern Shore natives—is cozy like grandma's house, with lots of round tables, comfortable captain's chairs, and authentic nautical decor. If there's a line, take a seat on the church pew just inside the front door and contemplate offerings on the specials board. Much of the ever-changing menu is Eastern Shore authentic, and many dishes are made using Grandma Gaskill's recipes. In the winter, savor Fisherman's Stew, made with local clams, fish, oysters, scallops, and shrimp in a tomato broth. Spring brings swelling toads, considered a delicacy in these parts. Here, the firm, mild-flavored fish—not actual toads—are served fried, stuffed with crab, or sometimes in toad scampi. This Southern-friendly spot even offers up homemade pecan pie.

Cape Charles Coffee House, 241 Mason Ave., Cape Charles, VA 23310; (757) 331-1880; capecharlescoffeehouse.com; Coffeehouse/Salads/Sandwiches; $. Cape Charles, a tidy little town near the southern tip of the shore, dates back to 1884. The waterfront "downtown" still has a quintessential small-town feel with wide sidewalks fronting the brick storefronts of the business district. Cape Charles Coffee House, circa 1910, was originally a bank. The tin ceilings, gleaming wood floor and Tiffany chandeliers contrast with a thoroughly modern menu of lattes and mochas, bagels, lox and cream cheese sandwiches, and a house favorite, chicken salad studded with walnuts and cranberries. There also are wines from nearby Chatham Vineyards. On a sunny day, request that the staff pack a picnic lunch—a service gladly provided. The town's charming, hardly-ever-crowded Chesapeake Bay beach is a short stroll away. Sunsets there are stunning.

Chesapeake Grill, One Island on the Chesapeake Bay Bridge-Tunnel, Virginia Beach, VA 23451; (757) 318-4818; virginia-originals .com; Sandwiches/Steaks; $–$$. This classy-but-casual restaurant has the most unusual location of any restaurant in Virginia—the southernmost, manmade island along the 17.6-mile Chesapeake Bay Bridge-Tunnel. The view is spectacular, especially since new owners opened up the interior with more windows in 2010. Diners can watch cargo ships, Navy vessels, and sailboats maneuver the waters where the Atlantic Ocean meets the Chesapeake Bay or spy on local anglers who camp out on the busy fishing pier to make their own fresh catches of the day. Inside, you can have breakfast, lunch, or dinner. The menu is split between grab-and-go fare such as burgers and sandwiches and sit-down dishes such as jumbo lump crab cakes. Before you go, check out the Virginia Originals gift shop, which features artwork and wine.

The Great Machipongo Clam Shack, 6468 Lankford Hwy., Nassawadox, VA 23413; (757) 442-3800; thegreatmachipongoclam shack.com; Seafood; $$. Hope you followed that advice about bringing a cooler and an appetite. Here, you'll want both. In the brightly colored dining room with fish on the walls, the friendly waitstaff can hook you up with classic fried and broiled seafood platters named for local sea captains. The dishes are served, if you please, with sweet potato fries sprinkled with cinnamon sugar, an Eastern Shore favorite. The restaurant's Bayside Seafood Cake—a riff on a traditional crab cake that adds fish, shrimp, and scallops to the mix, is a best bet on a bun. Then walk over to the retail section, where big boat coolers are stocked with fresh, local seafood, such as backfin crab, glass pints of oysters, and such. Local wines, too.

How to Appreciate an Oyster

The latest phase in the oyster craze is the "merroir-terroir tasting," events where wines are expertly paired with oysters and discussions run deep about terroir, the characteristics of the place where the grapes were grown, and "merroir," the same for the sea. Surprisingly, the tasting methods are similar. To savor an oyster on the half shell, start by deeply taking in the aroma. Then tip the shell to sample the "liquor" surrounding the meat; the salinity of the juice is the most apparent flavor. Oysters harvested from the Atlantic side of the Eastern Shore are much saltier than oysters grown on the Chesapeake Bay side. The farther up north on the bay you go, the "sweeter"—or less briny—the sea. Next, take the oyster into your mouth and work it around a bit. Go ahead, chew with your mouth open, breathing in fully to experience the complex flavors. Slurping is fine. Pay attention to the adductor, the dime-sized shaft of muscle that attaches the oyster's top shell to the bottom. It has a somewhat stringy texture and a hint of sweet. Finally, turn the shell upside down and inhale. If there's some mud on the shell, chill out. It's part of the experience—the merroir, if you will. Those who savor oysters, ostreaphiles, are like oenophiles, or wine aficionados. They use words like woody, forest floor, geranium, copper, bronze, and grass to describe the flavor. Sink into a dozen raw ones, and you will, too.

Island House Restaurant, 17 Atlantic Ave., Wachapreague, VA 23480; (757) 787-4242; theislandhouserestaurant.com; Seafood; $$. There's something magical about dining seaside—sunlight sparkling off the water, gulls arcing across the sky, the tinkle of waves on the shore. Life slows down; perspectives change. The Island House Restaurant is a couple of miles east of the main road, but it's a delicious detour to a special spot. It's modeled after the long-gone Parramore Island Life Saving Station and perched at the edge of Wachapreague Harbor. Try the Oysters Parramore, freshly shucked in a salty brine and topped with crab. Then, tweak your perspective even more by climbing the spiral staircase that leads to the lookout tower and a panoramic view of one of the country's last, vast undeveloped coastlines.

Little Italy Ristorante, 10227 Rogers Dr., Nassawadox, VA 23413; (757) 442-7831; francolittleitaly.com; Southern Italian; $$. Fed up with finfish and bivalves? Pull up to the white brick building at the Nassawaddox stoplight for an Italian-style antidote—a plate of veal-stuffed cannelloni or garlicky broccoli rabe with sausage, perhaps? Proprietors Franco and Cathy Nocera recently celebrated their restaurant's 20th anniversary. Portions here are huge, and this is the place on the Eastern Shore for pizza. There's plenty of pasta and pizza to please the gluten-free crowd, too.

Machipongo Trading Company, 13037 Lankford Hwy., Machipongo, VA 23405; (757) 678-0005; esvamtc.com; Casual American/Coffeehouse/Sandwiches; $. Talk about repurposing. This micro breakfast and lunch spot was once a Texaco gas station. Now, it's the place to feed your conscience as well as your appetite. A simple menu of sandwiches and burritos at breakfast or wraps and paninis at lunch is rounded out by freshly made smoothies and locally roasted coffees and lattes. Most ingredients, as well as ready-made provisions, are from local sources. Grab a sack of Pungo Creek Mills Heirloom Cornmeal, grown and ground right up the road. Or some locally made treats for your canine sidekick. Or a piece of artwork or jewelry for your crib. The pace is unrushed, and free Wi-Fi makes the little dining area a great spot to fire up the laptop and post your latest Eastern Shore adventure to Facebook.

Saigon Village Restaurant, 4069 Main St., Chincoteague Island, VA 23336; (757) 336-7299; on Facebook; Vietnamese; $. There's a happy aromatic marriage of mild curry and tart lemongrass that greets you in this tiny eatery. The menu is traditional Vietnamese, with stir-fried, noodle, and soup dishes, though *pho* is surprisingly absent. But the soups are worth a visit and offer a nice departure from the standard seafood fare found elsewhere on the island. Two stand out: The cellophane noodles come with chicken and shrimp and a gingery wallop offset nicely by fresh cilantro, and the white asparagus and crabmeat is an egg-drop variety that offers a twist on the crab flavors you get used to around the bay. The shrimp rolls, wrapped in fresh rice paper, are a refreshingly light way to start a meal. Though much of the restaurant's business is takeout, the dining room offers nine tables. If the weather's fair, take your food outside to the nearby seaside picnic tables and enjoy local life on the water.

Sea Star Cafe, 6429 Maddox Blvd., Chincoteague Island, VA 23336; (757) 336-5442; on Facebook; Sandwiches; $. This bright turquoise take-out sandwich shop is a great place to grab a bite before heading to nearby Assateague Island, where the wild ponies made famous in the books of Marguerite Henry roam. The shop shares its name with one of Henry's books—Sea Star was a pony known as the "Orphan of Chincoteague." Sandwiches come on fresh bread and croissants or in pitas and wraps, and the menu offers seven vegetarian and vegan options. The Key West, where avocado and Muenster cheese mingle on wheat bread, is a veggie favorite, and meat lovers flock to The Virginian, with beef, turkey, and ham sharing space on sourdough. You also can create your own combination. Customers order from a window on the side of the shop, and no indoor seating is available. Don't come when you're in a rush; the food is made to order and can take some time, though a few outdoor picnic tables and benches give you a place to linger.

Sunset Grille, 32246 Lankford Hwy., Kiptopeke, VA 23310; (757) 331-4229; on Facebook; Casual American; $$. No need to ask, "Where's the party?" On spring and summer weekends, the best party in these parts is right on the beach at Kiptopeke, just behind the sombrero-shaped Sunset Beach Resort Hotel. Locals float in by boat, drop anchor, and wade ashore for burgers, oyster po' boys, and wings. It's the best way to arrive, but strolling in from the hotel works just as well. The natives are friendly and talkative. The music is often live, and the beer always ice cold. Dine in the sand, under a market umbrella at a picnic table on one of the decks or inside the restaurant. And don't hurry off. They don't call this place the Sunset Grille for nothing. Be sure to stay for the show.

Tammy & Johnny's, 27352 Lankford Hwy., Melfa, VA 23410; (757) 787-1122; Casual American; $. You could go for the sweet potato sticks, a cup of clams, batter-dipped and fried string beans, barbecue, or a burger. But what you really should get at Tammy & Johnny's is fried chicken. It's lightly seasoned, with a craggy, crunchy, crispy crust, served hot as the dickens. Bite in, and it fairly falls off the bone. Get a snack and a biscuit, light with buttery tops. The flavor will make it easy to ignore the bare-bones dining room with its fast food–like palette of orange and brown and oldies rock music. And do take note that the bird is just as good cold the next day, so you might want to tuck some into that cooler of yours.

Landmarks

AJ's on the Creek, 6585 Maddox Blvd., Chincoteague Island, VA 23336; (757) 336-5888; ajsonthecreek.com; Seafood/Steaks; $$–$$$. A staple on Chincoteague Island since 1985, AJ's offers seafood, charbroiled steaks, and pasta dishes for dinner and seafood and

sandwiches for lunch. In the evening, the setting on Eel Creek is romantic, with candles providing ambient illumination in the low-lit dining
room. The seafood bouillabaisse—with its mix of clams, crabmeat,
mussels, oysters, scallops, and shrimp—is a house specialty, Use the
crusty yet soft French bread to sop up the rich, garlicky broth. The oysters in Champagne sauce showcase local bivalves in a graphically plated
dish that shows off the scallion-and-bacon toppings. For Caesar salad
lovers, you get the often overlooked option of anchovies. On weekends,
the bar offers entertainment, and it's not unusual to hear strains of Jim
Croce or Joni Mitchell tunes coming from the lounge.

Bill's Prime Seafood & Steaks, 4040 Main St., Chincoteague
Island, VA 23336; (757) 336-5831; billsseafoodrestaurant.com; Sea-
food/Steaks; $$–$$$. The black-vested and bow-tied waitstaff, along
with the Dale Chihuly–inspired orange-and-clear-glass chandelier, gives
the dining room an air of sophistication, but Bill's is a friendly place
where locals and tourists have been gathering for breakfast, lunch, and
dinner since 1960. You'll want to use your fingers to
devour the mini loaf of honey bread topped with
honey butter. The menu is simple but tasty, and
you can't go wrong with the Chincoteague oysters
and ham, which combines two salty Virginia favorites. As a side, try the Granny Smith apple coleslaw
for the perfect counterpoint. If you're adventurous,
begin the experience with an oyster shooter, which layers a bivalve, cocktail sauce, and vodka in a drink that's meant to be
downed in one shot.

Exmore Diner, 4264 Main St., Exmore, VA 23350; (757) 442-
2313; exmorediner.com; Casual American/Seafood; $. It's a diner,
a real one, opened in 1954 and dishing blue-plate specials ever since.
There's a row of booths along the front and a row of barstools at the
worn, white Formica counter. A constant stream of locals file in and

A Pearl of an Oyster

It used to be that Virginia oysters went pretty much by two basic monikers based on size, standard and selects, and were sold in jars or burlap sacks. Today, branding is fast becoming business as usual for the burgeoning ranks of Virginia oystermen. Following a period of devastating disease, the state's oysters have made a comeback. Recent harvests are the biggest in decades. Barcats, Cherrystone, Choptank Sweets, Nassawaddox Salts, Pleasure House, Shooting Points, and Yorksters—the commonwealth has all those and scores more. It's commonplace in coastal Virginia for ostreaphiles—or oyster lovers—to request oysters by name. Chalkboard menus at raw bars run several bivalves deep. Chefs develop favorites, and nothing else will do. **The H.M. Terry Co.** of Willis Wharf has been marketing the Sewansecott brand of bivalves for more than a century. Hog Island Bay, where the family's oysters and clams are cultivated to market size, is so pristine that it has been designated as a UN Biosphere Reserve. Sewansecotts have a deep cup that's perfect for slurping on the half shell. The shape is the result of several passes through a tumbler, where the oyster's "bill," or sharp outer edge, is chipped off. Inside is a mound of plump, firm meat in a shallow pool of clear, briny juice known as "liquor." Tip one back and slurp it up, and a bright brininess gives way to a rich oyster flavor tinged with sweet. Mountains of Sewansecotts are shipped to large markets, and the variety has been featured as the "Oyster of the Month" at New York City's venerable Grand Central Oyster Bar, where patrons happily pay a few bucks apiece for them. Now here's a tip: Drive over to Willis Wharf, park in the crushed-oyster-shell parking lot and ask for a box of bivalves at the front counter of the big, gray shucking house. For a fraction of the big-city price, you'll get enough for a feast or a roast. Clams, too. And one heck of a view.

out for breakfast, lunch, and dinner. If it's spring and the epicurean gods are smiling upon you, the special board will list "drum ribs," meaty swords from the mighty fish, breaded, fried and flaking right off the bone. Don't think of getting anything else. Other times of the year, savor what might be the last honest $5 crab-cake sandwich on the planet or some biscuits and gravy for breakfast. Wash it all down with a giant tumbler of Southern-style sweet, sweet tea.

Mallard's on the Wharf, 2 Market St., Onancock, VA 23417; (757) 787-855; mallardsllc.com; Neo-Southern/Seafood; $$$. He sings, he cooks, he writes books. That's Chef Johnny Mo, "The Musical Chef," who also sends elegant platters of duck, tuna, and porterhouse pork chops out of his creekside kitchen and then often emerges in chef's whites to serenade guests with his acoustic guitar. The food at this former general store, circa 1842, is far more refined than many an Eastern Shore eatery. Fried chicken livers, a gas station staple in the South, peek from underneath a roasted wild mushroom demi-glace and are perched on a pillow of mashed potatoes and wilted spinach. Tuna gets a yuzu glaze; filet mignon, a lobster cream sauce. Fresh mahimahi fish tacos, served at lunch with lime and spicy mayo, leave locals and food critics drooling.

Sting-Ray's Restaurant, 26507 Lankford Hwy., Cape Charles, VA 23310; (757) 331-1541; cape-center.com; Seafood/Traditional Southern; $. A couple of years back, author Michael Stern of *Roadfood* fame met us at the ordering counter of Chez Exxon, what locals call this way laid-back, award-winning restaurant inside a gas station. Until then, the region had been absent from his best-selling food guides. Then, Mr. Stern bit into a freshly baked sweet potato biscuit with thin, hot slices of salty Virginia ham hanging out the sides. He found the combination "inspired," and he savored lots of other dishes that day—crispy fried seaside oysters, crab imperial, stuffed flounder, and marinated shrimp he labeled "snapping good!" A slice of sweet potato pie topped with damson preserves provided the tipping point and put Virginia's Eastern Shore on the "Roadfood" map. We suggest stopping, even if you don't need gas. And if you have room for them in the cooler, get a couple dozen sweet potato biscuits and some sliced country ham to go. You'll be reaching into that stash for a snack shortly thereafter.

Specialty Stores, Markets & Producers

A & J's Fresh Meat Market, 21067 N. Bayside Rd., Cheriton, VA 23316; (757) 331-2822; on Facebook. Fresh sage sausage—just all-natural pork, sage, salt, and pepper stuffed into casings—is what A & J's owner and butcher James Elliott is best known for. But need a frenched rack of lamb? Or milk-fed veal, organic chicken, custom cuts of Naturewell beef or some freshly ground beef for burgers on the grill? He's your man. When you're nearing Cheriton, look for the red-and-black Jackson Hewitt Tax Service sign on the east side of US Route 13; otherwise, you might miss this humble market.

Becca's Cakes and More, 24399 Lankford Hwy., Tasley, VA 23441; (757) 789-3686; beccascakesandmore.com. We don't recommend this, but if you find yourself in a car with a piece of Becca's eight-layer Smith Island cake and no fork, by all means dig in with your fingers. The confections are that good. The cakes originated on Smith Island in Maryland, one of two inhabited landmasses in the Chesapeake Bay. Owner and cook Rebecca Eskridge Crutchley is from the other one, Tangier Island in Virginia, and grew up eating and making the cakes. She bakes each wafer-thin layer separately and offers her cakes in more than a dozen flavors, including Oreo and red velvet. Her shop, in a yellow house set back a bit from the road, has lunch items and a handful of tables where you can can gobble them down. The store is hidden from the road; just keep your eyes peeled for SMITH ISLAND CAKES, which overpower the word BECCA's on the small highway sign.

Blue Crab Bay Company, 29368 Atlantic Dr., Melfa, VA, 23410; (757) 787-3602; bluecrabbay.com. Just off the main road in Melfa, there's a cache of gourmet snacks that will have you reaching for your wallet when you walk through the door. The company, started in Pamela Barefoot's farmhouse kitchen, has amassed a constellation of awards for business acumen. But it's the addictive nut snacks, seafood soups, and clam-tinged Bloody Mary mixes that have caused Miss Pamela to ship her wares the world over. Her Sandbaggers—giant Virginia peanuts, a treat all by themselves!—are seasoned with sea salt and cracked pepper. They were honored in 2011 as a finalist in the nation's most prestigious specialty-food competition. Our favorite is Crab House Crunch, sweet peanut-brittle squares dusted with a crab-boil seasoning that combines many quintessential Virginia lowcountry flavors in a can.

Drizzles, 16 Strawberry St., Cape Charles, VA 23310; (321) 747-3042; drizzlesolives.com. Tasting shops that allow customers to sample exotic olive oils and balsamic vinegars from gleaming urns are popping up everywhere. Drizzles, in Cape Charles proper, does just that. The shop also offers a rainbow of peppercorns, salts, wild blueberry and sweet onion sugars, coffees imported from Honduras and Ethiopia, zany zebra-striped bowtie pasta, and more. It makes for great inspiration when you're cooking back on your home turf.

Gull Hummock Gourmet Market, 115 Mason Ave., Cape Charles, VA 23310; (757) 331-1500; on Facebook. The market recently moved into a bigger spot but still carries a solid selection of organic and Virginia products, including wines, cheeses, baked goods, and meats. Mingle with locals on Friday and Saturday afternoon, when owner Honey Moore uncorks select wines for afternoon tastings. At the checkout, take note of the counter made by a local artisan from wood that was cut from a tree up the road in Pungoteague.

Island Creamery, 6243 Maddox Blvd., Chincoteague, VA 23336; (757) 336-6236; islandcreamery.net. When summer's in full swing and tourists run amuck, you can easily find this ice cream shop by looking for the line that forms at the counter, continues out the front door, across the parking lot and down the street. Otherwise, look for the multistory faux lighthouse that dominates the shop's architecture. Thirty-four ever-changing flavors of ice cream, sorbet, and frozen yogurt tempt you at any time, and the cheerful staff is quick with samples. The house specialty is Marsh Mud, a double chocolate decadence that tastes like chilled brownie batter. Pair it with Iced Nirvana, powered by an in-house brew of espresso. Near the register, grab a bag of waffle-cone pieces for the perfect touch of crunchiness. Specialty and regular coffees and ice cream cakes are available, as is fudge that can be as traditional as cappuccino and as adventurous as lemon meringue cheesecake. Inside seating is available, but if the weather cooperates, head to the deck out front, where you can watch the parade of tourists on the town's busiest street.

Mr. Whippy, 6201 Maddox Blvd., Chincoteague, VA 23336; (757) 336-5122; misterwhippy.com. The enticing aroma of freshly made waffle cones hits you in the face, then gently embraces you as you enter this soft-serve ice cream parlor on the town's main drag. The menu beckons with more than 15 sundae options, 20-plus shakes, and a few sorbets. You'll be tempted to try a Cyclone, Mr. Whippy's own blend of ice cream and candies such as M&Ms and Snicker's candy bars. You won't be disappointed, but don't leave without becoming one with a waffle cone. You can opt for chocolate or vanilla ice cream, but the twist, which blends both, is perfect for indecisive types. The soft-serve is creamy and rich; the cone toasty and sweet. It's hard to wrap your head around this much gluttony, and it's hard to wrap your hand around the monster-sized cones. Enjoy the treats at one of the indoor tables or venture onto the deck for an alfresco adventure. A drive-through window makes it possible to stay in your car, though don't blame us if you can't enjoy the sweet scents.

Pickett's Harbor Farm, 3111 Pickett's Harbor Dr., Cape Charles, VA 23310; (757) 331-1610; pickettsharborfarms .com. A ways off the main road, on a lane with no stripe, is Pickett's Harbor Farm, where W.T. Nottingham and his family grow and sell a fine assortment of in-season produce inside their mercifully air-conditioned market. In the summer, you'll find peaches right from the tree, vine-ripe tomatoes, eggplant, melons, and paper sacks of green beans that are crisp, sweet and just perfect for snacking. Look beyond the crushed-oyster-shell driveway, and you might catch a glimpse of the farmer himself traipsing across the horizon on his tractor.

Quail Cove Farms, 12435 Machipongo Ln., Machipongo, VA 23405; (757) 678-7783; quailcovefarms.com. Here's a surprising shop on the US Route 13 straightaway. Bill Jardine grows organic sweet potatoes, a crop with a long Eastern Shore history. His sweet potatoes are usually stacked right inside the door of his family's retail market, which also stocks all-natural meats, organic bulk foods such as dried lentils and buckwheat groats, gluten-free baking mixes, Amish cheeses, and butter. We can't leave without grabbing a bag of Route 11 Sweet Potato Chips, made in Virginia from Jardine's organic spuds. And remember this advice when you're rooting through the sweet potato pile: The ones dripping sap from the ends will be sweetest of all.

What History Tastes Like

It's fortunate for us foodies that Bill Savage loves history and that his wife's a good cook. Otherwise, a flavorful link to this country's earliest cuisine might have been lost. See, Bill is a Civil War re-enactor. He's traced his family back to 1607, when the first permanent English settlement started at Jamestown. That lineage goes back to Ensign Thomas Savage, who settled on the Eastern Shore, cultivated corn, and shipped it back to the mainland colonists. At the turn of the century, Bill's great-granddaddy operated a gristmill in the small town of Painter, near the family farm. So in 2007, Bill couldn't resist buying a sack of corn from an Eastern Shore neighbor, who said that his grandfather had grown the variety Bloody Butcher back in 1870. Bill planted a crop. The seeds yielded tall stalks and cobs with oddly colored kernels—burgundy, blood red, purple that bordered on black, and calico with touches of butter, brick, and slate. At first, Bill thought he'd sell the cobs as decor, but competitors' cobs were cheaper. So he ground them up for chicken feed but, noting the sweet smell and unusual appearance, he gave some of the ground meal to his mother and his wife, Laurel. The women turned out pans of moist, sweet, faintly toothy cornbread, and a business venture was born. Today, the Savages plant acres of the heirloom corn each year, grind it on vintage equipment, and bag and number it by hand. It's sold in 2-pound paper sacks under the **Pungo Creek Mills** brand at small shops and some larger chains such as Whole Foods. Bill thinks of the cornmeal as a "taste in time," a direct link to the flavors of the past.

Wine, Cheese & More, 4103 Main St., Chincoteague, VA 23336; (757) 336-2610; **winecheesemore.com.** Virginia varietals from wineries such as Chatham and Holly Grove vineyards share shelf space with those from around the world in this shop nestled in Chincoteague's historic downtown. A small selection of local microbrews are chilled near the back of the store. In between is a case of cheese, and consider yourself lucky if the Dorothea Potato Chip Goat variety is in stock; it often sells out as quickly as it comes in. The aisles are filled with pastas, gadgets, foodie gifts, and even pure Mexican vanilla, as well as a line of jams and jellies that carry the Chincoteague Island label. That brand's FROG Jam sounds off-putting, but its name is an acronym for its sweet and tangy flavors: figs, raspberries, oranges, and ginger.

 *Wineries*

The Eastern Shore is a designated American Viticultural Area. Three wineries produce varietals, including Chardonnay, Merlot, Cabernet Franc, Cabernet Sauvignon, and Petit Verdot.

Bloxom Winery, Mason Road (Va. Route 681), Bloxom, VA 23308; (757) 665-5670; **bloxomwinery.com.**

Chatham Vineyards, 9232 Chatham Rd., Machipongo, VA 23405; (757) 678-5588; **chathamvineyards.net.**

Holly Grove Vineyards, 6404 Holly Bluff Dr., Franktown, VA 23354; (757) 442-2844; **hollygrovevineyards.com.**

Farmers' Markets

Cape Charles Farmers Market, 110 Blue Heaven Rd., Cape Charles, VA 23310. Sat 1 to 5 p.m., spring through fall.

Cheriton Farmers Market, Main Street, Cheriton, VA 23316. Sat 9 a.m. to 1 p.m., summer.

Chincoteague Island Farmers Market, 4113 Main St., Chincoteague, VA 23336. Wed and Sat from 8 a.m. to noon, Apr through Sept.

The Onancock Market, corner of Market and Ames Streets, Onancock, VA 23417; onancockmarket.com. Sat 8 a.m. to noon, May through Oct.

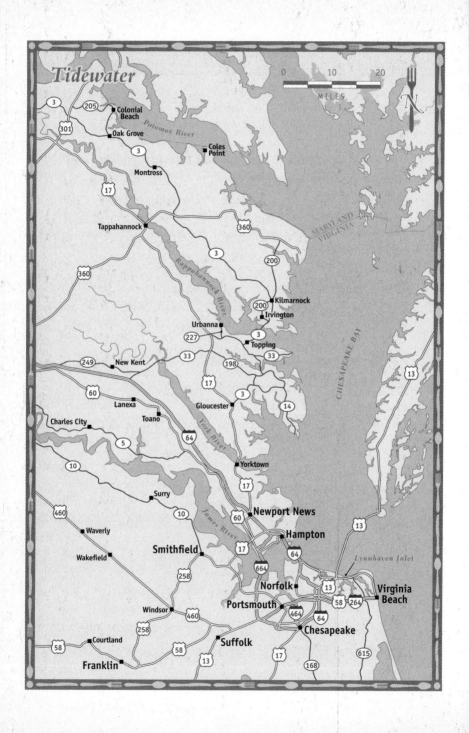

Tidewater

In 1608, the year after the first permanent English colony took root in Jamestown, explorers on the Chesapeake Bay witnessed a wondrous sight—an "aboundance of fish, lying so thicke with their heads above the water . . . neither better fish, more plenty, nor more variety for smal fish, had any of us ever seene in any place so swimming in the water." Lacking nets, "we attempted to catch them with a frying pan: but we found it a bad instrument to catch fish with."

Here's where America's foodways started. And no wonder. When settlers sailed into the eastern region of Virginia called Tidewater, they discovered a land with miles of Atlantic Ocean coastline, wetlands, brackish rivers, rich farmland, and part of the Chesapeake Bay.

"There were 15-foot sturgeon, oysters the size of dinner plates, and fowl darkening the sky," said Frank Clark, supervisor of historic foodways at the Colonial Williamsburg Foundation. "Compared with what they had in England, it was truly a land of plenty." For ship captains, "going to the Chesapeake was like going to heaven."

Tidewater's natural resources nourished the fledging nation and provided building blocks for all American foodways to follow. Early settlements gave way to plantations, where tables were set with melting pot menus. Dishes included quintessential Tidewater cured country ham and sweet potato biscuits; European classics such as French fricassees and Spanish *ropa vieja;* Native Americans' "three sisters" of corn, pole beans, and squash; and slave cooks' curries, peanuts, and okra from their Africa and the West Indies homelands.

Today, Tidewater's chefs and cooks take full advantage of the abundance, honoring the breadth and depth of this culinary birthright. Welcome to Tidewater, where you can taste the history.

Foodie Faves

Abbey Road Pub & Restaurant, 203 22nd St., **Virginia Beach, VA 23451; (757) 425-6330; abbeyroadpub.com; Beer Pub/ Casual American; $$.** This pub is the perfect place to come together near the Virginia Beach resort strip. You'll go away feeling fine. Owner Bill Dillon's love of The Beatles is obvious—from an outdoor mural that takes a few liberties in re-creating the *Abbey Road* album to the Fab Four paraphernalia that dominates the interior decor. Black-and-white photos of John, Paul, George, and Ringo are prominent, and posters take you back to yesterday, when the group was still touring and playing venues such as Carnegie Hall. It's a welcome change from the beach-themed bars that dominate the oceanfront area. The menu is extensive, with standard appetizer fare such as fried calamari rings and buffalo wings, burgers, and sandwiches, and entrees that include the signature shrimp scampi and Jamaican jerk chicken. After those hard day's nights on the beach, this place refreshingly offers breakfast until 4 p.m. The Yoko Ono plate and Beatles Burrito are hearty, and the french toast, gorgeously browned, melts in your mouth. If you want to embark on your own magical, if not quite mysterious, tour of the world's brews, more than 80 beers are available. If you'd rather twist and shout, there's live music most weekends and many weekday nights.

Anzio Turkish Italian Cuisine, 980 J. Clyde Morris Blvd., **Newport News, VA 23601; (757) 223-7311; facebook.com/Anzio TurkishItalianCuisine; Italian/Turkish; $.** Inside faux brick archways on one wall of this storefront eatery, an artist has painted boldly colored scenes of Turkey, with domed and sunbaked buildings. On the opposite wall, he has fashioned scenes of Tuscany. The somewhat crowded menu provides the same contrasts, with separate sections for Italian and Turkish fare. Here's where to get authentic Turkish and Eastern European foods such as *pelmeni* (Russian dumplings), borscht, and *morkovcha,* a crisp, shredded carrot salad seasoned with garlic and herbs that delivers an unforgettable explosion of exotic flavor. There are lamb gyros and shawarma, too. The Italian side of the menu is stuffed with stromboli, eggplant parmigiana, Alfredos, lasagna, and more. The scope and busy layout of the menu makes it almost exhausting to read. Persevere. It's worth the effort, and the pace here is unhurried.

The Art of Coffee, 15722 Kings Hwy., Montross, VA 22520; (804) 493-9651; theartofcoffee.biz; American/Coffeehouse; $. Who knew that a gas station could be retrofitted into a sunny, comfy cafe? At The Art of Coffee, the bones of the service station survive—gargantuan glass garage doors, pocked cement floors, and—what's that?—part of a car ramp. But there's nary a trace of grease nor gas. Rather, framed watercolors and photographs decorate the walls, and rooms are ringed with pottery, jewelry, quilted purses, and hand-hewn chairs. In short, there's plenty to look at while the cheery sandwich makers and baristas whir up a latte or flatten out your panini, which are named for famous artists such as Georgia O'Keeffe and Monet. The paninis come layered with fresh basil and mozzarella, or house-made sun-dried tomato spread, fresh spinach, and feta. A full breakfast menu features the usual morning fare, plus bone-in pork chops with eggs and eggs Benedict. Burgers, crab-cake sandwiches, and chicken salad round out the menu. On nice days, they open the garage bay door, so it's alfresco for y'all.

The Bier Garden, 434 High St., Portsmouth, VA 23704; (757) 393-6022; biergarden.com; Beer Pub/German; $$. This family-owned eatery is a mainstay of the restaurant scene in the historic Olde Towne district of Portsmouth. The Osfolk family—seemingly always on the premises—dishes out sandwiches, plates of schnitzel, sausages, and salads in a homey atmosphere that includes a covered porch and a couple of outdoor tables. But it's the beer at the bar—and the staff's encyclopedic knowledge of all things brewed—that has made this award-winning pub a local favorite. This place sports 20 taps of ever-changing kegs. Eight refrigerated cases behind the bar are stocked with ales and abts, pilsners, and bocks. The beer menu itself runs 20-plus pages long. If you're here near Christmas, call ahead for the date of the annual tapping party of a keg of Samichlaus, a strong lager whose name means Santa Claus. Then come early, because the house is always packed and the keg runs dry in no time flat.

Braise, 3333 Virginia Beach Blvd., Ste. 17, Virginia Beach, VA 23452; (757) 961-8131; facebook.com/braisevab; Seafood/Steaks; $$$. This restaurant, opened in 2013, brought Chef Bobby Huber back to the local culinary scene. Huber had gained a reputation after helming two local favorites, both now closed, under the name of Bobbywood and a stint at another area eatery. His new lunch-and-dinner place looks like a strip-mall storefront from the outside, but the interior is jewel-toned elegance, with soft lighting and sleek lines. The bar offers 20 seats at the L-shaped counter and a few tables, and a few private eating spaces are tucked off the main dining room. The waitstaff hums along in head-to-toe black punctuated by muted ties. Huber is a master at low-and-slow cooking, and the menu reflects that. A scallop appetizer, topped with spikes of crisply fried bacon, combines perfectly seared scallops with dabs of house-made apple butter and pimiento cheese. The Eastern Shore clams come on the half shell, with roasted garlic and fennel bulbs to boot. The entrees are primarily seafood and steaks, with some fowl and pasta thrown in. You can't go wrong with a standout from Huber's earlier days, the Bobbywood Filet. Served with a shock of "frazzled" onions on top, the dish reveals more and more surprises. It starts with the delicately battered and fried onions, then beef that has been braised for hours and finished on the griddle. That sits atop garlic mashed potatoes, and a red-wine reduction finishes the dish. The chef at times meanders through the dining room, tickling a baby and joking that, no, everything here isn't braised. Which wouldn't be a bad thing.

Byrd & Baldwin Bros. Steakhouse, 116 Brooke Ave., Norfolk, VA 23510; (757) 222-9191; byrdbaldwin.com; Seafood/Steaks; $$$$. It's all about the details—from the aging of the meat to the crispness of the linens—in this downtown restaurant that opened in 2006. The building's front is imposing, composed of white stone set off by four columns that flank granite steps, but inside the feeling is one of luxury. An attentive staff seemingly glides over the hardwood floors in this elegantly restored, turn-of-the-century structure, turning up just in time to refill water glasses, remove those pesky crumbs, or bring another glass of wine. The menu tempts you from the start, with prime beef tartare, brought to life with Spanish capers, and a traditional preparation of French onion soup. The beef and white bean chili, with chocolate undertones, is a revelation. For entrees, you can try seafood, lamb, or chicken, but the steaks, aged for at least 21 days, are what turn locals into loyals. The cuts are classic—filet mignon, New York strip, porterhouse, rib eye, and T-bone—and the flavors are rich with a hint of nuttiness. You'll get a steak knife, but you'll be tempted to dig in with just a fork. A great finisher is the unusual key lime pie, which resembles a cheesecake but bursts with citrus freshness. The extensive wine list makes choices difficult—more than 1,000 bottles are on the premises—but at times the suave atmosphere calls out for something retro, like a classic Manhattan or martini, shaken, without a hint of fruit juice.

Pickin' by the Dock near the Bay

It's a must-do summer activity for serious seafood lovers in Tidewater—heading to a crab shack and spending a few hours "picking" blue crabs. It's an art when it's done well, and those born here start young. The "come-heres"—as the natives call those who've relocated to the region—have to catch up. One of the best ways to do that is to spend an afternoon or evening at a Virginia Beach eatery on the banks of Lynnhaven Inlet.

The inlet's waters flow into the Chesapeake Bay to the north, and it's the bay that gives birth to blue crabs. In these parts, they're a delicacy akin to lobster. Some prefer to devour them as fried softshells, shortly after they molt and their fresh outer coating has not yet hardened. Others opt for crabmeat in cake form, either broiled or fried, seasoned with Old Bay. There's nothing wrong with either style, but for true-blue fans, steaming the shellfish in a pot of vinegar-seasoned water is the only way to go.

The resulting heat turns the blue beauties into red-orange affairs ready for eating. You can do this at home, but most head to their favorite local hangout.

On the Lynnhaven's jagged eastern shore, you can find three such joints, only a few doors apart: **Bubba's Seafood Restaurant and Crabhouse** at 3323 Shore Dr., **Chick's Oyster Bar** at 2143 Vista Circle, and **Dockside Restaurant** at 3331 Shore Dr. Each has its own staunch fans, who are loath to set foot in one of the competitors.

What they all share is an experience characterized by the food, the view, and the atmosphere.

Let's start with the crabs themselves. They don't give up their meat easily, unlike snow crabs that allow large chunks to be easily removed. With blue crabs, you have to work for your reward, so if you're ravenous, it's best to order some shrimp or clams or oysters to tide you over.

It's a messy process, and the waitstaff will layer your table with a sheath of brown paper and drop off a slew of napkins or your own roll of paper towels.

There are several ways to go about this, and the hardcore swear by their own method. Whichever approach you use—and it's best to be shown how to do this by someone who knows—you'll eventually get inside the shell. You'll see some feathery gills, which should be removed. You'll find some mustardy-looking goop, which is actually part of the crab's digestive system. Some pickers discard it quickly; others consider its strong taste a delicacy and savor it.

Next up is finding the meat and extracting it. This is picking, and it takes some doing. You're working with your fingers, looking for pieces as you pick your way through the crab's inner crevices. You'll pull out sections of precious meat as large as an almond; others will seem like mere threads. You can dip your handiwork in malt vinegar, melted butter or Old Bay seasoning, but the firm meat of the blue crab is so intoxicatingly sweet that it needs no condiments or seasonings.

As you've probably figured out, this can be a slow process, so you'll need something to do as you proceed. That's where a nice setting comes in, and Bubba's, Chick's, and Dockside have the same hypnotic one.

They all offer westward views out onto the water, where the local boat traffic comes and goes. A yacht, a power boat, a fishing vessel, then another and another, make their way in and around the inlet. Sometimes a boat docks at your eatery, and the passengers will disembark so they can join your eating frenzy. Sometimes, the vessels are served dockside—orders taken first and then food brought out by waiters who hand it to those aboard. From time to time, an enormous cruise boat passes by, and the packed tourists wave frantically to anyone ashore. If it's evening, the sun sets in the background, adding pinks and oranges and reds to a sky that is giving up its blue just as the cooked crabs have done.

You're happy to share this moment with those around you, and there's a spontaneous camaraderie often forged among those crab pickers. They'll gladly help newcomers get started, share a laugh with diners at other tables or nod approvingly when you've pulled the biggest piece of meat yet from your crab's body.

At some point, bite by bite, your hunger starts to abate. Steadily, the pile of cooked crabs on your tray begins to shrink, and the paper bag or bucket that holds your discarded shells fills up.

When you're finished, you waddle out to your ride, happy and stuffed. A summer rite, done the right way.

Captain Groovy's Grill & Raw Bar, 8101 Shore Dr., Virginia Beach, VA 23518; (757) 965-4667; captaingroovys.com; **Eclectic; $$.** It's true, the pedigree of the place is a bit sketchy—a former Laundromat, 7-Eleven, and general store in the slowly gentrifying, once terrifying East Ocean View area of Norfolk. Ignore all that. The sign out front, a fish wearing sunglasses, is more revealing of the ever-changing rainbow of dishes dreamed up by Chef David Watts, a longtime Tidewater restaurateur with experience in the West Indies. Themed special nights at this ultra-casual eatery might have waitresses bringing out sushi or Cajun food, while the regular menu includes a Cuban Panini stuffed with house-smoked pork or the Tahitian Tuna with a schmear of honey-wasabi sauce. Burgers go from traditional to the Karma Burger, a patty of fresh salmon chunks seasoned with Asian chili sauce and sesame seeds. It's best cooked rare. There's no better whole fried flounder and the nachos—topped with shredded chicken from every part of the house-smoked bird—basked in the winners' circle honors in a region-wide contest.

Car Wash Cafe, 481 N. Main St., Kilmarnock, VA 22482; (804) 435-0405; facebook.com/carwashcafeva; **Casual American; $.** How about coffee and a car wash? Two eggs over easy and a car wash? A crab cake and a car wash? This eatery looks like a Shell gas station with the iconic orange-and-yellow trim on cinderblock, but gone are the pumps and convenience store. Forget about a roller dog and a bag of chips with a moon pie on the side. Instead, 10 tables, 4 barstools and an open kitchen have been added, and the place is one of the more popular breakfast and lunch spots on the state's Northern Neck, the uppermost of three pieces of land that jut toward the Chesapeake Bay. After the first full moon in May, which marks the beginning of soft-shell-crab season, get Chesapeake Benedict, eggs given the traditional Benedict treatment but served with a fried soft-shell crab on top. The specials list, which can run nearly as long as the menu, might include a grilled ahi tuna sandwich, cucumber gazpacho, or liver and onions. Locals rave about the sweet potato fries and she-crab soup.

Catch31 Fish House and Bar, 3001 Atlantic Ave., Virginia Beach, VA; (757) 213-3474; catch31.com; Seafood; $$$–$$$$. You can't make reservations for this one, so the lines at this ocean-side restaurant can get long when the tourists swoop in. While you're waiting, you can study the chalkboard that details the day's fresh fish and raw bar offerings. That will take you a while. At one end of the space, an inviting bar offers a lift of spirits as well as spirits themselves. Splashes of blues are prevalent throughout the airy dining area, located in the first floor of the Hilton hotel, and the views are hypnotic. Look one way, and you're gazing at the boardwalk, the sunbathers, and the seemingly endless Atlantic. Glance the other way, and the cooking staff toils feverishly in an open kitchen. The menu—no surprise here—is heavy on fish, and the options don't stop there. Once you've chosen your temptation, you have to decide how you want it cooked: grilled, broiled, blackened, or bronzed, a lighter version of blackened. A delightful dessert turns crème brûlée on its head, using caramel corn for the crunch usually provided by the torched sugar topping. The waiters are a blur, but they take time to walk you through the menu and keep you satisfied. The restaurant offers breakfast, lunch, and dinner, calling it quits for only a few hours each day.

Circa 1918 Kitchen + Bar, 10367 Warwick Blvd., Newport News, VA 23601; (757) 599-1918; circa1918.com; facebook.com/ circa1918; New American; $$. It seems a mistake, the name Circa 1918, as though the sign maker jumbled the numbers and got away with it. Jamestown—America's first permanent English colony—is a county away, and historical Williamsburg just beyond that. Shouldn't the name be 1819, back when the USA was brand new, the year that Thomas Jefferson founded the University of Virginia? Turns out, the sign maker was right. Etched in script on the glass storefront of this hip, 38-seat Hilton Village gastropub is the history of this English-style hamlet and the nation's first federal war housing project, now listed on the National Register of Historic Places. The menu dishes up new- and old-school offerings with modern American verve. Here, chicken 'n' dumplings and vegetables come with a slick of jalapeño-honey glaze. Spicy meat loaf—a sturdy slab made with bison, not beef—is a destination dish for the restaurant, and so are frequent wine dinners. And don't ignore the specialty cocktail list. The Ava Gardner—a raspberry-blueberry vodka martini—honors the actress's local roots. The parents of the silver-screen star ran a boardinghouse in Newport News, circa 1935.

Citrus, 2265 W. Great Neck Rd., Virginia Beach, VA; (757) 227-3333; citrusvb.com; Casual American; $. Long before Guy Fieri stood stove-side and chatted with owners Lance and Cheri Shores, legions of locals flocked here for the Tidewater-centric menu of ultra-fresh salads, sandwiches, and breakfast food. Sure, there are all the usual morning offerings—french toast, omelets, and such—but autumn might bring pumpkin pancakes with a pecan glaze. In the spring, when seafood lovers crave the start of soft-shell crab season, Citrus is among the first to find the papery-shelled crustaceans. They're served Benedict-style—a hunky fried soft-shell, a pair of poached eggs and a satiny Hollandaise sauce on an English muffin topped with tomato. The dish is a seasonal rite of passage for regulars. Guiltless yet satisfying offerings include dishes that bring together scrambled egg whites, swiss cheese, avocado, hummus, cucumber, and tomato atop toasted rye. That leaves room for the signature mimosa, made with a blend of freshly squeezed orange juice, mango pulp, and pineapple juice. A generous pour of Champagne assures that it keeps its fizz to the finish. Summertime mimosas might be flavored with cantaloupe, honeydew, or watermelon juices. Real foodies can skip the made-in-China souvenirs of their summer vacation and bring back a gallon of sunshine in the form of a jug of Citrus's mimosa mix.

Conch & Bucket, 13 E. Queens Way, Hampton, VA 23669; (757) 864-0865; on Facebook; Seafood; $$. Simple preparation is key at this seafood-centric eatery just blocks from the working docks in Hampton. It's an airy, open spot with exposed brick walls and a long bar inside and a charming outdoor patio out back. About that bar, it's made with 40,000 bright copper pennies and took 23 days to complete. But we digress. The seafood, the seafood. Don't miss the crunchy potato chip–crusted crab cake with a generous serving of pimiento cheese rice pilaf. It's like two Southern treats on a single plate. The crispy, golden crust of the cake cracks open to reveal a moist, lightly seasoned crab interior that plays nicely with the spicy-sweet jalapeño-pineapple salsa. The creamy pimiento cheese rice pilaf is akin to risotto, but a touch of acid makes it a tad edgier than your average comfort food. The macaroni and cheese, on the other hand, is quintessential comfort food—cheddar cheese and elbows baked and served bubbly with the all-important browned edges. Get it plain, or with veggies, with bacon, with smoked country ham, or with shrimp and crab. Occasionally, another Southern treat, hummingbird cake, is on the menu. This delicate layer cake combines moist banana-pineapple-pecan cake with cream cheese icing and a raspberry drizzle.

Country Boy's Barbeque, 20 W. Windsor Blvd., Route 460, Windsor, VA 23487; (757) 242-8180; countryboysbbq.net; Barbecue; $. Barbecue on brioche? Trust us, this is worth a swerve off the blacktop. Usually, pulled or chopped 'que gets piled on plain white buns. But owners Danny and Heather Thornton didn't like how the bottom of the bun disintegrated, so Heather started baking brioche. Now their award-winning, hand-pulled, Eastern-style 'que—cooked over local hickory in a massive, custom-made smoker in the screened porch beside the dining room—gets piled on these. Everything here

Chesapeake's Tattooed Chef

Some days, when the lunch crowd descends on **Cotton Southern Bistro** at 648 Grassfield Pkwy. in Chesapeake and the wait staff wades in the weeds and the cook line goes nuts, Chef-Owner Jeff Brown can be found in a Virginia Beach tattoo studio. There, his head rests on his backpack, his sleeves are rolled up and punk rock plays on the radio.

During these times, Cotton's staff knows not to dial the boss man's cell. And when he returns to the restaurant, rested, they can admire the latest addition to his full-sleeve, farm-to-fork tattoo. Or, as Brown likes to joke, his "farm-to-arm" tattoo.

The tat begins at Brown's left wrist—"at dirt level,"—with beets, bell peppers, pattypan squash curling up his forearm and cherry tomatoes ripening on the vine. Brown's beefy bicep is bisected by a Carolina split-rail fence, where a crop of corn stands tall. Beyond that stands a big red barn, based on one in rural Chesapeake, and, beyond that, on Brown's shoulder, a bright blue sky. But wait. There's more. Underneath his arm is a butcher's diagram of a pig and a knife, fork, and unfinished spoon that disappear into the armpit region. At press time, yet to come were crowder peas, okra, and carrots, with the fringed tops curling across the "ditch," or the crook of the arm, which Brown expected to be the most painful part of the process.

Brown is a graduate of the Culinary Institute of America who completed an externship at the French Laundry in California. He returned to Tidewater with a farm-to-fork philosophy and in June 2011 opened Cotton on land where he once shot quail. His tat doesn't distress customers. These days, Brown says, it's more likely that a waitress will breeze through the kitchen hollering, "Hey Chef, table 36 wants to see your tattoo." So if you want to take a look, just ask.

is made from scratch—the slaw, the desserts, the mac 'n' cheese, the baked beans, and even the bread-and-butter pickles. Other offerings from the smoker include baby back ribs, beef brisket, and chicken wings. Portions are huge and the Thorntons are as friendly as can be. Settle onto one of the tractor seats at a table and soak up some serious Virginia hospitality.

Cul's Courthouse Grille, 10801 Courthouse Rd., Charles City, VA 23030; (804) 829-2205; culscourthousegrille.com; Traditional Southern; $$. Go ahead, walk on in. This place smacks of someone's house, but it's actually an ultra-casual restaurant. Here, you might find the owner sharing a quesadilla with his family while trying to dissuade out-of-state customers from begging for the coconut cake recipe, which in itself is worth a visit. The building, circa 1872, is the Nance-Major House and Store and an official Virginia Historic Landmark, thus its sloping, wide-planked floors. The menu ranges from fried green tomatoes and butterbean hummus to standard sandwiches, which are catapulted from the ranks of ho-hum by Miss Viv's homemade bread. Many menu items are named after locals. Consider Wilder's Catfish Sandwich, which honors L. Douglas Wilder, Virginia's first African-American governor, who lives just down the byway. Now about that coconut cake. It's three moist layers of white cake with ample icing, made even more memorable by—what? A sheet of lemon custard? Cul isn't telling. It's made by a lady who goes to his mom's church. He'll sell you a whole cake or a slice. But not the recipe.

Cutty Sark, 4707 Pretty Lake Ave., Norfolk, VA 23518; (757) 362-2942; on Facebook; Casual American; $. "What can I get you, hon?" That's how you'll likely be greeted at The Cutty, as locals call it, a vestige of Norfolk's old Ocean View section along the Chesapeake Bay. It's a friendly, order-pad-in-the-waitress's-back-pocket sort of place.

The restaurant is attached to an actual marina, and you'll have to pass through a corridor of boats perched high on cradles in varying states of disrepair to get to the door of this breakfast, lunch, and dinner eatery. The menu features a solid line of burgers, fried seafood baskets, crab cakes, chicken fingers, and hush puppies. The eatery also is a well-known morning-after spot, where the hungover are handled with a breakfast combo of comfort food, hair of the dog, and sweet Southern charm. The best of the former is Bite the Dog, a bargain-priced picker-upper platter. It's heaped with a palm-sized rib eye cooked on a flattop, two eggs, grits or hash browns, buttered toast (or biscuits, if you're lucky), and either two Bloody Marys or two screwdrivers on the side. The drinks, served in plastic tumblers, pack the octane of a 1.5-ounce pour of Aristocrat vodka, maybe more if your waitress deems it necessary.

Dancing Tomato 205 Business Park Dr., Virginia Beach, VA 23462; (757) 499-0000; dancingtomatovb.com; American; $. There's no way you'd happen upon this 11-seat micro-cafe located in a nondescript office building off a nondescript road in a nondescript corridor of Virginia Beach. But your palate will be rewarded for a short detour off the interstate. Here's where lunch hungries are quashed with soups and sandwich creations such as The Betty, a schmear of roasted nuts mixed with cream cheese topped with bacon and tomato on raisin bread or wheat panini. Or the Dixie Chicken, chicken salad made with homemade chow chow, celery, and bacon. If the special is avocado chicken salad, just get that. Dancing Tomato's signature roast beef, fennel-crusted pork loin, and grilled chicken breast are cooked in-house, and the collard salsa has a reputation all its own (see recipe on p. 256). Owner Laura Parker serves up everything with a great, big smile.

Doc Taylor's, 207 23rd St., Virginia Beach, VA 23451; (757) 425-1960; doctaylors.com; Casual American; $. This breakfast and lunch spot opened at the Virginia Beach oceanfront nearly 20 years ago to a line out the door and enduring success. It's a rare spot in the heart of the beach resort area where the past has been preserved, both in venue and menu. The two-story, circa 1939 clapboard cottage is the former home and office of the late Dr. Waller Taylor Sr., hence the name. The downstairs rooms and front sunporch are today a year-round favorite of locals, who come for pancakes, big breakfast sandwiches, burgers, and Sunday brunch. Several menu items are named for locals. You'll find Doc Conkwright's Cobb Omelet, Corpsmen Ken's Ham & Cheese, and the award-winning Scotty's Biscuits & Gravy. The latter is offered in a trio of ways: with traditional pork sausage, chorizo, or andouille. An extensive buttermilk pancake lineup features flapjacks five ways: banana, chocolate chip, granola, peach, and plain Jane. Perhaps the most popular sandwich is the Ray Ray, named for the cook—with a fried egg, bacon, cheese, and grilled Parmesan-coated tomatoes on an onion roll.

Eat, An American Bistro, 4005 Atlantic Ave., Virginia Beach, VA 23451; (757) 965-2472; eatbistro.net; Seafood/Steaks; $$–$$$. Big flavors emerge from the kitchen of this tiny eatery at the Virginia Beach oceanfront. Here, Chef-Owner Erick Heilig wakes up Oysters Rockefeller with a dusting of fennel pollen and sends out plates of carpaccio made with pepper- and brandy-cured beef over pesto green beans. The Hasselhoff Burger—made with brisket and chuck and topped with truffle mayo and a fried egg—is a locals' favorite. So are the shrimp and grits, seasoned with sage. Don't ignore the specials; this chef has winning whims. It's also a good idea to come a bit before your reservation and repair to the bar, where Chad Cruea's inventive spirit saturates the cocktail list. This guy is so committed to bubbles that he once disappeared into a mechanic's shop and emerged with a two-part contraption that allows him to add a Champagne-like sparkle to most anything he sends across the rail. His passion fruit yuzu cooler easily tames the sizzle of summer.

El Desorden, 665 Newtown Rd., Virginia Beach, VA 23462; (757) 497-4141; eldesordenva.com; Colombian; $$. If it's Friday and you're here, quick, order a bowl of *sancocho El Desorden,* the soup of the day. It's a dish so anticipated by Latino regulars that they call ahead to reserve it. The immense bowl of *sopa,* really more of a brothy stew than a soup, has the soulful flavor of a first-rate chicken soup but comes packed with tender, slow-cooked peasant cuts of bone-in chicken thighs, pork ribs, and beef ribs with the membrane attached. All that is studded with bold chunks of plantain and yucca, discs of corn on the cob and a dish of not-to-be-ignored lime wedges on the side; just a squeeze or two gives the stew a lively Latino flair. If it's not Friday, there's plenty more equatorial fare to keep things interesting. Try the *bandeja paisa,* a staple of the Medellín region of Colombia, the native land of owners Harry Pacheco and Luzmila Arroyova. It's a jigsaw of flavors, with beans and rice, top round, garlicky Colombian pork sausage flecked with green onion, deep-fried sweet plantains, a flat corn cake, avocado, a sunny-side-up egg, and the Colombian version of bacon—a strip of pigskin with a thick rope of meat and fat that has been scored and then deep-fried so that it looks like a medieval crown.

The Farmer's Kitchen, 11601 John Tyler Memorial Hwy. (Va. Route 5), Charles City, VA; (804) 829-2175; Barbecue; $. When traveling along Virginia's highways and byways, take special note of metal barrels lying sideways that have been outfitted with smokestacks and mounted on wheels or legs. They're sure signs that committed barbecue men or mavens are nearby. The Farmer's Kitchen, a red trailer parked on the side of the road, has two barrels ensconced in its gravel-and-dirt lot. A single table stands beside the trailer, a simple thing with a quartet of folding chairs. But most people get eats to go. A line forms at the window, regulars who've come to get their fix of fried fish, chili dogs, and the house specialty, chopped barbecue. That dish is topped with a fresh, coarse, vinegary coleslaw and a choice of either the region's traditional vinegar-based sauce or a sweet red version more common in the state's western part. The girl at the window, in braided pigtails, suggested that combining the two is the best way. And so it is—some sweet and some spice to mix with the smoke. Wash it all down with expertly brewed, medium-sweet tea, and be on your way in a jiff.

Fin Seafood, **3150 William Styron Sq., Newport News, VA 23606; (757) 599-5800; finseafood.com; Seafood/Steaks; $$$$.** The waiter brings a basket, and you figure that it'd be better to stick to the no-carb diet and politely decline. Instead, you bite into a slice of the crusty-on-the-outside, fluffy-on-the-inside French bread, and it grabs you like no other loaf has. Finished with salt and black pepper, it's sweet and tangy and needs no butter. It's a great way to start a meal in this seafood showcase in the city's Port Warwick section. With its splashes of blues and aquas—and finishing touches like candlelit sea glass on the tables—the decor instantly takes you seaside, and the menu keeps you there. Through an opening, diners can watch Executive Chef Kenny Sloane, his mohawk on full display, as he and his crew whip up blackened swordfish or pan-seared crab cakes. He's constantly moving, but at times he slows down to surreptitiously watch as a patron takes that first bite after a dish is served. If it's the seared scallops, the reaction is usually a huge, satisfied smile—and a quick second nibble. The scallops are impressive—browned to perfection yet tender inside, enhanced by a truffle demi-glace and house bacon. You, too, will do your share of ogling, as artfully plated entrees that you failed to order make their way to nearby tables. If you want to try it all, or at least more of it in a single setting, consider a tasting menu that offers three courses at lunch and five or seven at dinner.

456 Fish, 456 Granby St., Norfolk, VA 23510; (757) 625-4444; 456fish.com; Seafood; $$$. Contemporary flourishes combine with a gentleman's-club feel in the dining room of this downtown eatery that once was a billiards parlor. Opened in 2003, the restaurant's interior features bursts of forest green amid tastefully placed wood, while ceiling fans add charm from above. A gleaming waterfall wall separates the dining room from the bar. As the names implies, seafood is the star, and a good place to start is with one of the signature dishes, the potato chip-encrusted crab cake, available as either an appetizer or an entree. It sounds odd at first, mixing delicate crabmeat with ordinary potato chips. Then you bite into one of the cakes, and you're sold. The saltiness of the coating explodes in your mouth, mellowed quickly by the sweet firmness of the shellfish. The white truffle remoulade keeps you coming back for more. The fried calamari and fried oysters, both lightly battered and exquisitely fried, are popular appetizers with locals. The salad offerings range from a classic Caesar to a prosciutto-and-field-greens mixture set off by a white balsamic and peppadew vinaigrette. A few steaks grace the menu, but remember the name: You're really here for the fish.

Freemason Abbey Restaurant and Tavern, 209 W. Freemason St., Norfolk, VA 23510; (757) 622-3966; freemasonabbey .com; Casual American/Seafood; $$–$$$. It looks like a church, and that's because it was, originally built for Presbyterians in 1873. Since 1990, this downtown fixture has been the home of the Freemason Abbey, and many who dine there consider the she-crab soup to be a religious experience. Inside the stone building, tables fill the center of the large space and booths line the side walls. Seating rims the outer edge of the second story but leaves the middle open, which allows your eyes to gaze upward at the old church's high ceiling and the intricate stained-glass windows that add ambience. The restaurant is a casual place where shorts and flip-flops mingle with suits and ties. The most-sought-after dish is the aforementioned soup, with its rich creaminess enhanced by sherry and lumps of crab. The dish has won raves from regulars and slew of local awards. Our tip: For just a little extra, opt for the crock rather than the cup. Don't stop there. Offerings called Lunch in a Flash provide soups, salads, and sandwiches that are perfect weekday options for those in a hurry or who work nearby. At night, the dinner menu is a mixture of steak and seafood, and the entree of two lobster tails is a favorite. Cap it all off with a piece of Bailey's pie, a silky cheesecake made with Bailey's Irish Cream liqueur and an Oreo crust. You'll be in heaven.

Handsome Biscuit, 2511 Colonial Ave., Norfolk, VA 23517; handsomebiscuit.com; Neo-Southern; $. Early in 2013, after closing his Norfolk restaurant, one Norfolk chef went a little crazy, renovated a shoebox of a building in an aging, edgy neighborhood and torpedoed tradition. At Chef David Hausmann's new spot, Handsome Biscuit, sweet potato biscuits—once the strict domain of salty country ham or perhaps a pat of butter—are topped with all manner of things. The Shorty, crowned with an over-easy egg and cheese, is just the beginning. Moving further from tradition, the PB&JB comes with peanut butter, house-made berry jam and salted butter. Even further out is Mr. Close Love, topped with roasted pork shoulder, sweet hot mustard, and cucumber. Hella Fitzgerald comes with a jazzy combo of fried chicken, bacon, cheddar, and sausage red-eye gravy. The biscuits are made from scratch, as are the jams and everything that's pickled. The ingredients are local, and there's usually a line. While waiting, it's fun to watch diners at one of the eatery's four tables as they ponder how to tackle their towering biscuits, which stand three-plus inches tall. With a squish? A fork? Layer by layer? Businessmen, better tuck in those ties.

Harper's Table, 122 N. Main St., Suffolk, VA 23434; (757) 539-2000; harperstable.com; Pork/Steak/Seafood; $$–$$$. This 90-seater is a surprising find in the laid-back downtown area of Suffolk. The restaurant is upscale, contemporary, and cozy, with a menu that offers unique spins on Dixie cuisine. The lengthy bar buzzes on Friday night, as workers celebrate the beginning of the weekend with libations from the extensive wine list or the creative cocktail menu. A favorite is the Table Tea, a strong potion of bourbon, sweet tea (is there any other kind down South?), lemon, and peach bitters. The restaurant's namesake is Chef-Owner Harper Bradshaw, who formerly toiled at the city's highly acclaimed Vintage Tavern restaurant. His penchant for regional dishes is apparent from the start. Begin with a pork belly biscuit, sold individually, which combines the salty earthiness of the pig and the sweetness of strawberry jam in a light buttermilk biscuit. Bradshaw's artfulness comes through on the plates, beautiful to behold but even better to bite into. The Chesapeake Bay rockfish is moist, almost creamy, and made richer by a country ham butter sauce. The Downtown Suffolk BBQ Plate puts pulled shoulder pork front and center, and the sea scallops get a kick from the chorizo and smoked tomato. The entrees come with side dishes, but you can also order fries, grits and other options for the entire table. A fun ending is the cola float, a dessert that takes the childlike ice cream-and-soda idea to an adult level.

The Highlander, 676-B N. Witchduck Rd., Virginia Beach, VA 23462; (757) 962-7963; thehighlander-afinebritisheatery.com;

British; $$. Here's a wee spot where the English is lilting and the tables are always set for tea. At The Highlander, fish-and-chips, the British equivalent of America's burger and fries, are the house specialty, and this place does the dish right. A fat, fried fillet of haddock or cod comes with freshly cut chips—think french fries, not Ruffles, cut fatter than usual and fried golden brown, but without the crunch. A splash of malt vinegar moves these chips out of the fast-food nation. Recently, rocker Ted Nugent sought out the dish and found it rockin' good. The restaurant's culinary canon—replete with battered fried puddings (that's sausages to us Yanks), savory stews, and mashers—is first-class comfort food. Leave room for the Knickerbocker Glory parfait, just like the one Harry Potter ate.

Jammin' Jerk BBQ, 148 Burnetts Way, Suffolk, VA 23434; (757) 923-2934; jamminbbq.com; Jamaican; $$. The Suffolk location of this nine-table storefront is a true Jamaican restaurant smack dab in the middle of Virginia peanut country. In the kitchen, a wall of rough-hewn green logs tower beside the smoker, both essential elements in the iconic Jamaican dish called jerk, the core of the Island Krave menu. Montego Bay native Dorothy Lovell rubs her own blend of spices into raw chicken or pork and leaves it in the smoker for hours. But instead of sending a plate of mouth-scorching meat to every table, Lovell holds back on the heat, instead delivering intensely flavored meats that are pleasing to less-tolerant palates. Customers get their Jamaican groove on by dabbling in those little pots of sauces served on the side. Other dishes, such as oxtails, come hot from the pot with a concentrated beef flavor made silky by the smattering of fat and the marrow of the star-shaped bones. Roti, a traditional dish of stew wrapped in a thin sheet of bread, comes carnivore- or vegetarian-style stuffed with chickpeas. Chicken curry is offered daily, and goat curry is a frequent special. One element absent is island time—service is swift, but without the slightest bit of pressure to move on. The Norfolk location, **Island Krave,** opened in September 2013 and is located at 222 West 21st St.; islandkrave.com.

He Works for Peanuts

He's one of the world's most famous advertising icons—a long-legged legume outfitted in a top hat, spats, a monocle and a cane. He's Mr. Peanut, and he has ties to Suffolk, the western Tidewater city of 86,000 known as the "Peanut Capital of the World."

Planters Nuts, originally called Planters Peanuts, was founded in 1906 in Pennsylvania by Italian immigrant Amedeo Obici. Ten years later, his company sponsored a logo contest, and a 14-year-old schoolboy came up with a Peanut Man. An artist added the finer touches, and a legend was born.

By this time, Planters had built a processing plant in the heart of Virginia's peanut-producing country, and Obici and his wife relocated to a farm there in 1924. The company grew, and the Suffolk plant became a major employer. Obici repaid his good fortune with generous donations to numerous causes in his adopted community, and he and his wife became revered. A Suffolk hospital today carries the family name.

An updated company factory was built in Suffolk in 1994, and the **Planters Peanut Center** at 308 W. Washington St. in Suffolk offers a taste of the company's products. Planters, through corporate mergers, is now owned by Kraft Foods. Other peanut processors have opened in the region, however, and Planters isn't the local economic force it once was.

Through it all, Mr. Peanut has endured. In 2006, the company asked online voters whether a bow tie, cufflinks, or a pocket watch should be added to his outfit. The public liked him just the way he was.

The character has been enshrined on Madison Avenue's Advertising Walk of Fame, and a poll by the American Association of Advertising Agencies found Mr. Peanut to be the third most popular ad creation of all time, trailing only the M&M characters and the AFLAC duck.

Tourists in downtown Suffolk can visit a statue of the revered icon at the corner of Main and Washington Streets, where he rests, appropriately, on a pedestal. They can pause, take a photo or two and—if the idea doesn't feel too nutty—tip their hats to the hardest-working fictional peanut around.

Jessy's Taqueria, 3201 E. Ocean View Ave., Ste. 104, Norfolk, VA 23518, (757) 531-0033; Mexican; $$. Speaking a bit of Spanish is helpful when dining at Jessy's, but it's not mandatory. This no-frills, authentic Mexican taqueria serves food that is a revelation to those who equate the cuisine with the gloppy, cheesy, Americanized versions. Each dish on the menu has been photographed and is posted above the ordering counter, so gringos need only point. This is a good time to be adventuresome. Start with the guacamole, a destination dish for locals that comes four ways: regular, chipotle, *queso,* and jalapeño. Then, have a beef taco stuffed with steak, cheek, or tongue. Or try an enchilada or poblano with house-made mole. Wash it down with flavored water that's a Mexican staple. Ever-changing flavors include cantaloupe, lemon, mango, orange, pineapple, and watermelon, all made with fresh fruit. There's a full Mexican market, bakery, and butcher shop attached, so schedule time for browsing.

Leaping Lizard Cafe, 4408 Shore Dr., Virginia Beach, VA 23455; (757) 460-5327; on Facebook; Casual American; $. A restaurant without a freezer? No fryer? No flattop grill? An eatery with a chicken coop? That's Leaping Lizard. Need we say more? The quaint, yellow cottage that houses the cafe is a bit hard to spot, and regulars would rather keep it that way. Owner Bill Prince, a gracious, soft-spoken man, embraced the local-food movement long before it moved mainstream. His mantra is "seasonal fare from the local farms of tidal Virginia." There's not a bad choice on the menu, which features inventive seasonal salads, chicken, and fresh—not canned—tuna salad plates, wraps and signature sandwiches served on toasted, house-baked rosemary bread with potato salad. A favorite is the oven-roasted turkey, Surry ham and cheese, made with one of Virginia's finest cured hams. The sweet potato biscuit and soup combines the soup of the day with a freshly baked sweet potato biscuit topped with said Surry ham and

homemade peach jam. On a pretty day, dine outdoors under the towering tree-tops. In the spring, a little farmers market is open out back. A Guy Fieri favorite.

Leila's Mediterranean Kitchen, Deli & Grocery, 5045 Virginia Beach Blvd., Virginia Beach, VA 23462; (757) 644-6912; leilasmed.com; Mediterranean; $. Leila's is not well known among the area's mainstream restaurant crowd. In fact, we almost didn't include it because, well, there are only five booths in this authentic eatery, and we'd like to be able to settle into one whenever we have a craving for a *manakish*. It's an astonishingly flavorful Lebanese-style pizza—think thyme, sesame seeds, and olive oil on a thin crust. Other favorites are the hand-rolled grape leaves or a supper of *mekanek,* which is Lebanese sausage sauteed with olive oil and lemon. Order at the counter, then, while waiting, browse the compact grocery that occupies most of the space. It's crammed with bulk beans, flours, jams, marmalades, and spices, and the refrigerated case at the back holds imported cheeses, pita breads, sausages, and more. Somehow, the place even manages an olive bar, featuring Leila's very own brand. And, yes, there is a Leila herself, who is often back in the kitchen cooking up the flavors of home.

Lendy's Cafe, 1581 General Booth Blvd., Ste. 101, Virginia Beach, VA 23454; (757) 491-3511; on Facebook; Casual American; $. There's a facet of Virginia Beach that's not mentioned in glossy travel brochures. It's the deafening roar of Navy jets streaking across the sky as they take off and land at Naval Air Station Oceana Master Jet Base. Lendy's, just a few miles from there, is a hangout of members of squadrons who like their wings searing hot, their beer ice cold and the atmosphere familial and friendly. Burgers and standard sports-bar fare grace a menu emblazoned with a picture of a Navy jet and an aircraft carrier, but it's the wings that Lendy's has earned a rep for. Get 'em hot, killer, atomic, suicide, or below hell. "If you can't hang," the menu says, "we have BBQ, garlic, Parmesan, teriyaki, and wimpy." The winners of many a local contest, they're all good.

Luna Maya, 2010 Colley Ave., Norfolk, VA 23517; (757) 622-6986; lunamayarestaurant.com, Mexican; $$. Start with the guacamole, legendary in the Tidewater area, with its burst of avocado goodness enhanced but not overpowered by cilantro and cumin. Or if you're daring, try the souped-up, serrano-pepper version. Either way, you'll want to pace yourself, or you can easily fill up before your meal arrives. This cantina is the dream of sisters Karla and Vivian Montano, who have adapted South American family recipes handed down from their mother and grandmothers. They've created a casual restaurant warmed by a brick wall and orange decor. The friendly fare makes you feel right at home, from the surprisingly sweet tamales Luna Maya to the spicy *taquitos con carnitas*. Vegetarians have more than a handful of offerings, including burritos, enchiladas, and quesadillas. When the weather is fair, outdoor seating lets you take in the view of Norfolk's bohemian Ghent section. End with a drink—such as the cantina's twist on a margarita that has been sweetened with mango or sangria that will have you fishing every last piece of fruit from the pitcher.

Mannino's Italian Bistro, 4402 Princess Anne Rd., Ste. 107, Virginia Beach, VA 23462, (757) 474-4446; manninositalianbistro .com; Italian; $$. A few years back, a father from Palermo and a son with a degree from the Culinary Institute of America started turning out fine Italian fare in a storefront behind
a Hess gas station, and in 2013 they opened their third location in Portsmouth to feed a growing fan base. Specialties of the house that father-and-son team John R. and John M. Mannino have built

include the mile-high lasagna Bolognese, homemade egg noodles that are layered with Bolognese sauce, ricotta, and house-made mozzarella and béchamel and topped with a plum tomato sauce. Italian favorites are always simmering stovetop, but the chef also has a way with local seafood; fresh fish with an Italian twist is a mainstay of the chalkboard menu. The restaurant's she-crab soup, a point of honor for many a Tidewater chef, is a perennial winner in local contests. The thick, ecru-colored dish is packed with fat spoonfuls of lump crab, crab, and more crab, with a hint of spirituous Marsala. For lighter appetites, opt for the roasted garlic antipasti plate—a fat fist of roasted garlic, house-made mozzarella, prosciutto, roasted red peppers, olives, and a crusty sliced loaf that comes with a dish of high-test olive oil for dipping. With a nice glass of red, it's a meal in itself. **Additional locations:** 1608 Pleasure House Rd., Virginia Beach, VA 23455; (757) 226-0019; 606 High St., Portsmouth, VA 23704; (757) 966-7522.

Martin's Soul Food, 800 Baker Rd., Ste. 88, Virginia Beach, VA 23462; (757) 305-9555; Soul Food; $. A constant sizzle and pop comes from the kitchen of this small, storefront shop where owner Tim Martin spends just about every afternoon and evening. He's at the stove, frying up whiting snacks, gizzards, and chitterlings, and turning out pots of collards and pans of spot-on macaroni and cheese that, despite legions of fans, he says is still not as good as his mom's. Martin offers a menu that stays true to his roots, using recipes he learned from his mother, Orla, and his father, the Rev. Ernest Martin, a local pastor for nearly half a century. The restaurant, Martin's third, gets right to the heart of soul food. Newbies unfamiliar with the cuisine can get their sustenance from Martin's meat loaf, big slabs served with ketchup or gravy. The menu above the self-serve counter also lists turkey chops, chicken livers and onions, oxtails, and pigs' feet. More adventuresome eaters should try the latter, also known as trotters, a silky, savory dish that is considered a delicacy in Europe.

Merroir, 784 Locklies Rd., Topping, VA 23169; (804) 758-2871; on Facebook; Neo-Southern/Seafood; $$. We like a spot where the oysters are offered by the name of the creek where they came from. That's because we know that "merroir," a watery version of terroir, affects the flavor. We like it even better when you can order a dozen raw or mixed, and even better still when the bivalves are paired with a carefully curated list of craft beers and wines. This chic little artisanal tasting room offers all three in a retrofitted bait shack on the banks of the Rappahannock River. The menu is short, but oh-so-tempting. Try a sampler platter of a dozen expertly opened oysters (no shell, fully detached, the juicy "liquor" intact), raw or roasted. They range from salty Witch Ducks, a regular at the Grand Central Oyster Bar in New York City, to sweet Rappahannocks. Then dive into a bowl of clam-and-lamb stew, or pork belly sausage with pimiento and cheese. If the wind's not blowing, relax at a table out on the patio behind the place and take in a grand view of the "rivah." That's what they call it around here.

99 Main Restaurant, 99 Main St., Newport News, VA 23601; (757) 599-9885; 99mainrestaurant.com; Eclectic; $$$–$$$$. Billed as the city's first fine-dining room, 99 Main graciously accommodates cravings for fancy dining, casual dining, and even alfresco dining out on the quiet sidewalk under the shade of a pair of stately twin oaks. The restaurant sits on a side street in Hilton Village, a sort of English hamlet built to house shipyard workers during World War I that's now on the National Register of Historic Places. One side of the 75-seat restaurant is sunshiny yellow with white tablecloths, fresh flowers, and a wall of windows that disappears in fine weather. There's an open kitchen on the other side, where lights are dimmed, The Doors might be playing on the sound system and locals sit in comfortable, high-backed booths or perch at the four-seat bar and savor the chef's French-inspired cuisine. Don't miss Roasted Oysters "99" Style, served piping hot on the half shell and topped with a mild horseradish *glaçage* and a rustic dice of salty house-made bacon. Lamb shanks come braised with porcini mushrooms. For the past couple of years, the fall menu has featured an über-popular pumpkin, duck, and curry soup. Be sure to note the fishes of the day. If you choose one, ask the chef to cook the fish the way he likes, and instead of choosing from the three condiments—mint-almond pesto, chipotle-orange butter, or the mildly spicy cucumber chutney—get all three.

Olivia's in the Village, 6597 Main St., Gloucester, VA 23061; (804) 694-0057; oliviasinthevillage.com; Italian/Seafood/Steaks; $$. Gloucester Courthouse, on a tidy main street lined with locally owned shops, is the seat of one of the country's oldest counties. After touring the historic structure at one end of the street, head to Olivia's to contemplate it all over a platter of seafood crepes, the dish that earns the restaurant rave reviews. Thin crepes come filled with a Tidewater trinity of shrimp, crab, and scallops and are topped with a rich lobster cream sauce. The lasagna—a traditional preparation with Italian sausage and cheeses that is finished with a bright, fresh marinara sauce—can sate the heartiest of appetites. The steaks and burgers come cooked the way they're ordered, and there are plenty of choices for the salad set. And if you've not yet bit into a slice of quintessentially Southern lemon chess pie, this is the place to get started.

Passion, The Restaurant, 1036 Volvo Pkwy., Chesapeake, VA 23320; (757) 410-3975; passiontherestaurant.com; Seafood/Steaks; $$$. Nestled into a nondescript strip mall in this suburban city, this restaurant offers an air of sophisticated casualness and—yes, we'll go ahead and say it—a passion for Southern goodness. Customers enter through an area of sidewalk seating and are greeted by the bar, which can be tough to pass up. A half-wall hides the small yet airy dining area, a contemporary space whose walls are adorned with works by local artists. The menu fashioned by Chef Garrett Barner, updated to include some Asian touches, relies on local ingredients. The tapas can double as appetizers, and the macaroni and cheese is a welcome indulgence, with its white cheddar punch lifted by white truffle oil. Truffle oil is again on display in the fries, which regulars find tough to share with others at their table. The humorous Not Your Grandma's Spaghetti and Meatballs substitutes blackened scallops and strips of squash for the dish's signature parts. The menu's tour de force is the rack of lamb, with a five-pepper glaze that combines bell and jalapeño peppers with two kinds of vinegar and dark corn syrup. That specialty is available as either a tapa or an entree. The best plate not on the menu, though it's a recurring special, is Duck Two Ways—crispy sliced breast meat accompanied by a confit leg and thigh, surrounded by a ginger plum sauce that will have you scraping the plate for every last bit.

Pearl French Bistro, 703 Thimble Shoals Blvd., Newport News, VA 23606; (757) 223-5370; pearlfrenchbistro.com; facebook.com/ PearlFrenchBistro; French; $$$$. Fine French restaurants seem to pop up in the most unexpected places in this state. This little gem is tucked into a grid of office buildings and offers a respite from chains with its Parisienne charm and fare. The chef-owner, Ihsan Korkmaz, is a native of Turkey who worked in the kitchens of **The Trellis** (p. 128) and **Le Yaca** (p. 124)—two of neighboring Williamsburg's finest restaurants—before he attended Le Cordon Bleu cooking school in Canada. Today his ever-changing lunch and dinner menus offer traditional and contemporary versions of French standards. The menu might feature sauteed quail with white bean risotto or a chicken breast with chocolate sauce and pearl couscous. Check ahead for the dates of frequent tastings of wine and Champagne that are paired with thoughtful creations from the chef.

Pho 79, 1445 Sam's Dr., Chesapeake, VA 23320; (757) 547-4800; eatpho79.com; Vietnamese; $. The name of these restaurants hint at the history of the founding Vo family: 1979 was the year members immigrated to the United States from Vietnam. Starting first at the Virginia Beach Boulevard location, the family opened an eatery that gained fans and since has been expanded to four other sites. At each, the specialty is *pho,* a revered dish in the Vos's homeland. It's a brothy soup with rice noodles, served steaming hot, with sides of fresh basil, jalapeño slices, a tangle of crunchy bean sprouts and fat, juicy wedges of lime. The meat options for the soup are many: round steak, brisket, tripe (the edible meat from a cow's stomach), flank steak, soft tendon, and chicken. You can choose small or large portions, but be careful: The former is about the size of an adult's head. The star of the dish is the aromatic broth, which is long-simmered with cinnamon, cloves, star anise and ginger. It's spicy but not hot, seasoned but not salty. The waitstaff is glad to help novices maneuver the dish, explaining how to add the accompaniments and offering a warning to go easy on the hot sauce until you know what you're doing. **Additional locations:** 723 W. 21st St., Norfolk, VA 23517; (757) 333-4266; 12551 Jefferson Ave., Ste. 213, Newport News, VA 23602; (757) 877-1213; 4816 Virginia Beach Blvd., Virginia Beach, VA 23462; (757) 687-7844; 507 Hilltop Plaza, Virginia Beach, VA 23454; (757) 644-6799.

The Public House, 1112 Colley Ave., Norfolk, VA 23517; (757) 227-9064; publichouseeats.com; Casual American; $$. The sign above the door to this bar in Norfolk's Ghent section says Victuals and Libations. That's a fancy way of saying "food" and "drink," but this gastropub is anything but fancy. It's a place with an inviting bar and a welcoming staff that will help you pronounce "quinoa" if you're having trouble with the word. The look of the menu sets the tone, with funky typography that resembles old-time newspaper ads and playful reminders such as: "Public House Rule 4: Remember, friends don't let friends drunk dial." Some of the cocktails, including beer-based ones, feature bitters made by owner Karl Dornemann. The Norfolkhattan, for instance, is a play on a traditional Manhattan that combines root and orange bitters with bourbon. Appetizers are a mix of the indulgent— duck-fat fries and the slightly less so tempura-treated asparagus fries. Entree favorites for lunch and dinner include the Blue Collar Mac and Cheese, with its base of cheddar and mozzarella, and the White Collar version, with more upscale goat cheese, Black Diamond white cheddar, and fontina. For those late evenings, a welcome after-midnight portion of the menu lets you embrace some victuals as well as libations.

River Stone Chophouse, 8032 Harbour View Blvd., Suffolk, VA 23435; (757) 638-7990; riverstonechophouse.com; Steaks; $$$$. This premier restaurant, from the team that brought the stellar **Vintage Tavern** (p. 90) to Suffolk, pampers its guests from the moment they arrive at the impressive Arts-and-Crafts-style building. The interior is spacious and romantic, with much attention paid to table placement so each feels private and intimate. A stone fireplace warms the interior on cool evenings, and a patio lets cigar smokers light up on the premises. It's the kind of place that will reserve a dish for customers if they mention that it's a favorite while making reservations. And it's that brand of service that has won this restaurant a loyal local fan base. The raw bar is impressive, often featuring local seafood, such as prized Sewansecott oysters from the state's Eastern Shore. The steaks are the heart of the entree menu, and the rib eye, aged for at least 28 days, has a somewhat nutty, deep flavor and dissolves in your mouth. The other steak offerings are traditional—filets,

New York strips, Kansas City strips, and porterhouses—and the cuts are generous. The menu also features lamb, chicken, and some seafood options, but beef is the way to go. Our favorite sides, a five-cheese macaroni and cheese and sherry-flavored mushrooms, pack enough punch to share plate space with the sought-after steaks.

The Route 58 Delicatessen, 4000 Virginia Beach Blvd., Loehmann's Plaza, Ste. 156, Virginia Beach, VA 23452; (757) 226-8493; 58deli.com; Jewish Delicatessen; $$. It's as though the iconic Stage Door Deli in New York City touched down in Tidewater, and that's just how owner Jeff Goldberg planned it. Just inside the door of the storefront shop, guests are wowed by a revolving case filled with mile-high pies and cakes, most imported from New York City. Waitresses zoom around carrying plates heaped with all the requisite deli food—bagels, matzo ball soup, smoked fish platters, brisket, knishes—and sporting T-shirts that say, "If you finish, we made a mistake." That sets the tone for a super-sized culinary adventure, just like up north. Try the Super Reuben, nearly 5 inches tall, stuffed with house-cooked corned beef and served with a whole pickle. The cook doesn't weigh the meat, but Goldberg estimates that each sandwich tips the scales at about a pound to a pound and a half. There also are authentic Brooklyn egg creams. While you wait, read Jeff's report cards, which are posted on the walls and provide proof that elementary-school antics can be overcome.

Salacia, 3001 Atlantic Ave., Virginia Beach, VA 23451; (757) 213-3473; salaciavb.com; Seafood/Steaks; $$$$. This is a space where small children aren't allowed and where grown-ups come to be pampered. Named for the goddess of saltwater, this restaurant is next door to Catch31 on the first floor of the Atlantic-side Hilton Hotel. While Catch31 is spacious and teems with activity, Salacia is intimate and embraces its guests like a warm beach towel after a chilly ocean swim. A fireplace, ringed in blue tiles, highlights a wall of wood, and the dark blue–tinted glass on another wall keeps the atmosphere cozy. The round tables are preset in cobalt blue and white, and armrests enhance the comfortable chairs. Fish is the specialty, with offerings such as lobster, salmon, and mahimahi, but steaks, found under the "Butcher's Cut" portion of the menu, share center stage. A couple of surf-and-turf options let you try both. Fries, baked potatoes, and vegetables are available on the side. Wine and beer can quench your thirst, and an extensive cocktail and martini list lets you partake of such daring libations as a Kiwi Kiss, a gin-based drink flavored by apple schnapps and its namesake fruit. Go ahead—we're all adults here.

SeaSide Restaurant, 201 Wilder Ave., Colonial Beach, VA 22443; (804) 224-2410; seaside-va.com; French/Thai; $$. Colonial Beach, a river town on the shores of the Potomac, looks like a corn dog–and–fish taco kind of place. Yet, it's home to this tiny eatery that specializes in French and Thai dishes. How'd that happen? A few years back, the owners, Thailand natives, wanted to introduce their homeland's food to the town, but few who lived there knew what the cuisine offered. Locals seemed somewhat familiar with French, and the chef knew both, so the owners offered both. Now, the restaurant's a popular spot for townspeople and Northern Virginia foodies who don't mind driving for a few miles to get here. Dishes such as the *pla kra prow* marry local ingredients with Thai techniques. The flounder is fried whole and then spiced with chiles, basil, bell peppers, and topped with a basil sauce. Francophiles might start with shrimp bisque or escargots served with asparagus before moving on to coq au vin or ahi tuna loin au poivre, flavors from near and far.

Six Little Bar Bistro, 6 E. Mellen St., Hampton, VA 23663; (757) 722-1466; littlebarbistro.com; Eclectic; $$–$$$. Here's a hip little joint on a quaint little seaside street lined with antique shops and emporiums. The bistro's a bit hard to spot, as there's no sign out front and the top of the brick building says only "Fuller Building 1918." Inside, a wood bar runs the length of one side of the restaurant, while tables line the other. Tiers of upturned scotches and whiskeys above the bar attest to the serious attention to spirits, as does the long list of specialty cocktails. The vibe is ultra-casual and the food ultra-eclectic. It's all about small plates and nibbles, and the menu is organized by "hot" or "cold." Go as light as edamame with smoked sea salt and lemon or lump crab and smoked gouda–stuffed jalapenos. More substantial appetites are sated with a pair of Cuban pulled-pork sliders, served with a side of slightly sweet carrot slaw and a tiny bottle of Tabasco on the plate. While waiting for your order, the snarky cocktail menu makes good reading. The last item: Shut the Hell Up and Go Home. It's a glass of water, and it's on the house.

Small's Smokehouse and Oyster Bar, 2700 Hampton Blvd., Norfolk, VA 23517; (757) 626-3440; smallsodu.com; Barbecue/Seafood; $–$$. Guests feel right at home at this barbecue-and-seafood place, and that's just the way owners John Small III and his son Logan want it. They've opened a restaurant on the same street where John's grandfather once ran a hardware store, and Grandpa Small, decked out in his high school football gear, can be seen in a photo on one of the coral-colored walls. That's just one of the homey touches found here. The menu highlights two local favorites, oysters and other seafood that come primarily from the state's Eastern Shore, and vinegar-based barbecue smoked exquisitely by Chef Kenny Anthony. The bivalves can be ordered on the half shell or steamed, and the former swim in their own "liquor" while the latter come out slightly firm from the heat. The barbecue, smoked and seasoned expertly, gets its kick from its North Carolina–style vinegary sauce. Sides such as onion rings and fries complement a meal, and the collards forgo the usual pork addition in favor of chicken. A small, square-shaped bar offers a communal spot to grab a drink, and students from nearby Old Dominion University sometimes camp out there.

Smoke, 10900 Warwick Blvd., Newport News, VA 23601; (757) 595-4320; smokenn.com; Barbecue; $–$$. Big 'ol smoker out back with a stoking shovel? Check. Smoky aroma in the dining room? Check. Friendlier-than-family servers? Check. It seems that Smoke should be out in the country somewhere, but it's plopped down in front of a shopping center in the 'burbs. The easiest way to find it is to follow your nose. The respectable menu includes all the requisite barbecue items—pulled pork and chicken sandwiches, racks of baby back ribs and such. The place earns extra stars for offering smoked meat loaf, sliced beef brisket, and beef short ribs, which are not always found in barbecue joints. The barbecue is North Carolina–style, slow-smoked and seasoned with a vinegar-pepper sauce. It's put to good use on sandwiches, platters, and even nachos. Don't miss the Smoke Belly, with its thick, Asian-spiced, smoked and cured slices of meat fanned out atop a light cucumber salad. It's an appetizer that leaves room for the main event. And check the specials board for interesting additions, such as panko-fried frogs' legs.

Smoked From Above, 3376 Princess Anne Rd., Ste. 201, Virginia Beach, VA 23456; (757) 499-4959; smokedfromabovebbq.com; Barbecue; $. After opening their first location in 2005, Tidewater natives Lee and Michelle Holland smoked the competition in a regional rib contest and have defended their title ever since. These veterans of the national competitive barbecue circuit start with whole pecan logs loaded into a Southern Pride smoker. The racks, about 64 at a time, get a custom dry rub and are smoked from 2½ to 4 hours. Then, they're finished in a convection oven with a slightly sweet sauce. The Hollands do this about four times a week to keep up with demand for the restaurant's most popular dish, alongside its barbecue. The latter comes two ways: either with beef or chicken and the slightly sweet house sauce or with pulled pork finished classic Carolina-style, with a pepper-spiked vinegar. Get the latter on a sandwich dressed with coleslaw, and you'll get a bite of barbecue heaven. Around here, we don't even care if it's from Eastern Carolina. It's just plain good.

Som Bao Cafe, 2476 Nimmo Pkwy., Virginia Beach, VA 23456; (757) 430-1066; sombaocafe.com; Laotian/Thai; $$. This 11-table cafe—filled with the scent of kaffir leaves, basil, and spice—is named for Somdee and Bao Phoutasen, who secreted their family out of Communist Laos nearly 40 years ago. The restaurant is their children's way of honoring their parents. The menu is a carefully curated collection of authentic Laotian dishes. First-timers might want to start with *thom khem*—pork, chicken, or beef with a hard-boiled egg in a broth that has the cuisine's signature combination of tang, sweet, and spice. Or experience the Lao Platter, a feast for two featuring whole tilapia in a salty-savory broth; Laos *larb,* a heap of tangy-spicy minced chicken laced with the exotic flavor of kaffir leaves; and Lao jerky, thin slices of dried, marinated beef with no heat at all. Each platter comes with a small dish of slow-roasted chile sauce, a smoky, searing condiment made by Bao and well known in the local Laotian community. On the side is a woven basket filled with sticky rice. To go totally Laotian, pinch off a walnut-sized hunk of rice, dip it into Bao's sauce and use it as a utensil to eat the meal.

Someplace Different, 213 Virginia St., Urbanna, VA 23175; (804) 758-8000; pine3.info; on Facebook; Barbecue; $$. Urbanna is famed for its oyster fest, but now that this quirky eatery has moved from a soybean field on the outskirts of town to town proper, Urbanna's getting kudos for 'cue. We fairly fainted when Dan Gill, the owner, pitmaster, raconteur, ice cream maker, and scribe, opened a bread warmer drawer to reveal neat racks of mahogany baby back ribs seasoned and smoked right on the premises. There's pit smoked chicken, roast beef, and tri-tip, too. That all goes just right with the joint's signature jalapeño hoe cakes sweetened with molasses and a side of Gill's stories about everything from how he came to be a cook to a treatise on umami. Save room for the creamiest ice cream and the dreamiest flavors—grasshopper, chile, and butter pecan. If you're anywhere near here, don't miss this one.

Sonoma Wine Bar & Bistro, 189 Central Park Ave., Virginia Beach, VA 23462; (757) 490-9463; sonomatowncenter.com; European; $$$. This restaurant has become a popular lunch spot for those who work nearby and a dinner destination for those taking in a show or shopping in the Town Center of the state's largest city. Try for a table by the window—the one in the back corner is especially nice—or one of the cushy seats by the fireplace. Or opt for outdoor seats, with their close-up view of one of the nearby fountains. As the restaurant's name implies, wine is a signature here. More than 70 varieties are available by the glass, and there's a cozy bar to imbibe at. But don't overlook the food. The spinach salad balances the bitterness of endive with candied walnuts, currants and Granny Smith apples. Seafood and steaks are abundant on the often-changing entree menu. Molecular gastronomy is behind the Turtle Parfait, a dessert that is almost too beautiful to eat. But you'll dive in once you get a whiff of the chocolate ganache concoction, which features white chocolate, cream spiced with cognac, cloves and cinnamon, caramelized pecans, and coffee caviar.

Swan Terrace, 5641 Indian River Rd., Virginia Beach 23464; (757) 366-5777; foundersinn.com; Seafood/Steaks; $$$. Diners find a timeless elegance here, whether enjoying lunch or dinner from ornate wooden chairs by the indoor fireplace or alfresco on the terrace. The sunken dining room offers views of the open kitchen and of the courtyard, where you can marvel at the manicured lawns and gardens of Regent University. If you're lucky, you'll catch a glimpse of the restaurant's namesake waterfowl in the nearby lake. The restaurant is located in the Founders Inn and Spa, part of evangelist Pat Robertson's Christian Broadcasting Network, but long gone are the days when alcohol wasn't served. Executive Chef Scott Simpson relies on local ingredients for a menu that's upscale without being fussy. The Southern shrimp cocktail offers a surprise: twin fried green tomatoes and a Cajun remoulade sauce join the jumbo shrimp on the platter. The entrees change with the season, but making regular appearances are such Tidewater specialties as peanuts, which have shown up in a pesto paired with lamb chops. On the first Monday of each month, the chef offers Mouth Watering Mondays, a prix-fixe menu that lets him experiment with dishes such as an achingly tender braised American Wagyu short rib served over potato hash with fried parsnips. The communal seating for the monthly events is limited, and the tastings are popular, so make reservations well in advance.

Tides Inn Market, 200 N. Irving Ave., Colonial Beach, VA 22443; (804) 214-9352; on Facebook; American; $. All day, nearly every day, the offerings change at this gourmet bakery and sandwich shop in Colonial Beach, a throwback of a place with a beach-y, small-town vibe. Arrive in the morning, and a plate of blueberry scones and tall pound cakes might tempt from the glass showcase. Return at lunch to find lemon chess pie and a basket of freshly baked rustic loaves on the counter. The chalkboard menu always includes some sort of fresh, locally sourced salad, quiche, and wraps. Somehow, owner Caitlin Davis does all the baking, cooking, cashiering, and serving. She even writes the menu on the chalkboard in curlicue script, and she does it all with a smile. The Culinary Institute of America–trained baker also offers occasional baking classes and weekend wine-and-tapas nights featuring cheeses and salamis, as well as a respectable selection of beers. Get your order to go and eat it on the Potomac River beach, just a few blocks away, or in the charming dining room, with its exposed rafters and whitewashed farmhouse table. The dining room, circa 1906, was originally the garage of the adjacent Tides Inn Bed & Breakfast, run by Meghan Davis, Caitlin's mom.

Trilogy Bistro, 101 Granby St., Norfolk, VA 23510; (757) 961-0896; trilogynorfolk.com; Tapas; $–$$. Crab cakes and fried green tomatoes are as common in Tidewater as pesky mosquitoes on twilight nights, but that doesn't mean they're all created equal. Chef Todd Leutner, who with Vincent Ranhorn has opened this and other area restaurants, has elevated both dishes beyond the frequently seen run-of-the-mill versions. Those two local specialties are centerpieces of a tapas menu that includes a Bloody Mary flank steak, an Indian-style pork loin, and a jumbo crab-filled shrimp. The crab cakes come alive with a mango-basil gastrique and horseradish-bacon aioli that provide equal doses of sweetness and saltiness. The biscotti-encrusted green tomatoes are delicately fried and topped with a cream cheese mousse, corn salsa, and scallion aioli. The martini list is long and includes one, The Isabel 9/18/03, that has turned a natural disaster, the 2003 hurricane that hammered the region, into a refreshing mix of rum, cranberry juice, and a splash of lime. The setting for all this goodness is the first floor of the Virginia Club in a historic former downtown bank building. The dining room feels rich, with ample wood and leather, and its high ceilings offer an air of openness. Floor-to-ceiling wine storage gives diners something to gawk at while they await their next dish.

Landmarks

Aldo's Ristorante, La Promenade Shopping Center, 1860 Laskin Rd., Virginia Beach, VA 23454; (757) 491-1111; aldosvb.com; Northern Italian; $$. The thoughtfully decorated dining room—with its palm trees, tiled floors, a flaming brick oven in the open kitchen—sets the mood for the award-winning fare at Aldo's, an upscale Italian restaurant just a few miles from the Virginia Beach oceanfront resort strip. Despite the elegant surroundings and well-heeled clientele, you can enjoy a dinner as simple as an authentic Caesar salad, a modestly priced pizza topped with house-made mozzarella and always-fresh arugula or jet-set it with a hand-cut filet topped with a cognac-peppercorn sauce. In-the-know locals love the veal chop, split and stuffed with spinach and mozzarella. It's wildly popular, usually available, but never on the printed menu. In the winter, try the hot buttered rum, made with real butter and dark rum. It's like cashmere in a glass. Get one, and join the locals crowding around the piano bar Fri and Sat nights.

Baja Restaurant, 3701 S. Sandpiper Rd., Virginia Beach, VA; (757) 426-7748; facebook.com/baja.sandbridge; Casual American/ Mexican; $$. The Baja, which is pushing 40, has the feel of a laid-back beachcomber. It's the southernmost bar and eatery on the Virginia seaboard, situated just before a 15-mile stretch of protected coastline that leads to the North Carolina border, where a fence—no kidding—juts out into the ocean. Surrounded by a neighborhood of beach houses built on stilts, this locals' favorite sits on the bank of Back Bay, and it's a sensational spot to cool off and watch the sunset. Signature dishes include she-crab soup, Bill's Bachos, classic nachos made with blue crab and chorizo, blackened scallop pasta, and seafood au gratin. Seafood, burgers, skirt steak, they've got you covered. When picking a table, don't stop at the dining room. Out back are an expansive covered deck and a grassy area, complete with waterfront tiki hut. Grab a chilly beer or a margarita and get set for a sunset. But note that in January, when the beach is deserted, the crew closes down the place for the month.

Belvedere Coffee Shop, 3601 Atlantic Ave., Virginia Beach, VA 23451; (757) 425-0613; belvederebeachresort.com/coffee-shop; Casual American; $. This classic breakfast-and-lunch-only diner, attached to its namesake oceanfront hotel, is hyper-local; many Virginia Beach residents who live away from the seaside are unaware of its home-cooked fare. Here, white-aproned cooks scratch spatulas across the flat-top griddle, while guests sit on spinning stools with backrests, sip coffee and watch from the nine-seat counter. Across the narrow aisle are five booths. There's a cash register at one end of the counter, and two walls of windows with a view of the beach and boardwalk. That's pretty much it, except for the line that forms outside most days in the summer and most weekends in the off-season. It's worth the wait. A favorite breakfast dish is the biscuits and gravy—twin biscuits, split, and covered in chunky, white, slightly spicy sausage gravy flecked with pepper. At lunch, order the patty melt, a quarter-pound burger topped with fried onions and swiss cheese on rye, toasted right on the griddle. Beware: Parking can be difficult during the summer tourist season.

Cafe Europa, 319 High St., Portsmouth 23704; (757) 399-6652; thecafeeuropa.com; French/Italian; $$$. You'll want to steal a kiss, or at least hold hands, in this intimate, elegant restaurant in the downtown historic district of Olde Towne Portsmouth, one of the nation's oldest neighborhoods. Towering flower arrangements, statuary, low lights, soaring dark-wood paneling, and exposed brick evoke the atmosphere of centuries-old European eateries. Tables are arranged in a series of rooms. Service is like a whisper, the pace unhurried, European-style. Co-owner Veronique Simko greets guests at the door with her French accent, while her husband, Mike, a former soccer star in Communist Czechoslovakia, turns out dishes that include tomato-gin bisque, duck with plums, and cinnamon-and-lobster ravioli.

Cellars Restaurant, 4001 Church Point Rd., Virginia Beach, VA 23455; (757) 460-2210; thecellarsvb.com; Neo-Southern; $$$. For sea-level dwellers, a basement in itself is a remarkable thing. But hidden beneath the impeccably restored Church Point Manor bed-and-breakfast awaits a genie bottle of a restaurant and lounge. Descend a narrow set of brick steps, the portal to the cellar dining room, and you'll find a cool and intimate space with low ceilings and brick walls and arches, awash in amber light. Beyond that, discover the six-seat, copper-topped bar, where a shallow gas fireplace flickers in the background. And beyond even that, through a narrow, curtained doorway, is yet another hidden chamber, this one rimmed with plush, pillow-strewn banquettes, a couple of small tables and, get this, a real wood-burning fireplace. Finding Cellars is like finding a secret garden, and it's the perfect setting for the fare, Southern favorites prepared with a French touch. The beef carpaccio is topped with truffle oil, arugula, Parmesan, and a perfectly poached quail egg; the fondue changes weekly. Tender cedar planked salmon comes with beluga lentils, crème fraîche, and caviar. Once a beacon, the manor house is now surrounded by a neighborhood of upscale houses and is a bit hard to find. Make the effort. It's worth it.

Charles City Tavern, 9220 John Tyler Memorial Hwy. (Va. Route 5), Charles City, VA 23030; (804) 829-5004; charlescitytavern .com; Neo-Southern/Seafood; $$$. Virginia Route 5, one of the state's official scenic byways, winds along the north bank of the James River past a necklace of Colonial plantations—Shirley, Sherwood Forest, Edgewood, and Evelynton—each open for public tours, places where you can get a taste of the genteel life in old-time Virginia. This chef-owned tavern, a century-old farmhouse turned restaurant, provides a relaxed historic setting, a perfect respite from all that touring. For the main course, linger over an appetizer of pecan-crusted baked brie. For dinner, try the braised heritage pork belly with a smoked Granny Smith apple gastrique, a marriage of two very Virginia flavors. The bourbon-pecan bread pudding with Jack Daniel's butter glaze has won regional honors. The screened-in dining porches face fields that stretch into the horizon, and the charming gardens are planted with iris, azaleas, and jasmine. Stately pecan, oak, and beech trees provide shade. Those porches recently won top honors from *Southern Living* magazine as one of the best places in the country to eat a crab cake on a porch. The tavern's version, chock full of crabmeat, is served with a ragout of sweet corn and Virginia ham.

Coastal Grill, 427 N. Great Neck Rd., Virginia Beach, VA 23454; (757) 496-3348; on Facebook; Seafood; $$. It would be easy to miss this place. The eatery is 3 miles from the oceanfront beaches, and the outside is as unpretentious as the name. Yet Coastal Grill has earned accolades for its seafood for more than two decades. It has been featured in *Esquire* and has won top honors locally for its fried soft-shell crabs and scallops. The preparation is old-school Tidewater. It's the best ingredients and the rapt attention of the chefs that assure perfection. Every. Single. Time. But Chef Jerry Bryan's restaurant is loved by locals as much for those dishes as for the daily blackboard specials, which always include a school of fresh caught fish prepared in inventive ways. The menu is rounded out with duck, lamb, and beef dishes. The famous roasted acorn squash side dish is not to be missed—except in March, when it's not offered. It's served Southern-style with a generous topping of brown sugar and butter. The place goes through about 600 bushels a year.

Coles Point Tavern, 850 Salisbury Park Rd., Coles Point, VA 22442; (804) 472-3856; colespointtavern.com; American; $. When heading to this Northern Neck outpost, keep the faith. The tavern, circa 1954, does exist, pretty much as it always has, a rambling wooden building perched over the Potomac River. It's on the way to nowhere else, so you gotta plan it. But the place is not for everyone. People who like eating on old fishing piers where locals pass time at the bar will like this spot, with its tongue-in-groove pine paneling and dining on the decks. But the way cool thing about Coles Point is that the parking lot is in Virginia, while the tavern is just past the shoreline where Virginia cedes its territory to Maryland. That means that certain types of gambling that Virginians hold no cotton to are fair game in the tavern. Plus, it also operates as a private, carry-out liquor store, another no-no in the commonwealth. The menu is standard bar fare—burgers, big old salads, and subs. But there's also some mighty fine seafood, such as the Ragged Point fish sub, made with either tilapia or rockfish, depending on the catch. When we ordered a crab-cake sandwich, the barman said, "That crab was swimming this morning." The cook formed it, smashed it down on a flattop grill, and served it up slightly browned. Chock full of shellfish, it's one of the best around. In the summer, bands play in the back room, and when the dance floor's full, the whole place sways.

Croc's 19th Street Bistro, 620 19th St., Virginia Beach, VA 23451; (757) 428-5444; crocs19thstreetbistro.com; American/ Mediterranean/Middle Eastern; $$. If you've got a green sensibility, then Croc's is your spot. It's the state's first certified "Virginia Green" restaurant, and the owners host a seasonal farmers' market in the parking lot. If you've got a sense of humor, Croc's also is your spot. Consider the Fizzcal Cliff reduced-price bar menu that was rolled out, well, you can guess when. Or the hugely popular Sunday "Drag Yourself to Brunch" shows. But if you

THE POWER OF THE CRUSH

There's an odd affliction among veteran barkeeps at **Waterman's Surfside Grille** at 415 Atlantic Ave. at the Virginia Beach oceanfront. After a few months behind the bar, the right arm grows stronger than the left. The cause: the Crush, Waterman's signature line of fresh-squeezed citrus cocktails. In a single year, bartenders make a half-million or more crushes. If they were balanced along the rail of the Chesapeake Bay Bridge-Tunnel, the cups would stretch from one end of the 17.6-mile span to the other. "It's just crazy; it's absolutely insane," says Waterman's co-owner Mike Standing.

The cocktail has inspired its own line of T-shirts and glassware, and a summer kickoff party called Crush Fest, which each April raises funds for local charities. Although there are imposters, Waterman's Crushes brim with sass and citrus. The recipe is a straightforward blend of the juice of one whole fresh orange or grapefruit with flavored vodka, orange liqueur, and a splash of Sprite. That's served over crushed ice in a 16-ounce plastic souvenir cup bearing the original Orange Crush logo. Bartenders make them in five seconds flat.

like fresh, eclectic food, Croc's is also your spot. The philosophy is hard-core locavore. The chef harvests dinner produce from the lush garden out back, supplements it with locally sourced provisions and turns out Middle Eastern food— pitas, hummus, and *kefta* skewers—and a good smattering of seafood dishes—think blackened tuna with the signature five-pepper sauce. For landlubbers, a standout is the Virginia pork chili verde, local pork, tomatoes, and peppers served over stone-ground grits with salsa. There's more. If you like the nightlife, Croc's is again your spot, with an ultra-local crowd, live music on the weekend, and an inventive cocktail list. Beet martini, anyone?

Doumar's Cones & Barbecue, 1919 Monticello Ave., Norfolk, VA 23517; (757) 627-4163; doumars.com; Barbecue/Ice Cream; $. This is the real deal: a 1950s-style drive-in. The best way to visit: a convertible, preferably a '57 T-bird, with the top down. Then the tough part: Do you park outside and wait for your order to be brought car-side, or do you venture into the quintessential diner with its black-and-white tiled floor and red vinyl barstools? Either way, it's a trip, but only on the inside will you get to see history being made—and take in the enticing aroma. It's there that you can watch as vanilla, sugar, flour, milk, and eggs become first batter, then waffles and finally ice cream cones. The warm waffles are hand-wrapped around a wooden dowel that creates a perfect shape to hold the cold treat. Legend has it that founder Abe Doumar made the world's first waffle cone at the 1904 St. Louis World's Fair. A year later, he came up with the waffle machine that his descendants still use today. The place also is known for barbecue sandwiches stuffed with pork, either minced or sliced, and you can't go wrong with either choice. Standard breakfast options are available, as are burgers, fries, onion rings, shakes, and other diner fare. And who knows, you might just run into the *Diners, Drive-ins and Dives* guy himself. Yup, Guy Fieri has visited—twice!

Fred's Restaurant, 107 S. Main St., Franklin, VA 23851; (757) 562-2919; gotofreds.com; Casual American; $. Franklin, located 40 miles from downtown Norfolk where suburbia has long given way to flat expanses of farmland, is the type of small town that still hosts its own Christmas parade every year, complete with Santa atop a fire truck. Fred's is another Franklin tradition, serving locals standard American fare for nearly 50 years. It's the kind of place where geezers gather at the bar for a beer in the afternoon and newcomers merit a sec-

ond look. But no worries, the natives are friendly and the food fast and filling. The Bowl-o-Breakfast—two eggs, grits, sausage gravy, and potatoes in a bowl topped with cheese—will fuel you clear to dinner. Or try the Brunswick stew, a native dish that's chock full of chicken and veggies. Wash it all down with sweet iced tea, or sweet-sweet iced tea. The place makes both kinds, about 25 gallons a day. Before leaving, check out the plaque on the wall that marks the high-water level following Hurricane Floyd in 1999, when all of downtown all but disappeared under floodwaters.

Greenies, 96 W. Ocean View Ave., Norfolk, VA 23503; (757) 480-1210; greeniesoceanview.com; Casual American; $. First know this: Greenies isn't as rough as it looks. Located in the heart of Norfolk's Ocean View section (which, oddly, hugs the Chesapeake Bay beaches with not one iota of ocean to view), this was once such a rough-and-tumble joint that nice folks stayed away. But as the area slowly morphs into a kinder, gentler place, roughnecks and rednecks and others mingle peacefully in the sun on the big bay-front deck. A big draw is the bargain-priced steamed shrimp, always on special, but the burgers also have quite a few fans. At night, the vibe is more bar than restaurant, and the crowd tilts toward the edgier side.

Il Giardino Ristorante, 910 Atlantic Ave., Virginia Beach, VA 23451; (757) 422-6464; ilgiardino.com; Italian; $$–$$$. You'll find more than a taste of Italy at this restaurant near the oceanfront. There's an actual piece of the Old World itself. The centerpiece of this dining space is a wood-burning stove brought back from Florence by co-owner Tony Gargiulo. That sets the tone for an authentic experience. The dining room is refined but casual, with ficus trees offering a bit of nature and tiny lights from the high ceilings providing a romantic twinkle. The bar offers more seating and, when tourist traffic is heavy, guests without reservations often end up there. A favorite dish is the *pollo alla sorrentina,* a juicy chicken breast combined with spinach, zucchini, prosciutto, and mozzarella that blends well with its side of linguine. Prosciutto shows up in two other signature offerings—the *capellini piselli e prosciutto,* which melds a tomato cream sauce with

THE TALE OF THREE CHICKENS

Giant roosters and an immense fry pan. Spot one of these on the roadside, and you'll have found some of the area's finest fried chicken. Each month, the state's largest newspaper holds food contests for various regional fare, and this trio of landmark eateries is always in the running for top fried chicken honors:

Golden Skillet, *3332 Victory Blvd., Portsmouth, VA 23701; (757) 487-7065; and 1130 Armory Dr., Franklin, VA 23851; (757) 562-2255.* "Tender as Quail! Tasty as Pheasant!" That's the slogan for Golden Skillet's fried chicken, a Virginia original that was first served in 1964 at the fancy Thalhimers department store tearoom in downtown Richmond. The chicken is brined in a salt and herb mixture before it's breaded and fried to a slight crunch in 100 percent peanut oil. The chain, with its signature skillet sign, eventually grew to 221 restaurants, but the take-out only Portsmouth and Franklin locations are all that's left here.

Moseberth's Fried Chicken, *1505 Airline Blvd., Portsmouth, VA 23707; (757) 393-1721; moseberths.com.* An 8-foot-tall rooster is perched atop this eatery, where the Moseberth family first cranked up

mushrooms and angel-hair pasta, and the *vitello rotini,* with its white wine sauce. Dessert is a treat visually as well as gastronomically, as the waitstaff cuts giant slices of house specials such as dense chocolate cake and New York cheesecake from an island and, if you're fortunate, brings them to you.

The Inn at Montross, 21 Polk St., Montross, VA 22520; (804) 493-8624; theinnatmontross.com; Neo-Southern; $$$. Here's a specimen of a Virginia specialty: a grand, old historic house turned into an inn and dining room, one of many such places where you can eat and imbibe on the very same spot the Colonials did. There's plenty of the fryers more than 70 years ago. Moseberth's recipe—unchanged for three generations—is simple, but there's always a line at the take-out counter. The chicken is coated in flour, seasoned with salt and pepper, and then fried to a moderate crunch in a mix of canola and corn oil.

Pollard's Chicken, *3033 Ballentine Blvd., Norfolk, VA 23509; (757) 855-7864; pollardschicken.com for other locations.* This fried-chicken place—opened more than 40 years ago when Betty Pollard persuaded her sons to open a fried chicken joint rather than a gas station—is the baby of the local bunch. Today, there are eight locations in Virginia Beach, Chesapeake, and in Norfolk, where a gigantic giant rooster rules the roost. At Pollard's, the breading on the bird is specially made by a flour mill, and the chicken is fried to an assertive crunch in pure vegetable oil with no trans fats.

Some proud Virginians claim that fried chicken was invented in the commonwealth. No need to go to fisticuffs over it. We're just saying that we fry up some mighty fine bird.

history on the Northern Neck of Virginia, where this inn is located; it's the birthplace of three presidents—George Washington, James Monroe, and James Madison—and also Robert E. Lee, a military leader of the Confederacy. The inn's foundation dates to the 1600s, and a tavern stood on this spot in the 17th century. The current structure, built in 1800, serves as a bed and breakfast with Colonial-style furnishings. The small bar and dining room opens on weekends for some of the Northern Neck's most upscale dining. Neo-Southern favorites include the jumbo sea scallops and grits, succulent seafood served atop stone-ground cakes with Granny Smith salsa and bacon. The beef selections change weekly, but it's from cattle raised just 20 miles up the road on land that was once part of the Monroe estate. Crab Cristo is a crab-salad sandwich deep-fried and served with blueberry jam. Don't forget to have a cocktail, served in mason jars with handles. When you're turning off the shimmering blacktop on a summer day, a strawberry mimosa would be a true friend.

Jade Villa, 353 Independence Blvd., Virginia Beach, VA 23462; (757) 473-2228; jadevillavirginiabeach.com; Chinese/Cantonese; **$$.** Walk into the Jade Villa and the staff instantly and unabashedly tags you as a beginner or experienced. Depending on the verdict, you might be presented with a menu of Americanized Chinese chow meins, lo meins, and shrimp with lobster sauce. Insist instead on the other menu, filled with authentic Cantonese specialties such as the house Cold Combination Platter with jellyfish, beef, cuttlefish and tender, savory boneless pig knuckle, or sliced conch, duck tongue, and tripe. On Sunday, the queue at the door starts building early for the dim sum service, small sweet and savory dishes offered on carts and ranging from sticky rice in lotus leaves to stuffed black mushrooms to eggplant stuffed with shrimp paste. Jade Villa's atmosphere seems a bit harsh, with its office-like lighting and no-frills furnishings. One mouthful and that won't matter a bit.

Kyushu Japanese Restaurant, 400 Newtown Rd., Virginia Beach, VA 23462; (757) 490-1177; kyushujap.com; Japanese; **$$.** Owner Mitsunori Ebigasako opened his place more than 20 years ago when sushi was as rare as a tidal wave in Tidewater. Until recently,

"Ebi's," as the locals call it, had none of the polish and gleam of the legions of newbie sushi bars, but recent renovations have it following suit. Thankfully, the food retains all the flavor of an authentic Japanese sushi bar and Ebi always seems to be

behind the sushi counter, wielding his knife and constructing artful rolls and eye-popping platters of the freshest seafood, both local and imported. Tidewater, home to several military installations, has a sort of built-in meter for whether sushi bars make the grade. Since so many residents have done duty overseas, when a sushi bar stays full of military, as Ebi's does, it's got to be good. He's even named a roll in honor of his uniformed clientele. The Navy Roll—raw white fish with *konbu* rolled in rice and seaweed. The popular Mermaid Roll keeps sushi newbies happy with wasabi-tinged rice and tempura shrimp, salmon, and crab laid end-to-end with a smattering of *tobiko* (flying-fish roe) rolled up and then topped with thinly sliced avocado and scallions. True to its name, the tail of a tempura shrimp forms the tail of the mermaid.

Lynnhaven Fish House, 2350 Starfish Rd., Virginia Beach, VA 23451; (757) 481-0003; lynnhavenfishhouse.net; Seafood; $$$. This casually elegant restaurant really is part of a fishing pier, perched over the Chesapeake Bay within sight of the Chesapeake Bay Bridge-Tunnel. Owned by the Kyrus family, the fish house has won numerous awards for its seafood dishes and service. Throughout 30-plus years, the restaurant has cultivated a following of locals and tourists alike, who crave the jumbo-sized hush puppies. At lunch, try the flounder sandwich, a generous portion of hot flatfish atop a Kaiser roll with romaine lettuce, a Jupiter-size slice of organic tomato and a lemon wedge with a stack of steak fries—crispy and brown—on the side. Start dinner with she-crab soup, rated one of the top in the region, and move on to the award-winning fried oysters. They're as good as they get.

The Monastery, 443 Granby St., Norfolk, VA 23510; (757) 625-8193; 443granby.com; European; $$$. The heavy wooden doors to this longtime downtown mainstay feel Old World, and that atmosphere continues as you enter the dining room. It's at first a visual experience, with dim lighting that sets a romantic mood, statuary that reminds you of a European garden and stained-glass windows that dot the exposed brick walls. And then your nose kicks into action, picking up the scent of freshly baked bread or the pungent strains of sauerkraut that punctuate some of the signature dishes. The bar is front and center, and a refined glass of wine or Champagne seems like the obvious drink choice. The restaurant is the second with this name opened by Anna and Adolf Jerabek since they fled Communist Czechoslovakia in 1967. They landed in New York City, where they set up their first Monastery on the city's West Side. In the early 1980s, they came to Virginia, where they offer goulashes, wiener schnitzel, bratwurst, and other dishes from their home continent. The Black Forest cake is an appropriate, and tasty, way to complete your visit.

Pierce's Pitt Bar-B-Que, 447 E. Rochambeau Dr., Williamsburg, VA 23188; (757) 565-2955; pierces.com; Barbecue; $. Three miles off Interstate 64 is what just might be the biggest barbecue pit in the whole state of Virginia. Looming from behind this blazing orange-and-yellow eatery is one mansion of a smoker, as big as a single-family home. Peek inside, and you'll find massive cinderblock pits, the embers ever smoldering. Tidewater people have been devouring Pierce's barbecue for 40 years, and in 2012 *National Geographic* named the spot one of the world's 10 best barbecue joints. In the world, mind you, so you really ought to stop for some of the pulled-pork barbecue. It's become a bucket-list kind of thing, and it's different from most of the vinegar and pepper–seasoned sauces you'll find around here. Offered on tables in squirt bottles, Pierce's sauce is smoky and delivers heat, but not quite a burn. The recipe goes back 80 years. Sweet potato sticks—crunchy on the outside, creamy in the middle—make a nice side dish. There are also ribs and pulled chicken and Pierce's own line of peanuts. Plus, out past the parking lot is the prettiest little picnic area in a patch of green grass shaded by stately old trees. An added bonus: Pierce's just might have the cleanest bathrooms in the state.

The Raven Restaurant, 1200 Atlantic Ave., Virginia Beach, VA 23451; (757) 425-1200; theraven.com; American; $$. This popular hangout for locals and tourists near the city's beach resort area is a comfortable place to get a bite. The staff—decked out in T-shirts and shorts during the long, hot months—engages customers in chit-chat, keeps your glasses full, and warns you that the side of broccoli is super-sized and suggests a half order. Burgers weigh in at a half-pound and are the most popular item, and plates of onion rings and fries seem to be constantly whizzing past your table. The dinner menu offers seafood and steak options for those with bigger appetites. The restaurant opened in 1968, after twin brothers Ricky and Bobby Dunnington returned from a tour of Vietnam, and local military personnel frequent it often. The owners' sense of humor shines through on the menu, which congratulates visitors for their "discerning taste, good looks, charming personality and appreciation of the finer things in life." The atmosphere is relaxed, with a durable green carpet that can withstand beach traffic and the persistent sand that comes with it. The bar runs almost the full length of the indoor area, and covered seating is available outside. The restaurant's name comes from the 1845 poem by Edgar Allan Poe, a onetime Virginian whose work is a favorite of the owners. If you'd like a keepsake of your visit, an adjoining retail shop offers souvenirs and a variety of T-shirts showcasing the restaurant's logo that features that ominous black bird that said, and we quoth, "nevermore."

The Smithfield Inn, 112 Main St., Smithfield, VA 23430; (757) 357-1752; smithfieldinn.com; Traditional Southern; $$. In the mood for a bit of history? Long before the Alamo, before the Declaration of Independence, and before the first muskets were fired in the Revolutionary War, travelers enjoyed Southern charm and hospitality at what is now the Smithfield Inn, circa 1752. Today, the grand old inn, with its wide front porch appointed with rockers and shaded by green awnings, is a showpiece of this quaint Southern town. Genuinely gracious hospitality, combined with authentic Southern fare, gives travelers a true taste of Tidewater. Talk about authentic, the inn's yeast rolls and sweet potato ham rolls have been made by Ms. Mozell Brown for more than 50 years. The menu in the elegant formal dining room offers dishes such as peach-glazed chicken and shrimp and grits, made with fried Smithfield ham and cheddar grits. In the less formal historic William Rand Tavern, lunch on a Virginia Reuben made with smoked Virginia turkey and pimiento cheese or perhaps, most memorable, the fried green tomato BLT.

Steinhilber's, 653 Thalia Rd., Virginia Beach, VA 23452; (757) 340-1156; steiny's.com; Seafood/Steaks; $$$$. Welcome to old-school Tidewater, circa 1939, where the waiters still wear waistcoats and bowties and where the award-winning, lightly fried jumbo shrimp served with the restaurant's signature sauce has been an addiction for generations of locals. Perched on a tributary of the Lynnhaven River, Steiny's, as locals call it, is an "occasion" restaurant for many. Nuptials are murmured on the sweeping expanse of lawn under the towering magnolia tree. Engagements and birthdays liven up the dining room, where a portrait of founder Robert Steinhilber hangs over the fireplace. Today, you're likely to be greeted at the door by his daughter, Jeanne Steinhilber, or her son, Brady Viccellio, and shown to a seat in the wood-paneled dining room or on a deck or terrace laced with potted flowers, kept cool in the summer months by market umbrellas and misters—

perhaps the area's finest alfresco dining. Following an iconic shrimp appetizer, seafood lovers can choose from fresh fish crowned with shrimp, crab, or oyster stuffing, lobster tails and

Moose & Deer & Buffalo—Oh My!

The historic Port Norfolk neighborhood harkens back to *Leave It to Beaver*-land with its tree-lined streets and American flags waving from porches of turn-of-the-century Victorian, Queen Anne, and Arts-and-Crafts homes. But there's a jungle in its midst, and it's not to be missed. Step into Stove (below), the restaurant, at 2622 Detroit St. and get ready to gawk. The shoebox-sized, eight-seat bar called **The Cougar Lounge** is an enclave of enormous, expertly mounted game heads—wildebeest, antelope, moose, deer, and an immense buffalo head—that ring the room. It's where award-winning and quirky chef-owner Sydney Meers frequently holds court. How the beasts came to be glaring from the walls of this Portsmouth restaurant is a mostly a mystery; the chef says that the animals came to him by way of a friend of a friend with an IRS problem, and he'll say no more. Have a drink and wonder, then venture into the dining room for a neo-Southern spread of Mississippi low-country shrimp and grits, house-cured ham, fresh seafood, house-aged steaks, artisanal cheeses, and swoon-inducing desserts, all prepared with a hyper-local, hyper-fresh seasonable sensibility. Much of the produce comes from Meers's home garden, which consumes his entire yard, complete with smokehouse and apiary, located just across the street.

étouffée. Best bets for meat lovers include the boneless New York strip served with a choice of a la carte toppings, such as bordelaise or a trio of those fried shrimp. Or try the bone-in veal chop, always tender and topped with roasted pecans, spinach, feta, and pancetta.

Stove, the Restaurant, 2622 Detroit St., Portsmouth, VA 23707; (757) 397-0900; stoverestaurant.com; Neo-Southern/Seafood; $$$. This quaint and quirky 32-seat restaurant in the heart of a historic, middle-class neighborhood is the daily obsession of Chef-Owner Sydney Meers, one of the area's best-loved restaurateurs. From Meers's own Southern folk artwork on the walls to a menu filled with house-made sausage and cheeses and house-cured hams, it's clear that the chef and restaurant have become one. The ever-changing menu of small and large plates combines flavors from Meers's low-country Mississippi roots with the best Tidewater foodstuffs and adds a shot of Creole here and there. If it's your thing, get the étouffée with shrimp, the "pork o rama" barbecue with Meers's intensely smoky signature "Smoochie Bear" ham or shrimp and grits, a mountain of okra, cold-smoked tomatoes, roasted fennel, house-made sausage, and Gulf shrimp atop a custom blend of grits that are simmered for hours in milk and water. Every neo-Southern meal comes with a side of Syd, who intermittently cooks behind the tiled half-wall of his open kitchen and repairs to the dining room to sip whiskey, neat, alongside dinner guests. Don't dare skip dessert. Cowboy Syd's Sextuple Truffle, dark and dense on a shortbread pecan crust, quashes all chocolate cravings. See Chef Meers's recipe for **Winnie Lee's Fried Chicken** on p. 251.

Surf Rider Restaurant, 8180 Shore Dr., Norfolk, VA 23518; (757) 216-7550; surfriderrestaurant.com; Seafood; $$. A blinding glare reflects off the boats at the marina adjacent to the Ocean View location of this local chain of seafood restaurants, which has a fierce loyal following—especially for its crab cakes. Around here, everybody's got a crab cake on the menu. But for legions of locals, Surf Rider's is only one they want. In this window-walled waterside eatery, you can order a crab-cake sandwich or a crab-cake dinner, broiled, but never fried, and seemingly made without any filler at all. They arrive on old-school metal broiling dishes atop black chargers accompanied by the signature side, an enormous bunch of broccoli, a generous cup of hollandaise and a pair of hush puppies. The fried shrimp ranks high, and so do the fried oysters. But if you're just passing through, get the crab cakes. See website for other locations.

Surrey House Restaurant, 11865 Rolfe Hwy., Surry, VA 23883; (757) 294-3389; surreyhouserestaurant.com; Traditional Southern; $$. You can get here from several directions, but the best way to reach this place is to take the free Jamestown-Scotland Ferry across the James River. The ride is about 15 to 20 minutes, enough time to let you slow down for a visit to this quaint Virginia town of 7,000. The restaurant is located in the Surrey Inn, a white, cupola-topped structure that looks like the down-home place that it is. The menu oozes Southern hospitality, and a must is the famous Virginia peanut soup. It's a creamy and crunchy concoction that shows off the area's biggest crop. From there, the choices get difficult, but it's a delicious problem to have. Fried chicken or country-fried chicken—you know, the kind slathered in gravy? Ham steak or pork chops? Crab cakes or catfish? What you choose doesn't really matter, because you're in the hands of seasoned country cooks. Time will speed up again when you leave, but while you're here, revel in the old ways.

Terrapin Restaurant, 3102 Holly Rd., Ste. 514, Virginia Beach, VA 23451; (757) 321-6688; terrapinvirginiabeach.com; Seafood/ Steaks; $$$$. This is one of the most exciting places to dine in Tidewater, just to see what Executive Chef Rodney Einhorn has cooked up this time. The meticulous master, who has helmed the stove at the prestigious James Beard House in New York City, is known for his penchant for detail and his creative uses of local ingredients. He'll take an ordinary oyster, add impossibly tiny bits of apple and a hint of vinegar, and the bivalve will explode in your mouth with a saltiness that is at once tart and sweet. (See Chef Einhorn's recipe on p. 245) You'll want to have it every time you come back, but it's best not to get too attached to any dish. The menu changes seasonally, and you'll want to go along on Einhorn's journey. Regional producers get billing on the menu, where Cromwell Farms' May peas sometimes are found in the salmon dish and Maple Leaf Farms provides the breast for the Duck Duo. The restaurant, just a few blocks from the Atlantic, is elegant and intimate. Wine pairings can be divine, but don't underestimate the bar staff. The mixologists elevate a simple Sidecar with a twist of ginger or combine gin and lavender syrup into a smoothly refreshing English Garden. Settle in and enjoy the ride.

The Tides Inn, 480 King Carter Dr., Irvington, VA 22480; (804) 438-5000; on Facebook; Seafood/Southern Traditional; $$$$. Although The Tides Inn—a marina, spa, and hotel—has been lauded by every elite travel magazine around, it retains the feeling of old Virginia. The staff provides gracious service at an unhurried pace that's not at all stuffy. Every door you walk through will be opened for you. Everyone will smile. The inn's signature restaurant is the Chesapeake Club. Here, on the banks of the Rappahannock River, oysters come carefully paired with Champagne or topped with caviar or pickled watermelon salsa. The flounder and rockfish are straight from the bay. And the fried chicken comes with a side of Miss Ann's greens, sweet corn pudding and tomato piccalilli. Take a moment to ponder the gleaming walnut lockers behind the hostess station. Long ago, they held the members' treasured liquor, when this was a dry county that eschewed alcohol. Each night, the inn's private yacht embarked on a ritual, called the Whiskey Run, setting sail for Urbanna, a "wet" county just across the way. These days, guests and nonguests alike are welcome to dine here, or just repair to the Terrace Lounge overlooking the waterfront and croquet lawn, and sit for a spell with a cocktail. There's no music on the terrace, so you can hear the gulls, the sailboat riggings, and the wind in the pines. It's a fine, fine way to pass an hour or so in the sweet Virginia breeze.

Todd Jurich's Bistro, 150 W. Main St., Ste. 100, Norfolk, VA 23510; (757) 622-3210; toddjurichsbistro.com; Seafood/Steaks;

$$$$. This upscale restaurant helped revive Norfolk's downtown culinary scene when it opened in 1992. Now in a more spacious and elegant venue, where beaded-glass light fixtures sparkle against the dark-wood interior, this bistro continues to serve some of the most creative dishes around. Executive Chef Todd Jurich is a whiz with local seafood, and he's won accolades from the *New York Times* for his talents. His pumpkin and crab soup, a fall favorite, is stunning when presented in a hollowed-out pumpkin shell. His spring roll appetizer, with its delicate mixture of roast pork and prawns, is the kind of dish guests crave weeks afterward. Entrees range from a grass-fed beef filet mignon to a meat-loaf-and-mashed potato combination that is at once homey and exquisite. Lunch options abound. The signature oyster stew is powered by a potato puree and smoked bacon, and the trio of juicy baby burgers comes with perfectly golden fries that almost steal the show. The bar is lively, especially when nearby offices close each weekday afternoon, and the waiters know how to describe a dish in such mouthwatering detail that you must have it. Until, of course, they talk about the next one.

Vintage Kitchen, 999 Waterside Dr., Norfolk, VA 23510; (757) 625-3370; vintage-kitchen.com; Neo-Southern; $$–$$$. A few years back, *Condé Nast Traveler* magazine named Vintage Kitchen "one of America's best new restaurants." It remains one of the area's finest, led by Chef-Owner Phillip Craig Thomason, a Tidewater native who graduated first in his class at Le Cordon Bleu and who possesses an unwavering slow-food sensibility. The sleek restaurant—think leather, copper, and burled wood—is on the ground floor of a tall, white-collar office building. Beyond the copper-topped bar, a glass wall leads into the main lobby, while a wall of windows in the dining room allows a panoramic view of dry-docked Navy vessels and pleasure craft plying Norfolk's harbor in the Elizabeth River. The menu is a who's-who of Virginia's finest artisan food producers; almost every offering details the source of the cheese, meats, and produce. At lunch, try the Three Little

Pigs—Gryffon's Aerie pulled-pork barbecue sliders with Surry sausage and Gwaltney bacon—or the half-pound burger, touted as one of the region's best. For dinner, a small plate offering transforms pedestrian food: buttermilk-fried popcorn chicken with five-alarm honey lacquer. Or savor the sea with Chesapeake Bay flounder with brown butter, hazelnuts, and savory lemon marmalade.

Vintage Tavern, 1900 Governor's Pointe Dr., Suffolk, VA 23436; (757) 238-8808; vintagetavernvirginia.com; Neo-Southern; $$$$. You'd be hard pressed to find a more gorgeous dining setting in Tidewater than this rustic charmer. Located in a stone structure than looks like a welcoming Southern home, the interior is accented with wood and a large fireplace, but your eyes keep going toward the view. The restaurant has ample windows onto the backyard patio, where diners can have dessert or sip a drink amid a garden, a stream, and a backdrop of trees and greenery that hide all hints of the outside world. The first appetizer sums up the tavern's appeal. It's called a Taste of Southern Goodness and, like everything that follows, local ingredients are on full display. The hearty appetizer features a pile of salty Virginia

 ham, sausage crafted on the premises, deviled eggs, house-made preserves, and buttermilk biscuits to wrap them all into. Pork, raised on nearby farms, is the centerpiece of many dishes, including the often-changing Route 17 Plate, where pig lovers can find pork belly,

pork loin, or pulled pork, and the baby back ribs, powered by a molasses barbecue sauce. Steak and seafood options—locally sourced, of course—provide further temptation. You're served by a team, so dishes and drinks are constantly coming and going. The high-ceilinged, spacious bar isn't a bad place to dine either, and the bartender's creative take on the ginger-and-bourbon Virginia Highball will make you want to kick back and stay awhile.

Virginia Diner, 408 County Dr. N., Wakefield, VA 23888; (757) 899-3106; vadinerrestaurant.com; Traditional Southern; $. Unless you are texting while driving—which in Virginia comes with a hefty new fine—there's no way to miss the Virginia Diner, a western Tidewater landmark that dates back to the Great Depression. Cartoon billboards as far as 7 miles out begin touting the peanuts, chicken, and speed of service until, bam, the white clapboard building with the arched roof and enormous asphalt parking lot comes into view. The campers, vans, and semis in the lot attest to the fact that it's a popular tourist spot. The breakfast, lunch, and dinner menus feature no-nonsense dishes, modestly priced meals of baked ham, fried chicken, breakfast biscuits, seafood, and such. They're served in a vast dining room with ice-cream-parlor settees, red-and-white checked tablecloths, and friendly, efficient service. Before paying at the register, stock up on the Virginia Diner's brand of peanuts—they're offered every which way, chocolate covered, salted, candied, brittled, spiced, in the shell, in cans, in bags—well, you get the idea.

Zoës, 713 19th St., Virginia Beach, VA 23451; (757) 437-3636; zoesvb.com; Steaks/Seafood; $$$$. This haven, one of the region's best places to please your palate, makes you feel all warm inside, with its dark wood accents, partially padded walls and romantic atmosphere. That's even before you've had a glass of wine, which you should, because Sommelier Marc Sauter is one of the best in Tidewater at pairing perfect sips with delectable nips. Executive Chef Jerry Weihbrecht more than keeps up his end of the bargain, sending out dishes that are breathtaking and oh, so good. One of his signatures is blue crab mac-n-cheese, which combines large lumps of the Chesapeake Bay delicacy with three kinds of cheeses. On his Chinatown shrimp tempura entree, he dusts the shellfish with delicate spices before finishing it, tempura-style, to a golden brown. The steaks, aged for 28

Politics and Planked Shad

In Virginia, we treasure tradition like newborn kin. If you happen to be in western Tidewater on the third Wednesday of April, you can savor two traditions at once. That's when the Wakefield Ruritan Club's annual Shad Planking takes place at the Sportsmen Club at 12205 Brittles Mill Rd. in Wakefield.

It's a rite of spring that mixes Virginia state politics with the start of shad-eating season. Now, shad is an oily and bony fish and is more prized around here for the roe, wobbly sacks of eggs that people fry, broil and fashion into rings. But planked shad is a rare treat, and a dying art.

The Ruritans get started before dawn cooking the shad the same way the Indians did, the same way Civil War soldiers did—split down the back, nailed to boards and cooked for eight hours alongside an open flame. The fishes are salted at the halfway mark to remove the oil and basted thrice with a special sauce that's a closely guarded secret of the club (we believe there's bourbon involved).

Because planked shad isn't the most beloved food, the club also plates up whiting and shad roe, aka "caviar of the commonwealth," hot from the fryer. Meanwhile, under the pine and oak, state Senate, House and gubernatorial candidates offer libations to potential supporters, a political tradition that dates back to Colonial times.

days, have a deep flavor that the chef lets speak for itself. The waiters are knowledgeable about all things Zoës—explaining that the name is pronounced "ZOE-ees," the same as one of the daughters of the original investors. The staff also takes time to expound on the dishes and offer recommendations. Really, all you have to do is relax.

Specialty Stores, Markets & Producers

Adams Country Store, 9243 General Mahone Hwy., US Route 460, Waverly, VA 23890; (757) 899-8651; adamspeanuts.com. While out in Western Tidewater, keep an eye out for a giant peanut shell, painted pale yellow with thick black spots and taller than any man. That marks Adams Country Store, a genuine country store where the rarefied aroma of salt-cured pork and pepper prevails. At the door, guests are greeted by a linoleum-lined pedestal of whole cured country hams, the fat-streaked, wine-colored meat wearing only a few flecks of salt and pepper—no cloth bags, no paper, no plastic. Beside those sit a grease-soaked cardboard box of hog jowls, $3 per pound; bags of boiled peanuts; fist-sized bottles of Coca-Cola; and Miller beer ponies. Wooden shelves are lined with all manner of Adams Peanuts. Lewis Adams fries the family's brand of cocktail peanuts to a satisfying crunch and packs them in the back of the store. In addition to his Peanut Cooker title, Adams is the clerk, marketer, and full-time docent, keeper of the pedigree of every knick and knack shelved between the cans of herring roe, pork brains, and Sun Drop sodas. Between ringing up customers and carving up hams (that service is on the house, a rare perk), he's glad to share the stories behind the display of colored cotton balls, mounted gape-mouthed bass, and chicken catcher. Prefers to, really. "If I have the time, I'll capture you," he says, almost apologetically. "I like to spend time with everybody."

A. Dodson's, 2948 Bridge Rd., Suffolk, VA 23435; (757) 483-1344; adodsons.com. Those who fancy themselves as gracious hosts or hostesses shouldn't miss a stroll through this shop, where the motto is "Being Southern Is a Beautiful Thing." The locally owned emporium is filled with beautiful things—fine clothing, baby gifts, unusual house bling, and over-the-top seasonal decor. But there's plenty to tempt the epicure, including a full line of hard-to-find Nora Fleming and French Bull serving ware, embroidered dish towels, whimsical coasters with sayings such as "How's Y'all's Mama?" and "Y'all are sweeter'n sweet tea." For those who imbibe, there are whiskey stones for the highball crowd and corksicles for the grape-minded. Don't miss the back room, where a cache of sale items is stashed. **Additional location:** 1611A Colley Ave., Norfolk, VA 23517; (757) 222-0254.

Artisan's Bakery & Cafe, 711 Washington St., Portsmouth, VA 23704; (757) 396-6313; artisansbakerycafe.com. If you find yourself in Olde Towne Portsmouth with an Old World craving, this bakery has got you covered. You'll have to venture a couple of blocks off main street proper to get to the stately Victorian that houses this European-style bakery, but it's a diversion worth taking. Walk into the front hall of what once was a grand old home, and you'll see to your right the bakers in the open kitchen who are forming baguettes and German rye loaves. The lunch crowd seated in the parlor to the left nibbles on open-faced smoked salmon tartines or Black Forest ham and Gouda paninis, all on freshly baked bread, of course. If you've got time for only one option, consider dessert in the form of a pear tart Bourdeloue or apple galette. And grab a few house-made pretzels for the road.

Bean There Coffeehouse, 1860 Laskin Rd., Ste. 122, Virginia Beach, VA 23454; (757) 422-JAVA (5282); and 223 East City Hall Ave., Ste. 101, Norfolk, VA 23510; (757) 623-JAVA (5282). Whether you're in Virginia Beach or Norfolk, bypass Starbucks and get your fix at Bean There. This locally owned shop serves only the highest-rated coffees. If you plan to sit for a bit, expertly brewed java drinks and teas are served in white ceramic mugs, just one way the shop stays green. Made-to-order cappuccinos and macchiatos honor Old World techniques, and the menu is rounded out with pastries, desserts, beer, and wine. The Norfolk location invites patrons to linger in a comfortable setting with whimsically mismatched furniture, while the Virginia Beach locale has a sleeker vibe. On any particular visit, you might happen upon game night, fondue night, or one of the weekly cuppings featuring some of the world's best joe.

Bella Monte International Marketplace & Cafe, 1202 Laskin Rd., Ste. 100, Virginia Beach, VA 23451; (757) 425-6290; bellamontevb.com. It's hard to think of a gourmet gadget or kitchen treat that is not tucked into this charming and ever-changing market near the Virginia Beach oceanfront resort area. It's where we've found mortars and pestles, both high-end and low, bouquet garni bags, European baking extracts, fine wines and cheeses, wood planks for grilling, aprons, kitchen rugs, top quality teas and coffees, the best Italian canned goods, French table linens, cookies, chocolates, and even artisan bacon and breads. It's a wonderland to get lost in. Don't miss the wine wall, where the price is right: three bottles for $22, one of the best-kept secrets in town.

Bergey's Breadbasket, 2207 Mount Pleasant Rd., Chesapeake, VA 23322; (757) 546-9225; bergeysbreadbasket.com. There's an old saying in the South that pie fixes everything. In rural Chesapeake, in the crumb-sized kitchen of this family dairy-turned-bakery, you can test that theory. The ever-changing, made-from-scratch pie menu provides seasonal doses of cure-all comfort food that locals will drive miles for. Fresh fruit pie season begins in May with the first blush of the strawberry crop. A month later, when local fields are picked clean, the bakers move seamlessly into blackberry pie season, with local berries, of course. In July, blackberry pie season morphs into peach. Sometime during peach pie season, blueberry pie season begins. Then apple pie season—overlapped with a short period of pumpkin pie—and then it's back to apple. A few winter months are filled in with coconut and key lime creations until the strawberries blush once more, and the cycle begins anew. The shop also has breads and fresh fruits and veggies, plus made-to-order milk shakes, voted among the best in the region.

Border Station, 101 Caratoke Hwy., Moyock, NC 27958; (252) 435-2665; and 4732 Battlefield Blvd. S., Chesapeake, VA 23322; (757) 421-2373. That bipolar address is no typo, people. Border Station straddles the Virginia–North Carolina border, physically and philosophically. It's located on the main road leading from Virginia to North Carolina's Outer Banks, and it's a pretty cool place to stop. Foodies flock to the aisles carrying Virginia and North Carolina foodstuffs—whole hams, peanuts every which way, hot sauces, saltwater taffy, Cheerwine, Sun Drop soda, and such. Don't miss the refrigerated case in the back filled with country curiosities such as souse, side meat, and slab bacon. Before leaving, have your picture taken straddling the state line, which is tiled right into the floor.

Bravo's Frozen Custard, 166 S. Rosemont Rd., Virginia Beach, VA 23452; (757) 313-6370; bravos-frozen-custard.com. Lucky for locals that a Wisconsin couple came here for vacation, fell in love with the beach, and returned to open an authentic frozen custard shop, just like the ones that blanket the frozen north. Frozen custard is kingly compared to its ice cream cousin. It combines whole eggs, real cream, and a minimum of air whipped into the mix. That makes for a dense, satisfying treat, so dense, in fact, that the shop's Blizzard-like concoction is called a "Concrete." The owners make three flavors of fresh custard daily: vanilla, chocolate, and the flavor of the day, which might be caramel cashew, Irish cream, or butter pecan. The little shop with a quaint collection of ladybug figures is located in an aging shopping center just off Interstate 264. Look for the gigantic inflatable ice cream cone out front.

Carolina Cupcakery, 2019 Colley Ave., Norfolk, VA 23517; (757) 351-1548; carolinacupcakery.com. Owner Dawn Eskins is serious about cupcakes. She's been on the Food Network's *Cupcake Wars*, she's written a book called *Cupcake Confessions* that details her career as a baker, and she's been known to employ power tools on her batter, which uses all-natural ingredients and can get stiff when refrigerated. She's 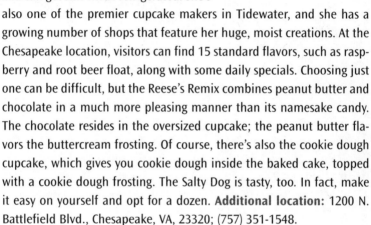 also one of the premier cupcake makers in Tidewater, and she has a growing number of shops that feature her huge, moist creations. At the Chesapeake location, visitors can find 15 standard flavors, such as raspberry and root beer float, along with some daily specials. Choosing just one can be difficult, but the Reese's Remix combines peanut butter and chocolate in a much more pleasing manner than its namesake candy. The chocolate resides in the oversized cupcake; the peanut butter flavors the buttercream frosting. Of course, there's also the cookie dough cupcake, which gives you cookie dough inside the baked cake, topped with a cookie dough frosting. The Salty Dog is tasty, too. In fact, make it easy on yourself and opt for a dozen. **Additional location:** 1200 N. Battlefield Blvd., Chesapeake, VA, 23320; (757) 351-1548.

Central Meats, 1120 Kempsville Rd., Chesapeake, VA 23320; (757) 547-2161; centralmeats.com. Earl Edmundson started this butcher shop in 1960 in neighboring Suffolk, then moved to this location 12 years later when a new highway overpass got in his way. The shop's showcase is the meat case, where 2-inch cowboy steaks might sit next to plump rib roasts. You're also likely to find pork chops, lamb chops, chicken, and bison. If you can't find it, ask. The staff will try to oblige. Same goes when you're not sure how to cook it. All the meat is butchered in the shop, as is smoked sausage. Cuts of beef and leaner bison can be purchased individually or, if you're a serious carnivore, package deals are available. The store also sells foot-long hot dogs,

A Family That's a Cut Above

For brothers Brad and Johnny Hardison, meat is a family affair. Brad runs the **Village Butcher** at 608 Hilltop W. in Virginia Beach. Johnny does the same at the **Country Butcher Shop** at the Virginia Beach Farmers Market at 3640 Dam Neck Rd. The men came to know the business from their father, J.T., who earned his butcher's license in the 1960s, and they've carried on one of dad's traditions. Their shops are known for their personal service. Need a thick steak for aging? They'll cut one for you. A crown pork roast? Of course. They specialize in grass-fed beef, which they insist is better-tasting and better for you. In each shop, refrigerated cases hold a wealth of uncooked goodness: giant T-bones, filets, rib eyes and prized Kobe beef, as well as roasts so robust they could flavor multiple pots. That's only the beginning. The center-cut pork chops stand an inch high; the cherrywood and slab bacon screams for a cast-iron skillet. The shops also stock exotic meats, so depending on the day, you can find alligator, bison, duck, elk, goat, kangaroo, lamb, ostrich, or pheasant. The brothers are proud of a homemade sausage that they boast will put Jimmy Dean's version to shame. There are also deli meats, cheeses, and assorted other products. But in the end, for both of J.T.'s boys, the important thing is getting to know their customers and giving them what they want.

cheeses, country and spare ribs, and a wealth of sausages, such as chorizo, sage, and a maple-flavored breakfast variety. Out front, you'll find ice, which can come in handy if you need to ice down that brimming cooler or if you've gone whole hog and bought an entire porker—yup, you can do that here—for an upcoming pig roast.

Delicate Oriental Grocery, 5394 Kempsriver Dr., Virginia Beach, VA 23464; (757) 216-2611; on Facebook. What strikes you first in the jam-packed Asian market is the scent. It's vaguely familiar, though out of place, and then it hits you: It's burning incense. It comes from an altar-like red bookcase near the back of the store, where statues of Buddha and other trinkets reside. The smell puts you at ease as you maneuver the aisles, starting with the produce section that is strong on Asian specialties such as Thai basil, bok choy, and Chinese spinach. The side of one aisle is devoted to every kind of rice and noodles you can imagine; the opposing shelves house hoisin, bean, and other sauces, along with flavored vinegars. A small spice section has star anise and dried banana flower among its offerings. The frozen compartments reveal duck, bangus (milkfish), chicken feet, and pork belly. Near the front of the store, you'll sometimes find coolers stocked with jumbo shrimp, their heads intact, or blue crabs. A back wall is filled with utensils for cooking and serving the ingredients you've purchased—steamers, woks, rice cookers, wonton spoons, and small, ornately decorated bowls for sauces. The checkout lines can get long, and be prepared: You can use a credit card only if you spend more than $15.

French Bakery & Delicatessen, 4108 Granby St, Norfolk, VA 23504; (757) 625-4936. Breeze through the double screen doors of the French Bakery, and you'll be instantly charmed by the old-fashioned decor: an antique Coca-Cola icebox, wrought-iron ceiling fans, and curving glass cases beckoning with éclairs, cookies, and the bakery's signature orange doughnuts. You might, or might not, be charmed by the persistence of the Habib family, which has owned the shop for nearly a century. So be sure to arrive with a bit of moxie along with that appetite. The bakery's signature orange juice doughnuts are a must at breakfast, or try any of the pastries in the case. These bakers are masters, and they use only the finest ingredients, facts that they'll remind you of when they ring you up at the register. At lunch, locals crave the pastrami sandwich, with its meat piled onto homemade bread, or the seafood or oyster sub, served on a disposable plate with nary a frill. Likely, you'll be prodded to add on dessert—we warned you—so save some resolve for that. Some offerings are absolutely breathtaking.

Grand Mart International Foods, 649 Newtown Rd., Ste. 105, Virginia Beach, VA 23462; (757) 490-7901; on Facebook. This huge supermarket specializes in Asian foods, and it's the place to go for produce of an unusual bent. Need some *manzanos,* those adorable yellow fruits that seem like miniature bananas? You'll find them here. Or some Korean yams, whose dull purple skin hides a striking violet interior? Yes, they're here, too. So are cactus fruit, cactus leaf, daikon, and jackfruit, along with more common fare such as bell peppers, onions, oranges, and radishes. The seafood section features more than 20 whole fish. Depending on the day, you'll find head-and-tail-intact red snapper, rockfish, or Spanish mackerel. The store's interior is where the processed foods are, and aisles specialize in different cuisines: Asian, Indian, Japanese, Korean, Latino, and Middle Eastern. The different varieties and flavors of soy sauces are simply overwhelming. There is also standard fare, but the big draw here are the items you can't find at your neighborhood grocer or chain superstore.

Grayson & Emma's Garden Spot, 28412 Southampton Pkwy., Courtland, VA 23837; (757) 653-9652; on Facebook. It certainly looks like a garden shop on the outside, what with all those rockers and Adirondack chairs sprinkled on the wide front porch and those hoop greenhouses out back. But inside, Grayson & Emma's is the place to savor some hard-to-find, purely western Tidewater treats. Dandoodle sausage, for instance, is always in stock. That's seasoned ground pork (is there any other way?) stuffed into a portion of a pig's stomach, tied off with a string. It's a tad troubling to look at, but dunk it into a pot with some greens or beans and it yields a singular flavor, different from greens seasoned with ham hock. Then, slice it up for a nice sandwich. A refrigerated case on one side of the shop offers home-cooked foods such as bread pudding, corn pudding, tomato pudding, snaps, corn and butterbeans, and collards, all sold by the pint and quart. A metal basket of pig's ears sits with a display of dried black-eyed peas, because, you know, they go together. A country cafe recently opened in the store and offers the option of savoring chicken and dumplings, local sausage sandwiches, and pimiento cheese right on the spot. At the register, grab a jack, a little fried pie filled with peach or sweet potato or some such treat.

Heritage Amish Bake Shoppe, 3600 Dam Neck Rd., at the Virginia Beach Farmers Market, Virginia Beach, VA 23453; (757) 716-3772; heritagebakeshoppe.com. This homey little bakery, run by a local Mennonite family, opened in 2012. Walk in, and you'll see women and girls in simple frocks and aprons greasing pans and crimping piecrusts. The bakery offers freshly made sourdough bread, pumpkin muffins, carrot-cake cupcakes, shoofly pie, and other homespun treats, in addition to jams, jellies, and bulk goods. Although a relative newcomer to an area studded with bakeries, the shop quickly earned a following and won a regional contest for its potato flake dinner rolls, a recipe that came from a church friend of owner Susan Kauffman. The shop's slightly sweet whole-wheat dinner rolls also wowed the judges.

A Ham with a Side of History

Out in the western Tidewater countryside, while whizzing past fields of peanut and cotton, you might notice a few big, blunt-cornered triangles hovering on the roadside. That's the shape of a whole country-cured ham tied in a cloth bag. One of the area's iconic images, it's been painted on a water tower, printed on business cards and T-shirts and fashioned into signs, including one that woos customers into **The Ham Shoppe of Surry** at 11381 Rolfe Hwy. in the small town of Surry.

It's a homey little shop with a highfalutin' clientele. The carmine cottage, with its wide front porch, houses the retail hub of Edwards of Surry, a family business that cures thousands of country hams right next door, and turns out all manner of bacon, sausage, and smoked turkey breast, too.

It all got started in the 1920s when S. Wallace Edwards captained the ferry that crisscrossed the James River—and is still in operation down at the end of the street. Captain Edwards sold ham sandwiches on the side to supplement his income, and later turned to curing whole hams. The shop is stocked with pork, jams, and jellies, and third-generation cure-master Sam Edwards III continues his grandfather's tradition of offering spot-on salty, savory country ham sandwiches (see his recipe for **Country Ham** on p. 254). They're perfect washed down with an ice cold drink known around these parts as "co-cola." Afterward, you'll want to tuck a pouch of Edwards's award-winning Surryano ham in the glove box. Sometimes called Southern prosciutto, it's on the menu at places like Husk Restaurant in Charleston, SC, and Manhattan's Momofuku Ssäm Bar, named one of the top 50 restaurants in the world. So get some of that, and a pound of Virginia bacon steak, dry-cured, hickory-smoked slices so thick that they can go right on the grill. Then, it's worth a drive up the street, on the right just past the stoplight, to see the company's original smokehouses, shaped like wigwams. Captain Edwards designed them that way to honor Native Americans who taught the settlers how to salt and smoke pork in the New World.

Jane's Sweet Potato Biscuits, 305 N. Main St., Franklin, VA 23851; (757) 653-6234; janesbiscuits.com. When we first met Miss Jane, back in 2005, she had just started rolling out, cutting and baking endless batches of sweet potato biscuits in her home kitchen, circa 1920. Word spread quickly about her sweet, dense and somehow-at-the-same-time light creations, made from scratch, every single one. Miss Jane expanded her home kitchen, then in 2011 opened up a storefront on Franklin's charming Main Street. She's added buttermilk cheese biscuits to her menu, hearty 3-inchers made with two Vermont cheddars. Her latest: cinnamon-pecan biscuits with a Grand Marnier glaze. Veer off the main road and pop in for a dozen, or better yet, a dozen dozen. The sweet potato–and–cheese biscuits will keep for months in the freezer, and what better way to remember a visit to Tidewater? Pair them with some Virginia ham. A little sweet, a little salt, a lot of heaven. If the habit sticks, Miss Jane's mail order operation is there for you.

Kitchen Barn, 1628 Laskin Rd., Hilltop West Shopping Center, Ste. 701, Virginia Beach, VA 23451; (757) 422-0888; kitchenbarnonline.com. In 1975, long before anyone uttered the phrase "Food Network" or "locavore," owner Joel Feldman opened his shop and stocked it with every conceivable item cooks might want, be they kitchen newbies or seasoned professionals. There's a wall of cookware, including Pillivuyt porcelain and imported Polish pottery (each piece numbered and signed), plus brands such as Le Creuset and All-Clad cookware. Visitors also will find stainless-steel strainers, cheesecake pans, bread pans, pepper mills, cookie cutters, butter bells, waffle irons, mixers, spatulas, whisks, and bowls. This shop is the area's go-to store for fine cutlery, including a respectable line of Japanese- and German-made knives. The place also offers a professional knife-sharpening service. Basically, the store's got everything from a $600 Bosch mixer to a $4 mini measuring cup, and it's all top-quality equipment.

The Kitchen Koop, 38 High St., Portsmouth, VA 23704; (757) 399-4475; kitchenkoop.com. The striped awning out front of this corner store in the historic Olde Towne section of Portsmouth harkens back to the mom-and-pop shops where you leisurely browsed the inventory while chatting with friends and staff members. Step inside, and you're back in the good ol' days, though the merchandise is thoroughly modern. It's a friendly place, where the sheer volume of the stuff makes you slow down and take a gander. If gadgets are your thing, spend some time near the wall where you'll find row after row of kitchen tools, from zesters to mango peelers. Brand-name cookware such as Cuisinart, Gourmet Standard, and Mauviel Copper calls out for a cook to take it home. And if you're looking for a high-end knife, the staff will remove the cutlery from the glass cases and let you give it a test drive. Some edible items are available, too, including coffee beans, jellies, jams, cooking oils, and bread mixes. And there's much, much more. Don't come when you're in a hurry; you can get lost amid the cook's bounty.

Laguna Bakery, 5394 Kempsriver Dr., Virginia Beach, VA 23464; (757) 366-0704. This strip-mall bakery, named after a province in the Philippines, bursts with exotic aromas, both savory and sweet. Once primarily the domain of baked goods, this Filipino shop now has expanded its line of hot food, which can be eaten at one of the three tables or purchased as takeout. The *pancit palabok* is a special, a noodle dish spiced with a shrimp sauce. Locals living nearby in the Little Manila section of Virginia Beach also crave the *lumpia*. If there's a pan of skewered coconut balls when you visit, grab one. The deep-fried treat is gooey on the outside, tender on the inside, and perfect to nibble on in the car. Dinner rolls, about the size of softballs, are one of the more popular baked goods, but you'll also find cream cheese rolls, mango and other fruit breads, and black bean rolls. The mung bean *hopia,* a flaky pastry filled with sweetened mung bean paste, is an acquired taste, but you'll have no problem gobbling down the dainty coconut macaroons.

O'DoodleDoo's Donuts, 1601 Bridge Rd., Suffolk, VA 23433; (757) 745-7323; odoodledoos.com. If the name of this doughnut shop in the northern part of Suffolk reminds you of the sound a rooster makes, there's a reason. Owner Reeva Luecke and her crew get up before the crack of dawn 7 days a week, except major holidays, to begin baking. Luecke chose the name for that reason and a few playful ones— she thinks it's fun, ridiculous even, to hear people try to pronounce it, and she wanted a name with a lot of O's because the letter looks like the specialties she sells. The shop, which opened in 2011, is ready for business at 5 a.m. sharp, and sometimes there's a line out front. You'd better get there early, because it closes when that day's inventory is gone or when the afternoon clock strikes 2. The flavors change daily, and the most popular are an old-fashioned sour cream and a classic red velvet cream cheese. Regulars also can't get enough of the doughnuts that feature bacon, such as cinnamon bacon, maple bacon, blueberry pancakes and bacon, chocolate bacon—well, if there's a flavor she can mix with the pork product, Luecke does it. She loves it when kids come in; they go wild over her whimsical creations. The Life's a Beach doughnut is one of those. It features a three-dimensional scene: graham cracker "sand" on one side, blue frosting "water" on the other, topped with an edible palm tree and fish. "This doughnut is about eating fun!" she says. The shop sells another original product that's almost as lip-smacking good as the doughnuts. Handmade lip balm comes in the flavors of her baked goods, so you can get a taste of red velvet, chai latte, and even doughnut glaze all day long.

The Perfect Setting of Virginia, City Center at Oyster Point, 701 Mariners Row, Ste. 112, Newport News, VA 23606; (757) 594-9515; facebook.com/ThePerfectSettingVA. If you're aiming to bring home some Southern hospitality, The Perfect Setting has all the necessary accoutrements. Let's start with the baby grand piano at the entrance, which hints at the elegance and taste within. For the more formal hostess, the shop offers the latest china patterns from Fitz and Floyd, embroidered table runners, napkins, and Waterford crystal. For the more casual host, whimsical beach-themed serving pieces from Mudpie and Vietri. Shelves are stocked with unique barware, deviled-egg plates, candles, and punch bowls. Plus, there's a floral designer on staff busy creating stunning silk centerpieces, a statement for any home.

Red Ribbon BakeShop, 5386 Kempsriver Dr., Ste. 108; Virginia Beach, VA 23464; (757) 420-6980; facebook.com/RedRibbon-VAB. This Filipino bakery in the heart of Virginia Beach's Little Manila neighborhood is part of a chain that began in California. The space is cheery, with walls of orange, mustard, and red. Nine white tables, flanked by orange chairs, and three booths invite you to sit a spell. But first you must check out the treasures near the back of the shop in the display cases—cakes and baked goods whose sight makes you ooh and aah. Slices of cake are available, but the whole ones are hard to pass up. The mango cake oozes with the tropical fruit. It's a chiffon confection layered and frosted with a mango cream filling and topped with more pieces of mango. The ube cake demands attention with the striking purple color it gets from its namesake yam. It looks as though it would be overwhelmingly sweet, but the taste instead is pleasantly mild. A favorite are the butter *mamons,* melt-in-your-mouth small cakes that blend white chiffon and butter. Specialty coffees give you something to wash it all down with.

Rowena's Kitchen, 758 W. 22nd St., Norfolk, VA 23517; (800) 627-8699; rowenas.com. This might just be the cutest little shop in Norfolk. A curvy walkway sashays through a patch of grass and posies and ends at the storybook entrance of Rowena's Kitchen, a locals' go-to spot for better-than-your-momma's pound cakes and other fanciful treats. Many a Rowena's addiction has started with her made-from-scratch, all natural almond pound cake topped with a generous drizzle of Rowena's lemon curd (which also tastes great on a spoon). The late Rowena is an actual person who started her baking business more than 30 years ago, inspired by three fruit trees in her yard. Her goods are now sold worldwide and have earned accolades from the likes of *Southern Living* and the Food Network. Yet, everything is still made by hand in the same kitchen where it all started. The little shop with the black-and-white-checked floor proffers bakers' racks of pound cakes (chocolate with raspberry curd, anyone?), tea cakes, cookies, curds, and unusual jams such as peach-orange-clove and carrot. Savory sauces, too, such as curry and Thai—but don't leave without a pound cake, at the very least a little one.

The Royal Chocolate, 164 Central Park Ave., Virginia Beach, VA 23462; (757) 557-6925; theroyalchocolate.com. Step aside, Mr. Wonka. This locally owned gourmet chocolate shop cranks out all kinds of chocolate-centric confections, most made in-house by friendly chocolatiers. Stop in for a leisurely romp with chocolate fondue, be it dark, white, or milk chocolate, or get some to go for your hotel room. Sparkling glass cabinets showcase a constellation of truffles. Fetching candy apples are first dipped in caramel, then in chocolate and finally sprinkled with cashews, coconut or cookies, or they're drizzled with white chocolate and tied with blue satin bows. But wait, what about chocolate bars from around the world? This could very well be the hardest decision you make in a day. In the summer, which around here can be blazin' hot, we recommend ordering up a frozen hot chocolate and taking your time. Check ahead for the dates of their frequent chocolate tastings.

The Sauce Shoppe, 3388 Princess Anne Rd., Virginia Beach, VA 23456; (757) 468-0913; facebook.com/TheSauceShoppe. Sam Esleeck, the gregarious owner of The Sauce Shoppe, stocks several locally produced barbecue and hot sauces in his store, which resembles a library with its floor-to-ceiling shelves of hundreds of artisanal sauces, rubs, and marinades from across the country. "And most are better than anything you get in the grocery store," Esleeck says. "Imagine a guy from Hunt's or Heinz stirring a 2-million-gallon vat of sauce. Then imagine a guy stirring 20 gallons." Some local brands you'll want to try: Admiral's Choice Pear Chutney BBQ Sauce, named in honor of an actual admiral (hey, it's a Navy town) and Esleeck's own Colonial Black Strap Virginia Bourbon Whiskey BBQ and Grilling Sauce, a thick, spicy, molasses-based sauce tinged with Virginia whiskey that is perfect on ribs. "Nothing else like it in the shop," Esleeck says.

Savor the Olive, 1624 Laskin Rd., Hilltop North Shopping Center, Virginia Beach, VA 23451; (757) 425-3866; and 419 W. 21st St., Norfolk VA 23517; (757) 624-3866; on Facebook. Who knew that olive oils develop flavors based on the soil, climate, and conditions where olives are grown and offer flavors such as eucalyptus, artichoke, pepper, grass, herbs, and even green banana? Or that fine vinegars can have the flavors of oregano, chocolate, and peach? Frank and Bonnie Lawrence do, and they search near and far for the best olive oils and balsamic vinegars in the world. Use the tiny pleated cups to savor the oil and the vinegar. It's a revelation, really.

Sugar Plum Bakery, 1353 Laskin Rd., Virginia Beach, VA 23451; (757) 422-3913; sugarplumbakery.org. Visions of baked goods will dance in your head after a visit to this locals' favorite. The bakery was founded in 1987 by a group of parents as a place where their adult children with disabilities could work. The not-for-profit bakery continues that mission today, and about half the staff have a mental or physical challenge. The display cases hold a wealth of sweetness. Cookies are sold by the pound, and the options include the Chesapeake, with chocolate chips, coconut, and walnuts, and standbys such as sugar, oatmeal raisin, pecan sandies, chocolate chip, ginger snaps, and triple chocolate. But it's the baked nuttiness of the peanut butter cookies that remain one of our favorites. The signature cakes include the Mozart, a yellow variety with raspberry and Bavarian cream fillings, and the Trazom, a chocolate cake with the same goodness inside. In all, more than 20 cakes are sold, as are cupcakes, scones, cannoli, brownies, doughnuts, and pies. A rack holds fresh English toast, challah, and other freshly baked breads. A cafe section offers salads and sandwiches, but whenever we venture toward it, we're reminded of the adage, "Life's uncertain; eat dessert first." So it's the baked sweets that command our attention and cause preschool boys to gleefully shout "Baker-yyyy! Baker-yyy!" as they run around the store on a sugar high.

Swagat's Spices & Indian Specialties, 309 Aragona Blvd., Virginia Beach, VA 23462; (757) 490-3374. Aisles and aisles of exotica await at the area's largest East Indian market. Even the most elusive ingredients can be found here. Although there is a language barrier, the staff will usually work with you to find exactly what's needed, be it ghee, naan, paneer, produce, spices, teas, even henna. For cooks just beginning a foray into East Indian ways, there's a continent of inspiration along an aisle of boxed "kits" for dishes such as *shai paneer masala,* with shopping lists for everything else that's needed printed right on the box. Two things to consider before leaving. Should you buy one of those CDs near the door to set the mood for your at-home East Indian feast? And should you grab a Samosa, a deep-fried triangle pocket filled with exotically spiced meat? Why not do both?

Taste Unlimited, 3603 Pacific Ave., Virginia Beach, VA 23451; (757) 422-3399; tasteunlimited.com. Part sandwich shop, part gourmet food market, Taste Unlimited has celebrated the region's cuisine since its first store opened in 1973. The best place to start is with a taste: Try a sandwich or wrap—turkey, ham, or roast beef—with the house dressing that locals adore. We don't know the recipe, but the dressing perks up everything it touches with its hints of mayo, steak sauce, spicy brown mustard, and Worcestershire sauce. You can eat in the dining area, but then it's time to browse. The stores are known for carrying products produced locally and around the commonwealth, such as Virginia peanuts, Taste of the Bay cheese straws, and cookbooks. A refrigerated section holds sassy Southern pimiento cheese, Brunswick stew and French herb cheese spread, all house-made. At the Pacific Avenue location, nearest the oceanfront, a dispenser lets you refill your empty bottles with an item that isn't from around here—olive oil from the Laconia section of Greece. Before you go, indulge again, this time in one of the gelatos. Our choice: sea-salt caramel. **Additional locations:** 4097 Shore Dr., Virginia Beach, VA 23455; (757) 464-1566; 1544 Laskin Rd., Ste. 110, Virginia Beach, VA 23451; (757) 425-1858; 717 N. Eden Way, Ste. 600, Chesapeake, VA 23320; (757) 424-4583; 6464 Hampton Blvd., Norfolk, VA 23508; (757) 623-7770; 702 Mariners Row, Newport News, VA 23606; (757) 596-8651.

TBonz and Tuna, 429 Dock St., Tappahannock, VA 22560; (804) 445-8862; tbonzandtuna.com. Stop in for a sammy stuffed with Boar's Head meats, and you'll wish you'd brought the cooler. This gourmet meat and fish market is owned by a local meat cutter who earned his chops in area supermarkets and now offers a place to get cut-to-order free-range chicken, organic chicken, pork tenderloin, baby back ribs, pork chops and pork ribs, either country or western style. Want a 1-inch-thick T-bone? Got you covered. A 2-incher? No problem. If you're in the market for seafood, what you want is likely lurking on ice or in the freezer case. Think alligator sausage, sushi-grade tuna, frogs' legs, crayfish, lobster tails, stone crabs or locally fresh-caught fishes, soft-shell crabs, hard crabs, and shrimp—steamed in-house. Beer and wine are available, too. Boaters will appreciate the location, just across from a public boat ramp. Just haul the cooler across the street, and the friendly staff will hook you up.

Terebinth Patisserie & Bistro, **717 Eden Way N., Ste. 610, Chesapeake, VA 23320; (757) 410-0900; terebinthlove.com.** It's hard to believe you're in the midst of the Greenbrier strip-mall section of Chesapeake when you enter this eatery, which opened in 2010. It's a calming space, with mustard-colored walls, high ceilings, and padded black leather chairs and banquettes. Light jazz is the soundtrack, and there's a coffee-shop feel. Customers are reading books, checking e-mail, or engaging in conversation. First, you must decide what to eat. If it's before 3 p.m., you could go savory, with a panini or a salad or the macaroni and cheese. Or you could indulge in one of the temptations displayed in the pastry case, where jewel-toned French *macarons* and red velvet cake share space. Or you could opt for the Elvis, a peanut butter and banana cupcake. If you're a first-timer, you get a free *macaron,* with its flaky shell that gives way to a soft, chewy center that holds a delicate raspberry, Earl Grey tea, or other flavor. Lattes are served with a design that has been etched with cocoa in the frothiness that sits on top.

Uncle Chuck's Seafood, **3640 Dam Neck Rd., Virginia Beach, VA 23453; (757) 263-4788; on Facebook.** A crooked crosshatch of coolers sits out on the front porch of this seafood shop at the Virginia Beach Farmers' Market, which is open year-round. Other coolers await inside, where owner Chuck Macin, more seafood curator than fishmonger, offers up backstories on all he sells, including several types of Eastern Shore oysters, local fishes, and more exotic offerings such as sweet shrimp from Argentina or Arctic char and other fishes from far-off lands. Another cool thing about Uncle Chuck is that he's a heck of a cook and can offer suggestions on what to do with all he sells. And don't think about leaving without asking what Virginia cheeses he might have on hand in that little refrigerator on the back wall.

Welton's Seafood Market, 3621 Pacific Ave., Virginia Beach, VA 23451; (757) 428-6740; weltonsseafood.com. The seafood is excellent, but it's the service that keeps 'em coming back. At the tiny structure that houses the store in Virginia Beach, owner Richard Welton or daughter Ashley usually is behind the fish case. At the larger Norfolk venue, friend John Crooks mans the counter. At both places, customers get to know their fishmonger, who returns the favor. And at both locations, there's not a hint of fishiness in the air. In Norfolk, Crooks will ask questions about your preparation plans. If he doesn't have the seafood you're after, he's been known to call competitors or to offer a substitute, then grab a whole fish and carve perfect fillets for you on the spot. Want oysters? He'll let you examine them up close before he packages them for you. Considering a halibut dinner? Crooks will ask when you plan to make it and, if you say 3 days out, he'll smile and gently suggest that you wait awhile to make a purchase. That's because more than three-fourths of Welton's inventory is local and most of it is freshly caught, from the waters off North Carolina to the nearby Lynnhaven Inlet. For non-local varieties, the owner is careful about his suppliers; the salmon, for instance, is raised in Canadian freshwaters. Both stores have Facebook pages and do a pretty good job of keeping them updated, which lets you know what's on ice before you get there. And if the name Welton rings a bell to locals, that's because Richard is a descendant of one of the families that ran the Smith & Welton department stores for more than a century. **Additional location:** 100 W. 20th St., Norfolk, VA 23517; (757) 622-2702.

Westmoreland Berry Farm & Market, 1235 Berry Farm
Ln., Oak Grove, VA 22443; (804) 224-9171; westmorelandberryfarm
.com. Got kids? Take 'em here, because they will never forget the Goat
Walk. It's a singular spectacle to see the farm goats traipse along a
narrow bridge high above the main road to reach the feeder on the
other side, which human kids are welcome to operate. Post-gawk,
ride the spotted Cow Train. Or hop on a hay wagon for a ride to the
pick-your-own fields, which, depending on the season, might be flush
with strawberries, raspberries, blackberries, or pumpkins. Refuel at the
Eagle Cafe with a ham sandwich on rustic bread or a fresh berry sundae
made with real ice cream churned just one county over. Or just savor a
scoop of black cherry, cappuccino, or honey cake. Then walk it all off
at the adjacent 729-acre Voorhees Nature Preserve on the banks of the
Rappahannock River. Four miles of moderately challenging, wooded
trails wind through the Nature Conservancy property, and bald eagles
frequently soar overhead. Then, check out the farm market for fresh
produce, jams, jellies, and such. Open spring through fall.

Wineries, Breweries & Distilleries

Back Bay Brewing Co., 630 N. Witchduck Rd., Virginia Beach,
VA 23462; (757) 513-3359; backbaybrewingco.com.

Beach Brewing Co., 2585 Horse Pasture Rd., Ste. 204, Virginia
Beach, VA 23453; (757) 563-2337; beachbrewingcompany.com.

Brass Cannon Brewing, 8105 Richmond Rd., Ste. 105, Toano,
VA 23168; (757) 566-0001; facebook.com/BrassCannonBrewing.

ON THE VINE

The three wineries in this region produce white varietals such as Chardonnay and Vidal Blanc, reds such as Cabernet Franc, Chambourcin, Merlot, and Norton, and fruity varieties such as blueberry and strawberry.

Chesapeake Bay Distillery, 2669 Production Rd., Virginia Beach, VA 23454; (757) 692-4083; chesapeakebaydistillery.com.

New Kent Winery, 8400 Old Church Rd., New Kent, VA 23124; (804) 932-8240; newkentwinery.com.

O'Connor Brewing Co., 521 W. 25th St., Norfolk, VA 23517; (757) 623-2337; oconnorbrewing.com.

Pungo Ridge Winery, 1665 Princess Anne Rd., Virginia Beach, VA 23456; (757) 426-1665; pungoridgewinery.com.

Saude Creek Vineyards, 16230 Cooks Mill Rd., Lanexa, VA 23089; (804) 966-5896; saudecreek.com.

Smartmouth Brewing Co., 1309 Raleigh Ave., Ste. 300, Norfolk, VA 23507; (757) 624-3939; smartmouthbrewing.com.

St. George Brewing Co., 204 Challenger Way, Hampton, VA 23666; (757) 865-7781; stgeorgebrewingco.com.

Two Fathers Brewing Co., 2016 Belvidere Rd., Virginia Beach, VA 23454; twofathersbrewing.com.

Chesapeake Farmers' Market, two locations: **Battlefield Park, 120 Reservation Rd., Chesapeake, VA 23322; Chesapeake City Park, 900 Greenbrier Parkway, Chesapeake, VA 23320.** Wed and Sat from 8 a.m. to 1 p.m., mid-June through late Nov.

City Center at Oyster Point Farmers' Market, 705 Mariners Row, Newport News, VA 23606. Thu from 10 a.m. to 2 p.m., May through Sept.

Five Points Community Farm Market, 2500 Church St., Norfolk, VA 23504. Thurs and Fri from 11 a.m. to 7 p.m., Sat from 9 a.m. to 5 p.m., Sun from 11 a.m. to 5 p.m., year-round.

Franklin Farmers' Market, 210 S. Main St., Franklin, VA 23851. Sat from 8 a.m. to 1 p.m., mid-May through mid-Oct.

Peninsula Town Center Farmers' Market, 4410 E. Claiborne Square, Hampton, VA 23666. Sun from 11 a.m. to 3 p.m., mid-May through Oct.

Smithfield Farmers' Market, downtown Smithfield. Sat from 9 a.m. to noon, late March through Oct.

Suffolk Farmers' Market, Suffolk Visitor Center Pavilion, 524 N. Main St., Suffolk, VA 23434. Wed from 3 to 6 p.m., Sat from 9 a.m. to 2 p.m., late April through late Nov.

Tappahannock Farmers' Market, 300 Prince St., Tappahannock, VA 22560. Third Sat of the month from 9 a.m. to 1 p.m., April through Nov.

Virginia Beach Farmers' Market, 3640 Dam Neck Rd., Virginia Beach, VA 23453. Mon through Fri from 8:30 a.m. to 5 p.m., Sat from 8:30 a.m. to 4 p.m. and Sun from 10 a.m. to 4 p.m., year-round.

Yorktown Market Days, 425 Water St., Yorktown, VA 23690. Sat from 8 a.m. to noon, May through Dec.

Williamsburg

Every American food lover should journey to Colonial Williamsburg, home to some of the nation's oldest eateries. And why not, on the way, prepare a toast? Then make your way to Raleigh Tavern, established in 1717, in the heart of the historic district, and remember statesmen such as George Washington, Thomas Jefferson, Peyton Randolph, and Patrick Henry, who on this very spot defied British rule and debated and advanced the ideals of freedom and democracy that the country was built on. You can't eat there, but you can savor the history.

Today, four other authentically restored taverns offer menus that hew to the hearty fare that the founding fathers dined on. Visit one, and drink to the history of the place. Over at the Governor's Palace and the Public Armoury, demonstration kitchens detail how it was prepared.

But a world of flavors awaits beyond the historic venues—first-class French dining, a swoon-inducing chocolate shop opened after a James Beard Award–winning chocolatier emerged from retirement; top-notch steakhouses; a Spanish *tienda;* a small green building where pies, savory and sweet, are the order of the day; and a place where the "canary" in the name refers not to wings but to wine.

Heck, in the summer you can even tie on a bib and tuck into a pile of steamed blue crabs, and toast again, but this time with a nice, big knob of backfin.

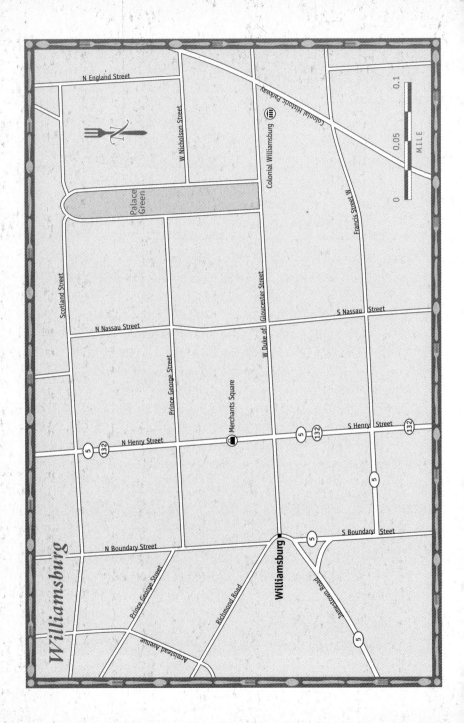

Williamsburg

N England Street
W Nicholson Street
Palace Green
Scotland Street
N Nassau Street
Prince George Street
Merchants Square
N Henry Street
N Boundary Street
Prince George Street
Armistead Avenue
Richmond Road
Williamsburg
Jamestown Road
S Boundary Steet
S Henry Street
S Nassau Street
W Duke of Gloucester Street
Francis Street W
Colonial Williamsburg
Colonial Historic Parkway

MILE
0   0.05   0.1

5 132
5 132
5 132
5
5
5

Berret's Seafood Restaurant & Taphouse Grill, 199 S. Boundary St., Williamsburg, VA 23185; (757) 253-1847; berrets .com; Seafood; $$–$$$$. After a day scouting Colonial Williamsburg's sights—the Powder Magazine, the grandeur of the Governor's Palace, the blacksmith shop—take off your tri-cornered hat and get some sustenance at Berret's, a 20-year mainstay of the Merchants Square dining scene that's open for lunch and dinner. Choose between the ultra-casual Taphouse, a covered, outdoor dining area open April through October, and the more formal indoor restaurant open year-round. The specialty of both sides of the house is seafood. Get your crustacean fix at the Taphouse with the Triple Crab, a meal that stars an award-winning crab-cake sandwich—with lots of sweet backfin—topped with a crab salad accompanied by creamy she-crab soup. Berret's is the rare restaurant that uses roe in its recipe, and the soup is topped, as it should be, with a dram of sherry. In high summer, order steamed crabs and pick them right there on the porch. On the more formal side of the house, choose from dishes such as seafood, sausage and duck gumbo, lamb, or steaks. Seasonal fishes are cooked in parchment—if it's summer, try the cobia if they have it. It's a star of the sea.

Blue Talon Bistro, 420 Prince George St., Williamsburg, VA 23185; (757) 476-2583; bluetalonbistro.com; French-inspired Comfort Food; $$$. Roosters rim the dining room of this cheerful, French-leaning, breakfast-lunch-and-dinner bistro in the heart of historic Williamsburg's Merchants Square. Open the menu, and it's obvious that a brigade of talented chefs staffs the kitchen. They're led by Executive Chef–Owner David Everett, whose love of comfort food and Virginia products blankets the menu. Feeling adventurous? Try the *pied de cochon*. Yes, yes, that's pig's feet, people. It's an old-school Southern dish borne out of poverty. It's also considered a delicacy in France, and it's rarely found on a restaurant menu. The impossibly thin crepes are filled with creamed chicken and mushrooms, and the seared duck breast comes with a cherry sauce. For a lighter appetite, there's pâté, ever-changing and made in-house. And make time for a cocktail. The Blue Talon has one of the most inventive mixologist staffs around, and the menu of libations changes seasonally (see the recipe for **Blue Talon Cocktail** on p. 258). The Bee's Knees combines dry gin, honey, fresh-squeezed lemon, orange bitters, and fresh cracked pepper and gets a shard of honeycomb for the garnish. Historic cocktails such as the Devil's Backbone even get their own gigantic ice cubes, a thoughtful twist that invites a lingering tête-à-tête.

Dudley's Bistro, 4904 Courthouse St., Williamsburg, VA 23188; (757) 566-1157; on Facebook; Seafood/Steaks; $$$$. Talk about a shock to the system. When we drove to the circa 1905 farmhouse in Toano where we'd always found Chef Jim Kennedy busy in his herb garden or planning the next big game and wine dinner, we found a pizza joint instead. After a few days of mourning, we happened upon Dudley's Bistro in the new-fashioned, nary-a-tri-cornered-hat-to-be-seen New Town section of Williamsburg. Could it be? One look at the menu and we knew Kennedy was back in the kitchen—panfried oysters with tomato jam, herb crepes topped with wild boar bacon, duck confit and tomato jam, pan-seared rainbow trout atop house-made shrimp ravioli, goat cheesecake for dessert. Not too long afterward, he appeared in the nine-table dining room chatting with guests as he always did at the old place, talking about game nights he's planning, featuring antelope, bison, duck, quail, and venison, as well as the herbs he's started growing in the alfresco area planters. Kennedy's ardent locavore sensibilities combined with a "simple is best" culinary philosophy and more than three decades in the kitchen make this a not-to-be-missed experience.

Fat Canary, 410 W. Duke of Gloucester St., Williamsburg, VA 23185; (757) 229-3333; fatcanarywilliamsburg.com; Seafood/ Steaks; $$$–$$$$. In Colonial times, wine was referred to as "canary," a nod to the ships sailing to the New World that stopped in the Canary Islands for that provision and others. At the Fat Canary, Executive Chef Thomas Power Jr. offers a menu so rich in provisions it would make those old-time sailors drool. Yellowfin tuna, tempura-style, gets its kick from wasabi, flying-fish roe, and daikon. It was a longtime special that has made its way onto the permanent menu. The 2-inch-high pork chop, with a caramelized sear and perfect pink center, comes with house-made applesauce and a goat-cheese soufflé. Other entrees include guinea fowl and quail. The restaurant's contemporary dining room, with tinges of apple green, is small, and it's best to make reservations because seats, especially on weekends, can be hard to come by. Wine is the obvious drink here, but the cocktails can be playful. Try a Katy Pear-y, a refreshing combination of pear cognac, pear liquor, lemon, and bitters. The chef's family owns an adjoining shop where you can stock up on cheese and wine, that namesake "canary."

Green Leafe Cafe, 765 Scotland St., Williamsburg, VA 23185, (757) 220-3405; greenleafe.com; Beer Pub; $–$$. Beer is plentiful here, and you can choose your quaff from a lengthy list titled "The Bible of Buzz." More than 60 drafts and 150 bottled varieties are available, and *USA Today* named the place one of the Top 10 bars in the country. You'll find Virginia brews, including Bud Light made at the local Anheuser-Busch plant and ales from Legend Brewery in Richmond, as well as American beers and a handful from Europe. At the

Scotland Street location, hundreds of decorative taps line the walls, and the decor mixes the old—ceiling fans and wooden booths—with the new—a disco ball dangling from above. The cafe is a popular hangout for students from the nearby College of William & Mary, and the menu offers appetizers, salads and sandwiches, as well as signatures such as beef brisket and Aussie chicken. There's a Hawaiian influence on a few selections, including a burger and crab cakes that feature pineapple salsa. It's a tomato-based condiment whose heat is tempered by the sweetness of the fruit. You'll be tempted to put the salsa on everything, except, of course, the beer. It's cold and frothy and goes down smoothly just as it is. **Additional location:** 4345 New Town Ave., Williamsburg, VA 23188; (757) 221-9582.

Honey Butter's Kitchen, 4680 Monticello Ave., Williamsburg, VA 23188; (757) 221-8038; honeybutterskitchen.com; Casual American; $–$$. This strip-mall restaurant oozes down-home charm and has the feel of 1950s diner, complete with Formica-topped tables and a ring of booths around the interior. There's an antique stove on display, and old cast-iron pots and pans adorn the walls. You expect to find a jukebox, but instead oldies and doo-wop are piped through the speakers. The eatery is the newest restaurant opened by owners Jason and Heidi Steeg, who also run the local Five Forks Cafe. Honey Butter's is a family place, where you can build your own breakfast or munch on lunch and dinner. Sandwiches include BLTs, Monte Cristos, and Reubens, and you'll want to try a side of Chesapeake fries, seasoned with Old Bay. Or opt for the garlic-fried potatoes, with a sweet roasted garlicky taste that complements rather than overpowers the spuds. The dinner menu offers Southern favorites, like pork barbecue and crab cakes, as well as roasted turkey and New York strip. The waitstaff oozes down-home charm, too, and is quick to offer suggestions when you're not sure what to order.

Opus 9, 5143 Main St., Williamsburg, VA 23188; (757) 645-4779; opus9steakhouse.com; Steaks; $$$$. Welcome to Williamsburg's finest steakhouse. Opus 9 sits in a commercial district of mostly mid-scale chain stores a few minutes from Colonial Williamsburg. While the surroundings lack the charm of the historic capital, inside the restaurant it's all contemporary elegance and fine food. Ol' Blue Eyes sings in the background, the black-and-white-clad waitstaff sport bow ties and cufflinks, and a baby grand piano stands ready for Sunday brunch when a jazz duo or trio sets the mood. The restaurant offers a quartet of signature steaks, most notably an unusual bone-in filet mignon served with Pommery mustard and fresh horseradish. The New York strip gets a classic au poivre preparation, and the Oscar 9 is a filet topped with fresh crabmeat and, here's the twist, a portobello. Steaks are cooked unerringly to order, and a choice of a baked white or sweet potato offers another nice touch. Seafood also comes expertly prepared, so why not start with lobster scampi?

Peter Chang, 1203 Richmond Rd., Williamsburg, VA 23185; (757) 345-5829; peterchangrestaurant.com; Chinese; $–$$. This is the second Virginia restaurant opened by Chinese-born chef Peter Chang, and it continues the tradition begun at the Charlottesville location of inventive dishes that go beyond the typical Chinese buffet. Chang has been called a master of peppers, and the spiciness of some offerings can surprise unsuspecting diners. The hottest dishes are marked on the menu, and they often come with a warning from the waitstaff: If you can't stand the heat, get out of the Szechwan. The duck in a stone pot combines intense chunks of duck meat with strips of tofu in a rich broth that's spicy but not scorching. Nothing is more dramatic than the bamboo fish, a dish plated with pieces of ornamental bamboo and flavored with cumin, pepper powder, green scallions, and cilantro. **Additional locations:** 2162 Barracks Rd., Charlottesville, VA 22903, (434) 244-9818, peterchang-charlottesville.com (see p. 188); 11424 W. Broad St., Glen Allen, VA 23060, (804) 364-1688, peterchangrva.com; 1771 Carl

D. Silver Pkwy., Fredericksburg, VA 22401, (540) 786-8988, peterchangs chinese.com; and 3364 Princess Anne Road, Suite 505, Virginia Beach, VA 23456, (757) 468-2222.

Landmarks

Le Yaca, 1430 High St., Suite 801, Williamsburg, VA 23188; (757) 220-3616; leyacawilliamsburg.com; French; $$$$. The roots of Le Yaca, a classic French restaurant near Colonial Williamsburg, go back to the French Alps and Saint-Tropez, where the first two Le Yacas thrived. The original Williamsburg location opened in 1980, and the restaurant moved to its new location in 2014. Le Yaca has thrived ever since a favorable review by Phyllis Richman of the *Washington Post* 4 years later. The white-on-white dining room and professional waitstaff set the stage for authentic French fare such as the lamb, which hangs roasting in front of the flames of the massive open fireplace. Start with a classic preparation of snails, a crab-filled crepe, or a fresh duck liver served with caramelized white peach and port wine sauce. For the main course, it's hard to bypass Dover sole meunière, starring imported sole, or twin lobster tails with a classic beurre blanc. Our favorite way to dine here is from the three-course prix-fixe lunch menu or the four-course menu at dinner. Bon appétit, either way.

Old Chickahominy House, 1211 Jamestown Rd., Williamsburg, VA 23185; (757) 229-4689; oldchickahominy.com; Traditional Southern; $. Of all things, it's the house's ham biscuits that have won this humble restaurant a starring role in glossy spreads in the likes of *Saveur* magazine. The white dough is rolled out to a particular thickness, cut into squares, baked, sliced and stuffed with Edwards's ham, which is cured in the next county over. Those lauded biscuits share the breakfast and lunch menus with all manner of low-country Virginia

There's Ham in Those Houses

By now, you've got to be wondering, what the heck's up with all the ham? Well, there's a reason that Virginia became the Country Ham Capital of the U.S. of A. The tailor-made weather made us do it.

See, in late December, when hogs reach slaughter weight, the first frost has usually passed and the insect population has been quashed. Hogs get slaughtered, and dressed out, and the hams get cloaked in salt and nestled in shelves in smokehouses for the winter months, when it's neither cold enough to freeze the meat nor warm enough for spoilage.

At spring smoking time, hams are hung from rafters, greenwood or fruitwood fires are stoked for a few days to flavor the meat, and 60-degree temperatures keep the houses from getting too hot. Finally, the fires are snuffed, and the hams are left dangling from rafters for months—or even years—and some say that the sweet Virginia breeze imparts a flavor all its own.

Colonial Williamsburg holds proof that we've loved country hams since the birth of our nation. Of the 88 original structures in Colonial Williamsburg, 12 are smokehouses, according to the *Colonial Williamsburg Journal*. Fifty more have been reconstructed, many on footprints of original buildings. We suggest that pork aficionados make a point of visiting the Governor's Palace, the Wythe House, and the Peyton Randolph House, where smokehouses are still in use.

Then, while wandering the byways of rural Virginia, try to spot old smokehouses behind aging farmhouses, square-ish, windowless structures with pointed roofs. Whoever spots the most gets treated to a salty ham biscuit. Now that's a prize.

comfort food—Brunswick stew, chicken and dumplings, hominy grits, and creamed ham on toast. The Chickahominy first opened in 1955, then following a robbery, the new place was built on Route 5, one of the main roads curling through the historic district. The building, with its deep front porch and wide barn-door entrance, was constructed partly with salvage from buildings dating back 200 years. It has the soul and feel of Colonial Williamsburg, although it's a short drive away. The warren of small rooms that make up the dining room feature roomy tables with brass candlesticks and ladder-back chairs. Curtains are swag brocade, the accents are authentic, and the service is as sweet as the tea. Reservations are recommended, but even if you're asked to wait a spell, time moves quickly while rooting around the adjacent antiques shop. And here's a perk: The restaurant collects the scraps of country ham left on the cutting board, packs them into Styrofoam cups and sells them for about $3. Back home, you'll find a million uses for that pure gold ham dust.

Regency Room at Williamsburg Inn, 136 E. Francis St., Williamsburg, VA 23185; (757) 229-2141; colonialwilliamsburg .com; New American; $$$$. Nothing is left to chance at this elegant restaurant that's part of the Williamsburg Inn, built by John D. Rockefeller and opened in 1937. The setting, not surprisingly, is a favorite for weddings and receptions. The structure's graceful portico entrance welcomes guests to the Southern hospitality they'll find inside. The restaurant's service is impeccable, and the dinner menu is decadent, with appetizers such as oysters Rockefeller—of course—and crabmeat Randolph. Entrees are New World, such as the locally sourced crab cakes, and Old World, such as chateaubriand and pork tenderloin schnitzel. There's a caviar menu, where you can order roe from American paddlefish, American hackleback, or a couple of kinds of sturgeon, and a French press menu, where you can get the inn's signature coffee roast or blends from around the world. Sunday offers a lavish brunch.

EATING THE COLONIAL WAY

Four taverns in Colonial Williamsburg, one of the region's most popular tourist attractions, offer visitors the chance to dine in re-creations of eateries that were gathering spots for colonists. Virginia's early leaders—George Washington, Thomas Jefferson, and Patrick Henry, to name just a few—often ate here when the town was the capital of the growing colony. Today, the servers dress in period costumes, and the taverns retain a rustic feel. At night, you'll be eating by candlelight; there was of course no electricity in olden times. Even the menus often feature early American spellings, so you'll find "salats," or salads, and Welsh "rarebit," or rabbit. Here's a taste of what's in store:

Chowning's Tavern, *109 E. Duke of Gloucester St., Williamsburg, VA 23185; (757) 229-2141.* This bar originally opened in 1766, when the restlessness of the Colonists hadn't yet reached fever pitch. Lunch and dinner are offered and, when the weather is nice, you can enjoy garden seating. The menu includes barbecue pork ribs, Brunswick stew, sandwiches, and a "soupe" of the day.

Christiana Campbell's Tavern, *101 S. Waller St., Williamsburg, VA 23185; (757) 229-2141.* The original was a favorite of George Washington, who liked the tavern's seafood, and he'd be happy in the replica that stands today. The menu includes crab, fish, scallops, and shrimp. End your meal with a Rummer, a potent drink of dark rum with splashes of apricot and peach brandies.

King's Arms Tavern, *416 E. Duke of Gloucester St., Williamsburg, VA 23185; (757) 229-2141.* The original opened its doors in 1772, and today King's Arms offers a menu heavy on Southern comfort foods. You'll find dishes such as peanut soup, pork chops, and seafood macaroni.

Shields Tavern, *422 E. Duke of Gloucester St., Williamsburg, VA 23185; (757) 229-2141.* You can feast on modern-day fare like Carolina-style barbecue sandwiches or try an 18th-century dish described as ale-potted beef with mushrooms, carrots, and pearl onions over mashed potatoes, which we today call pot roast.

Traditions, 310 S. England St., Williamsburg, VA 23185; (757) 220-7976; colonialwilliamsburg.com/do/restaurants/resort-restaurants/traditions; Neo-Southern; $$$$. Do not think hotel restaurant. Consider instead the possibilities that come from combining history and a talented chef. This restaurant, located inside the Williamsburg Lodge in the heart of Colonial Williamsburg, honors its historic setting by scouring local family farms and artisanal food producers to fill the larder, just as the tavern owners did in Colonial times. Much of the produce comes from the 90 acres of gardens in the historic district. Fishes are local, mushrooms from a grower a couple of counties over, and Executive Chef Rhys H. Lewis even manages to find enough of the elusive white Hayman sweet potatoes to turn them into dumplings and put them on the seasonally changing menu. That's the specialty of the house—old-school ingredients with a neo-Southern twist, artfully presented. Consider a starter of persimmon BBQ'd quail. Persimmons are native to Virginia—Colonials made beer from them—and a farmer tends a grove of them not too far from here. Order the braised pork shank, served with carrots, turnips, and greens, and you'll be eating like the royal governor. Check the restaurant's schedule for frequent wine and cheese or chocolate pairings hosted by the chef.

The Trellis Restaurant, 403 W. Duke of Gloucester St., Williamsburg, VA 23185; (757) 229-8610; thetrellis.com; New American; $$–$$$. This landmark, just a stone's throw away from Colonial Williamsburg, helped bring fine dining to the area when it opened more than three decades ago. You can eat in one of several rooms inside, opt for a spot at the bar or choose outside seating, where you can watch shoppers go in and out of the nearby Merchants Square boutiques. The menu, which changes often, relies on locally sourced foods for offerings that combine Southern comfort with

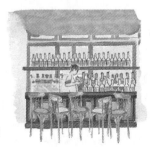

American favorites. You might find roasted quail with Edwards's sausage or a boneless rack of lamb with lamb sausage. For dessert, try the dish that the restaurant is best known for. Created by then-chef Marcel Desaulniers, Death by Chocolate is a stunner. It's a seven-layer chocolate torte, with a house-made white chocolate truffle, chocolate ice cream, and a rich, gooey dark chocolate sauce. If the name of the dessert is to be believed, it's not a bad way to go.

Specialty Stores, Markets & Producers

Aromas, 431 Prince George St., Williamsburg, VA 23185; (757) 221-6676; aromasworld.com. The name of shop refers to the tantalizing coffee smells that permeate this eatery and make their way outside, where guests gather around small sidewalk tables. Inside, you can get coffee drinks, as well as breakfast, lunch and dinner, and seating is available there, too. The decor is a cheery mix of reds and mustard yellows, and the chatter of students from the College of William & Mary and tourists provides a soundtrack. The place is usually packed, and you sometimes have to work your way to the counter to place your order. Once there, check out the display cases, where you'll find a variety of cakes—the peanut butter fudge is a must-try—as well as brownies, cheesecakes, cream puffs, éclairs, and muffins. The atmosphere is homey, and the staff knows the regulars on a first-name basis. The sign above the counter says it all: "Yummy food pickup here." Get yours with a cup of joe.

Carrot Tree Kitchens, 1782 Jamestown Rd., Williamsburg, VA 23185; (757)-229-0957; carrottreekitchens.com. This bakery started with Debi Helseth's obsession to create the perfect carrot cake. It was 1984, and she was challenged to come up with a better version by a restaurant manager. She did what any Southern girl would do; she called her grandmother and asked for the family recipe. By 1995, she had launched this bakery in Williamsburg—additional Carrot Trees would open in nearby Jamestown and Yorktown. Her line has expanded to other sweets, including brownies, lemon bars, pies, and specialty cakes, such as coconut and almond supreme. Sandwiches and other lunch items are available for takeout, or you can eat at one of the seven tables in the apple-green dining room. The carrot cakes remain a big draw. They're available in one, two, or three layers, and offered in two sizes, a standard 9-inch or a 6-inch "baby" cake. To name her bakery, Debi used words from her own history. The "carrot" part is obvious; the "tree" came from her wedding. She and her husband were married under a locally famous oak in nearby Colonial Williamsburg.

The Cheese Shop, 410 W. Duke of Gloucester St., Williamsburg, VA 23185; (757) 220-0298; cheeseshopwilliamsburg.com. Here's how we like to start a foraging session at The Cheese Shop: Walk right past the entrance, veer to the right, and descend the narrow brick stairway to enter the most glorious basement, with a faintly musty smell, where 4,000 wines, 140 craft beers, and a knowledgeable staff await you. Taste, smell, buy a bottle or case and then traipse up the staircase at the back of the Wine Cellar and—voilà!—The Cheese Shop. It's a full-service gourmet emporium with all sorts of chocolates, crackers, oils, pastas and a made-to-order sandwich shop at the back of the store. But the cheeses star here. Tastings are encouraged, and the cheese cutters behind the counter can expertly recommend a cheese to complement your wine haul or for a quick bite on the patio. Or better yet, do both! And here's a tip: On the patio, avoid the table nearest the trash can. A swarm of bees agrees that's the best place to dine.

Discover Teas, 1915 Pocahontas Trail, E-4, Village Shops at Kingsmill, Williamsburg, VA 23185; (757) 847-5190; discoverteas .com. Here's the plan: Drop the kids at Busch Gardens for a romp with the roller coasters and head across the street for a shot of zen. Open the door, and pause for a moment while breathing in the sweet, tannin-y aroma of the shop. Then head to the table in the center of the room, where dozens of loose teas are available for olfactory trial runs. Owner Kenneth Roberts stocks 100 loose teas, a blend-your-own tea bar, as well as every tea accessory imaginable. There's always a pot or two brewing, but call ahead for frequent tastings and the dates of Roberts's weekly tea appreciation classes. There's a second location 20 minutes east in Newport News.

Jamestown Pie Company, 1804 Jamestown Rd., Williamsburg, VA 23185; (757) 229-7775; buyapie.com. You can go savory or sweet at this little green cottage, where a steady stream of customers comes to get their daily pie fix. The pizzas feature a thick, fluffy crust, and some are topped with the green peppers, ham, mushrooms, and onions you've come to expect. Be adventurous. The River Crab Pie has giant lumps of crabmeat in a white sauce. The Chesapeake Bay offers bay scallops and shrimp. The Surry combines crabmeat and prosciutto. The potpies—including beef, chicken, turkey, and veggie—are deep-dished and deeply addictive. Sandwiches are available, and dessert also comes in a crust. Go nuts with pecan or peanut pie. Go sweet with a long line of fruit pies, including bumbleberry, cherry, raspberry, and strawberry. You can go whole hog with an entire pie, or go easy on your waistline with a single slice. But definitely go. There's no seating—this is a take-out place—so be warned: As you're driving away with your order, you'll be tempted to pull over and dig in on the spot.

La Tienda, 1325 Jamestown Rd., Williamsburg, VA 23185; (800) 710-4304; tienda.com. Don Harris fell in love with Spain while stationed there in the 1960s as a Navy chaplain. During the next decade, Don's naval career continued, and he and his wife, Ruth, moved their family to a small Spanish city. They loved the food, the people and the culture. Back in the States, they eventually opened La Tienda, which means "The Shop," to bring a taste of the culture they missed to their American counterparts. The store carries hundreds of products, from saffron strands, just perfect for paella, to a paella pan so large it could double as a coffee-table top. Two types of Spain's famous ham, or *jamon,* are available—a Serrano and an Iberico—as well as beans, breads, cheeses, crackers, and pasta. A wine room features bottles from Spain and beyond, and tastings are held every Saturday. Stop by the store on Friday afternoon for fresh paella or the following day for tapas. If you can't get there, you can order products from the store's website.

MAD About Chocolate, 204 Armistead Ave., Williamsburg, VA 23185; (757) 645-2995; madaboutchocolate.us. Sans the lure of the commonwealth's Colonial capital, a certain tribe of epicures still would make the pilgrimage to Williamsburg just to wallow in the chocolate-y goodness of this tiny, artsy, chocolate-centric shop. Marcel Desaulniers, world-renowned chef and chocolatier, emerged from a 2-year recess in 2012 to open the place with his artist wife, Connie. In Virginia, the sigh of relief was audible clear to the coast. Desaulniers is the James Beard Award–winning cookbook author of *Death by Chocolate,* named for the devastating signature dessert served at The Trellis Restaurant in Williamsburg. Desaulniers sold that place—and the dessert—before his short hiatus. No worries. There's plenty here to savor in the form of Desaulniers's scrumptious signature cookies, immense and ooey-gooey and virtually all of them warm from the oven. Frankly, my dears, it's a destination spot, a bucket list sort of place. Come ready to indulge. While you wait for your order, admire Connie's whimsical artwork, much of it for sale. A visit is worth every strained button, slimmed wallet, and extra mile on the treadmill.

The Peanut Shop of Williamsburg, 414 Prince George St., Williamsburg, VA 23185; thepeanutshop.com. This shop, in the Merchants Square shopping center near Colonial Williamsburg, carries all things peanut. You'll find barbecue peanuts, butter toffee peanuts, cinnamon peanuts, green-boiled peanuts, honey mustard peanuts, peanut butter straws, milk and dark chocolate peanuts—even dill pickle peanuts. We could go on. So it comes as a quite a shock when the clerk calls the busy store to attention and points out the most popular item: white chocolate cashew toffee brittle. What's going on here? Cashews? "If you live more than 2 hours away and came with a spouse or a friend, you have to get two of them," the clerk advises. "That way, there can be no argument in the car about whose can it is." While you're here, you also might pick up a package or two of peanuts.

Winery & Breweries

Alewerks Brewing Co., 189-B Ewell Rd., Williamsburg, VA 23188; (757) 220-3670; alewerks.com.

Anheuser-Busch, 7801 Pocahontas Trail, Williamsburg, VA 23185; (757) 253-3600; anheuser-busch.com.

Williamsburg Winery, 5800 Wessex Hundred, Williamsburg, VA 23185; (757) 229-0999; williamsburgwinery.com.

Farmers' Market

Williamsburg Farmers Market, 402 W. Duke of Gloucester St., Williamsburg, VA 23185. Sat from 8 a.m. to noon, Apr through Oct; limited dates in off-season.

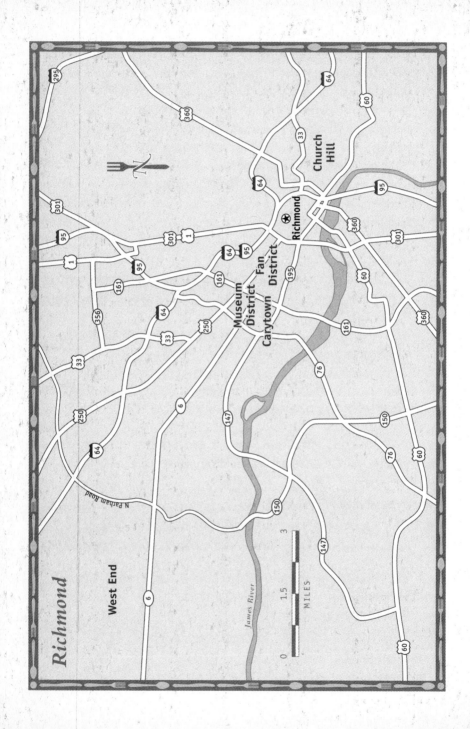

Richmond

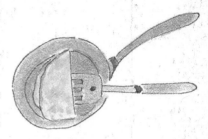

Small-town charm meets big-city cuisine in Virginia's capital, a city marked by gently rolling hills, a maze of one-way streets, and strongly defined neighborhoods. The food is Southern and so much more, where chefs put their own stamp on staples such as pork loins and shrimp and grits and use local fiddlehead ferns and grass-fed beef in creative ways. Many buildings in the heart of the city date to around 1900, and the best places to eat tend to be small eateries with tin ceilings, wooden floors, and exposed brick walls. One great restaurant is often only a few doors from the next, so here's an idea to savor as much of the city as you can in a short time: Consider having appetizers and cocktails at one place, moving elsewhere for entrees and devouring dessert at yet another. And, then, doing it all over again a few hours later.

Foodie Faves

Acacia mid-town, 2601 W. Cary St., Richmond, VA 23220; (804) 562-0138; acaciarestaurant.com; Seafood; $$$. You're in some of the best hands around at this contemporary restaurant in the city's Fan District. Executive Chef Dale Reitzer is a whiz with seafood, and he's a three-time semifinalist for the James Beard Foundation's best mid-Atlantic chef honor. He and his wife, Aline, opened Acacia—named for their dog—more than a decade ago in Carytown, and it continues to be a foodie favorite at its newer, more spacious location. The menu is loaded with locally grown and sourced food. The selections change seasonally, but you'll find appetizers such as squash blossoms filled with lobster and scallop mousse or oysters grown in the Piankatank River from nearby Chapel Creek Oyster Co. The crab cake is a specialty and one of the best in the state, a loosely held together concoction that overflows with large lumps of backfin and comes with a tantalizing bacon sauce. The wine list is impressive, and the cocktail menu is playful. Try a Monte Carlo, a mixture of bourbon, cognac, Aperol, and Italian bitters that is aggressive and soothing at the same time. A helpful waitstaff goes out of its way to answer questions and offer delicious-sounding descriptions of the dishes. That makes it difficult to know what to order, but when Chef Dale is cooking, it doesn't really matter.

Addis Ethiopian Restaurant, 9 N. 17th St., Richmond, VA 23219; (804) 308-3649; addisrichmond.com; Ethiopian; $$. It's hard to be territorial about your food when you're dining as this restaurant in the city's Shockoe Bottom section. Everything's made to share. The real treat is the *injera,* the airy and pliable Ethiopian bread made from flour milled from the tiny grain called teff. The discs are as big as a dinner plate, and they become your utensils. Just tear a piece off, and scoop up some lamb sauteed with garlic, jalapeño, onion, and rosemary. Or be brave and opt for a dish simmered in *awaze tibs,* a spicy sauce of red chile, garlic, and ginger. The *sambussas* are one of the signature dishes, an appetizer with spicy lentils inside crisply fried pastry shells. Entrees offer beef, chicken, lamb, and seafood, though many vegetarian options are available. The menu makes it easy for novices to try Ethiopian fare, and indicates the amount of burn you'll get from each dish. The waitstaff is quick to help, warning that the dishes labeled "hot" are just that. The restaurant has nine tables and four booths that line the front windows, where on summer weekends you can gaze at the goings-on at the 17th Street Farmers' Market across the street.

Aziza's On Main, 2110 E. Main St., Richmond, VA 23223; (804) 344-1523; azizasrichmond.com; Mediterranean; $$. This restaurant is Lebanese by day, Mediterranean by night, and charming always. With only 10 tables and a small bar tucked between brick walls, it's one of the hottest spots in town and was named Richmond's best restaurant by the local alternative weekly newspaper. Aziza is the name of the Lebanese mother of Rusty Fallen, who opened the place with her son Billy, the man behind Richmond's Billy Bread craze. They started small, offering only lunch. They added dinner and then pizza, which is made in the glowing brick oven near the rear, and finally Sunday brunch. The restaurant relies on locally sourced food, but the way it's put together here is far different from many of the neo-Southern restaurants now dotting the local scene. Lunch is Lebanese and might include tabbouleh or grape leaves. The pizzas range from traditional pepperoni and peppers to a prosciutto-and-arugula blend. The dinner menu is Mediterranean and changes often, but if they're available, try the octopus on house-made chitarra pasta with a vodka sauce or the gamey veal sweetbreads over garganelli pasta. They're unlike anything else you'll get in the city.

Burger Bach, 10 S. Thompson St., Richmond, VA 23221; (804) 359-1305; burgerbach.com; Gourmet Burgers; $$. It's hard to imagine another restaurant taking the humble hamburger more seriously than Burger Bach in the Carytown section of Richmond. A global search for the finest meats led the owners to a sustainable farm in New Zealand, where they found humanely raised Angus cattle and lamb grazing in the sunshine. They also found a name for the joint. Bach, pronounced "batch," is a vacation home, and that vibe has been captured in the laid-back feel of the place. Perch on a bar stool and, despite the bustle, the barman will suggest that he make you a fresh,

THE BEST BREAD IN RICHMOND

Few things make Richmonder foodies go as gaga as Billy Bread. A local urban legend, the bread has been part of the Richmond food scene since 1999, when it was first produced by Billy Fallen. The crust is crunchy, the inside airy and light. The hearty bread is made from hand-ground grains that include rye, spelt, hard red winter wheat, and wheat flour, and Billy says the yeast plays an important part in the texture and flavor. Billy fell in love with bread after tasting an amazing loaf years ago at a Vermont general store. He tracked down the baker, a Frenchman living in the area, and began an internship. Billy's now the master, and his bread can be found at some of the city's best restaurants, including Aziza's on Main, the restaurant he opened with his mother before leaving to concentrate on his dough. Some shops in Richmond and other Virginia cities also sell the bread. Billy has called his trademark "a naturally leavened, multigrained bread," but others say it's akin to French or sourdough. We just call it, simply, delicious.

pulpy juice, with or without spirits, while patrons around you order signature 6-ounce burgers "pink" or "no pink," the only way they're cooked. There's much more variety in the construction of the burgers. The Aucklander comes topped with avocado relish, uncured bacon, New Zealand Egmont cheese (a sort of Gouda-cheddar hybrid) and fresh, mixed greens. Lamb burgers get a kick from tzatziki, tarragon sauce, and sauteed mushrooms. Salads are made to order in big metal bowls right behind the bar, and check the restaurant's Facebook page for raw-bar happy hours featuring oysters from local creeks and rivers.

Can Can Brasserie, 3120 W. Cary St., Richmond, VA 23221; (804) 358-7274; cancanbrasserie.com; French; $$$. "A whirlwind of pleasures and vices." That's how a French artist characterized the scandalous cancan dance that challenged Victorian morality in turn-of-the-century France. It's the same spirit that endures in this little patch of Paris in the Carytown section of Richmond. On the sidewalk out front, a vendor's cart laden with fresh flowers is parked next to a violin-banjo duo. Inside the big, open, yellow-and-cream dining room, fresh loaves beckon from bakers' racks, and waiters in white, floor-length aprons deliver dishes of coq au vin, escargots, rabbit, and other properly prepared French dishes, many with a twist. That rabbit? It's served with a green apple-almond puree and pickled watermelon. Beyond the classics are hamburgers, topped with cheddar, gruyère or Roquefort and served with *frites,* of course. The salad of beets, topped with mâche, goat cheese, candied walnuts, and a shot of walnut vinaigrette, earned honors as Richmond's salad of the year in 2012. A light lunch—perhaps a salad and a split of Champagne—at the silver-topped bar that runs the length of the restaurant is a singular treat.

Capital Ale House, 623 E. Main St., Richmond, VA 23219; (804) 780-2537; capitalalehouse.com; Beer Pub; $$. It all started when the manager of Legend Brewing Co. in Richmond noticed an empty downtown storefront. He commenced to drinking beer with some entrepreneurial friends, and today the 115-year-old building is the flagship of Capital Ale House, the city's first serious beer pub. It's a wood-paneled place where you'll find aficionados hunched over the bar sipping on some of the 51 tap beers, 200 bottled beers, including a full page of Virginia microbrews. A well-thought-out menu lures newbies into the fold by organizing ales and lagers into four categories, such as "sharp & hoppy" or "malty & sweet." There are plenty of hard ciders for the hop-averse, and the hungry masses have not been neglected. Ho-hum bar food gets the boot in favor of dishes like chimichurri steak salad and Virginia chicken, which comes stuffed with corn bread and country ham with greens on the side. Wash it all down with, well, pretty much anything you can dream of. And take your time. The signature feature of the 60-foot-long bar is the frosty strip of ice that runs the length of it, there to keep your libation chilly cold.

Coppola's Deli, 1116 E. Main St., Richmond, VA 23219; (804) 225-0454; coppolasdelirichmond.com; Italian/Delicatessen; $. You know a place is good when folks who work at other restaurants recommend it. That's the deal with this deli, which gets heaps of high praise for its simple but tasty sandwiches. "It's the real thing," says a waitress who hops tables up the street. Coppola's is a classic delicatessen and market, where customers can get a mile-high club on three slices of wheat bread or a smoked turkey on a freshly baked roll. The corner eatery has a few tables on the sidewalk beneath its red-and-white-striped awning, but the real action is inside. You can shop the market area for deli meats, cheeses, wine, and other items, or order an Industrial and wait for the goodness to arrive at your table. This traditional Italian hero has salami, mushrooms, onions, peppers, lettuce, and tomatoes smothered in melted provolone. You even get a pickle on the side.

Edo's Squid, 411 N. Harrison St., Richmond, VA 23220; (804) 864-5488; Italian/Seafood; $$$$. You won't find a website for Edo's Squid, nor will you find it on Facebook. In fact, at night when it's open, it's pretty hard to find Edo's from the street, where it shares a down-trodden building with a sub shop that might or might not be shuttered. To get to Edo's, enter the door at the left corner of the building and ascend a narrow and steep staircase covered in cheap carpeting. It ends abruptly at a cache of paper towels and cleaning supplies stored

MEALS ON WHEELS, RICHMOND-STYLE

Maybe it's the idea of eating outside. Maybe it's the choices that range from oven-fired pizzas to homemade ice cream. Or maybe it's the festival atmosphere. Whatever the reason, the city's food-truck scene has exploded in recent years. On almost any day of the week when the weather gets warm, these trucks set up mobile food courts—sometimes outside a local brewery or farmers' market, other times at the Virginia Historical Society or a busy mall—and the city's hungry residents turn out en masse. You can find Asian-Mexican-American fusion tacos at **Boka Tako Truck,** with a bright yellow logo that makes it easy to spot. Or hop over to the **Pizza Tonight** unit, and get an artisan pizza fired in a mobile brick oven. The Margherita starts with a tomato sauce and is topped with mozzarella and basil; the Fig and Pig mixes fig preserves, prosciutto, and Gorgonzola. The Cajun influence is strong at **Curbside Creations,** where the po' boys offer alligator and shrimp. **Gelati Celesti** offers its heavenly ice creams from a food truck stamped with words such as "scrumptious" and "handmade." There are corn dogs at **Flynn's Foods,** Italian meatballs at **Meatball Co.,** crepes at **Paris Creperie.** And so much more. Most of the food is made to order, so lines can get long and patience is required. True fans recommend creating a meal from several trucks and, to save time, placing orders back to back from several units. Then all you have to do is wait for the goodies to get done, find a place to hang out, and enjoy the crowd.

against a wall. Go on. Open the unwelcoming door to the right, and there it is. It's a Richmond favorite, where a marble bust of Petronius, the ancient Roman "judge of elegance," guards the copper-topped bar, and the menu is scrawled on massive notepads hung on the exposed brick walls. Seafood offerings might include branzino and skate wing;

land offerings can be quail or lamb porterhouse. The chef also has a confident hand with simple, Italian classics. Start with the squid with arugula and beans, perfectly seasoned with garlic and olive oil. So what if the food you paid top dollar for comes on a chipped plate? The flavors make up for it. Petronius approves.

The Halligan Bar & Grill, 3 N. 17th St., Richmond, VA 23219; (804) 447-7981; Casual American; $. The first thing you notice when you walk into this bar is the fire truck in the wall. It's a real life-size 1973 Seagrave fire engine, with working lights and siren, that runs the length of the bar. The vehicle lets you know that this is as much a museum to firefighting as a place to grab a bite to eat. The restaurant is the inspiration of Shawn Gregory, a local firefighter, and his wife, Cynthia. Even the restaurant's name is a nod to firefighting—a Halligan bar is a tool used in rescue operations. The theme is carried out on the charred-looking walls, where firefighting memorabilia is displayed, and on the menu, which offers salads and wraps under a "Lites-N-Sirens" heading and fries and other sides under a "Flare Ups" label. The Wings of Fire are a locals' favorite, jumbo chicken pieces tossed in a variety of sauces. The house specialty is the Halligan sauce, but the 5-Alarm variety beckons those with a sense of adventure. Barbecue is another signature, and you can get it three ways—vinegary Carolina, slow-cooked Memphis, or dry-rubbed Texas. If you're in need of cooling off after all that heat, the bar has—no surprise—Hook & Ladder beers on tap.

Julep's New Southern Cuisine, 1719 E. Franklin St., Richmond, VA 23119; (804) 377-3968; juleps.net; Neo-Southern; $$$–$$$$. This corner restaurant in the city's Fan District is located in the oldest commercial building in Richmond, built back in 1817 when Virginian James Madison was president. Originally a lumber house, the structure since 2003 has been home to this celebration of Southern cuisine. It's an elegant and genteel place, with hardwood floors, an exposed brick wall and a spiral staircase that carries diners to seating on the second floor. Waiters, attired in white shirts and ties, take time to talk guests through the menu and offer suggestions. The fried green tomatoes, lightly breaded and perfectly fried, are touted as some of the best around, and they're accompanied by pimiento cheese and a peppadew aioli. The shrimp and grits are to die for. Executive Chef Randall Doetzer uses stone-ground grits from Wade's Mill in Raphine, adds andouille sausage, onions, peppers, spinach, and tomato, and finishes the dish with a lobster sauce that provides richness and creaminess. It's available as an appetizer and entree, and don't make the mistake of getting only the small portion. The rack of wild boar is a paean to Virginia, with its sides of sweet potatoes and oyster mushrooms. Ditto the Country Cioppino, with its blue crabs, crawfish, mussels, oysters, and sausage in a tomato broth with roasted fennel. Julep's is owned by Amy Ayers, whose sister restaurant, Mint, helps explains this one's name.

Kuba Kuba, 1601 Park Ave., Richmond, VA 23220; (804) 355-8817; kubakuba.info; Cuban; $$. The front door of Kuba Kuba faces a Fan District neighborhood of neat townhouses with tiny, manicured gardens. The unassuming entrance is nothing short of a portal to another world. Outside, it's all shady streets and chirping birds. Inside—bam!—it's like being shot straight into the Caribbean, with an explosion of colors, artwork, pots, pans, music, and flavor. Order a beer, and it comes in a can. Salads look like confetti on a plate. Whet the appetite with *camarones y mejillones de Kuba Kuba,* large shrimp and tender mussels in a savory sea of tasso ham and cilantro broth. The bread on the side, with the palm leaf baked into the top, certifies the authenticity of the family-owned, 15-year-old establishment. Said bread forms the base of the Cuban sandwich, made with slow-roasted pork and Smithfield ham. Kuba Kuba's *tres leche* cake has earned thumbs up from Food Network star Duff Goldman. It's so popular in Richmond that brides order it for their wedding day.

Pasture, 416 E. Grace St., Richmond, VA 23219; (804) 780-0416; pasturerva.com; Neo-Southern; $$. If there's something comforting about this restaurant, it's no wonder. Co-owner Jason Alley also runs the popular Comfort eatery in Richmond, and Pasture is his upscale version of a Southern food restaurant. The decor is mid-century retro, with sleek lines and low booths set amid a wood-and-white background with pops of turquoise. The restaurant began as a Southern tapas place but has added entrees to both its lunch and dinner menus. The tapas are still big hits, such as a spicy pimiento cheese served with Ritz crackers or the plate that features pickled cucumbers, beets, onions, and cauliflower. For a true Southern treat, try the fried peanuts. The pork rinds, airy and crunchy, are addictive, and that's even before you've dipped them into the accompanying guacamole. The seafood stew melds clams, shrimp, and seafood sausage in a tomato-saffron sauce, which you'll want to sop up with the locally famous Billy Bread. The dessert menu comes on a 4-by-6-inch recipe card, and includes yet another twist on grits—a rice grits pudding paired with a strawberry orange jam.

Rappahannock, 320 E. Grace St., Richmond, VA 23219; (804) 545-0565; on Facebook; Seafood; $$$. Smack in the middle of downtown Richmond, a couple of fourth-generation oystermen have opened a sleek raw bar and restaurant, creating an instant buzz that's grown to a roar. Brothers Travis and Ryan Croxton are perhaps the state's most successful marketers of oysters. Their company harvests from several Virginia waters and has trademarked names like Barcats, Old Salts, and Witch Ducks, a brand that New Yorkers slurp at the venerable Grand Central Oyster Bar. No surprise that it's this city's best oyster bar. Shuckers each day expertly pry open three or four brands of bivalves and send them out on the half shell swimming in pools of oyster liquor atop cracked ice with a speared lemon wedge. Don't miss the opportunity to savor, compare and contemplate the "merroir" of each one. But be sure to push away from the raw bar with room to wade into the rest of the menu, which updates the tired surf 'n' turf standard by combining the brothers' Olde Salt clams with smoked pork shoulder, braised kale, *sofrito,* and amontillado sherry. Pastured chicken from nearby Harmony Hill Farms goes on the wood-fired grill and is presented beautifully with toasted farro, favas, oyster mushrooms, and Castelvetrano olive tapenade. Local oysters, expert shuckers, and a wizard in the kitchen. No wonder the roar.

River City Diner, 7 N. 17th St., Richmond, VA 23219, (804) 644-9418; Casual American; $–$$. Located along the cobblestone streets of the city's historic river district, the River City Diner on 17th Street is an old-fashioned place with wood floors and Formica tabletops. Red squeeze bottles of ketchup adorn each table. Old advertising murals, touting Lucky Strikes and the People's Drug Store, remain on the exposed brick wall. The dining is split-level, and you can watch as your food is made in the open kitchen. Breakfast, lunch, and dinner are served, and the menu is typical diner fare, with a few Virginia twists. The eggs and crab cake, which is more of a patty, is nice way to start the morning. Tuesday is pasta night, Wednesday offers half-price burgers from 5 p.m. until closing, and highballs and beer are featured from 4 to 7 p.m. on Tuesday and Thursday during happy hour. End your visit appropriately with a milk shake, but opt for a flavor you might not have found in a diner in the 1950s, such as coffee, peanut butter and jelly, or pineapple. **Additional location:** 803 E. Parham Rd., Richmond, VA 23227; (804) 266-1500; 11430 W. Huguenot Rd., Midlothian, VA 23113; (804) 897-9518.

The Roosevelt, 623 N. 25th St., Richmond, VA 23223; (804) 658-1935; rooseveltrva.com; Neo-Southern, $$–$$$. If you had a Southern grandmother, albeit a hip one, she would serve you the kind of food you'll get at this corner restaurant in the city's Church Hill section. The place is homey, with its brown painted tin ceiling, four large ceiling fans, and worn wooden floor. Local historical photos, in black-and-white and sepia tones, dot the walls, and an intricate old map shows Richmond circa 1865, right as the Civil War was coming to an end. The fare is comfort food with a modern twist, and the man behind it is co-owner and chef Lee Gregory, a nominee for a prestigious James Beard Foundation award. The restaurant opened in 2011 and has become a locals' favorite for Sunday brunch. The 14 tables fill up quickly, and patrons order dishes such as the sausage corn dogs, three large links wrapped in corn batter and served with a heated maple syrup in a small cast-iron skillet. The crispy chicken thigh, perfectly crunchy on the outside and moist on the inside, comes with potatoes and a sausage gravy. The Bloody Mary, garnished with a slice of green tomato, has just the right amount of kick. Dinner entrees include trout and bluefish and pork tenderloin, and the wine list features only the commonwealth's best. The Seersucker cocktail is a treat, with bourbon, bitters, and a charred lemon cube mixed with a sweet tea syrup that oozes of the South.

Secco Wine Bar, 2933 W. Cary St. Richmond, VA 23221; (804) 353-0670; seccowinebar.com; New American; $$–$$$. This sleek restaurant shows how good simplicity can be. Try the fried chickpeas, lightly dusted and lightly fried, then seasoned with Middle Eastern Aleppo pepper, akin to paprika but not as smoky. Or bite into the fried Sicilian olives stuffed with Gorgonzola. Both appetizers have strong flavors despite few ingredients. They're the work of Executive Chef Tim Bereika, who also offers a make-your-own charcuterie board. For dinner, try one of the house-made pasta dishes or opt for small plates, such as the avocado-and-beet-topped bruschetta. A chalkboard above the recycled-wood bar details the wine offerings, and more than 25 varieties are available by the glass. Choices might seem difficult, but a knowledgeable waitstaff makes that decision simple, too, asking multiple questions about what flavors customers like and what dishes they're pairing the wine with. Owner Julie Battaglini's goal was a place that offered great wine, great cheese, and great company, and Secco lives up to that dream.

Stella's, 1012 Lafayette St., Richmond, VA 23221; (804) 358-2011; stellasrichmond.com; Greek/Small Plates; $$–$$$. This is Stella Dikos's third incarnation of her namesake restaurant, and many locals agree it's her best yet. It's a homey, rustic spot that feels as though it's been around for ages. But if you look closely, you can tell that it's only a few years old—check out the recessed lighting in the tin ceiling, which still retains its shine. The menu is definitely Old World, with moussaka, pastitsio, and spanikopitas among the offerings. Under the "meze" heading of the menu, you'll find dishes like fried calamari and the beef and lamb meatballs that are anything but small plates. Lunch, dinner, and Sunday brunch are offered, and you can find small-plate and drink specials from 4 to 6 p.m. on weekdays. The bar is marble-topped, as is a communal table for 16 in the restaurant's center. During dinner, old Greek movies play against a back wall, and the 1965 "Stella," a retelling of the Carmen story, is an appropriate favorite. Stella herself watches over the dining room from an artist's rendering near the front door.

Landmarks

Chiocca's Downstairs Deli & Bar, 425 N. Belmont Ave., Richmond, VA 23221; (804) 355-3228; Sandwiches; $. This restaurant opened in 1952, and it's still here in the basement of a structure at the corner of Belmont and Kensington. The red booths and bar stools seem original, as do many of the wall decorations, which include black-and-white photos and sports pennants. The bar is big, and the place can get rowdy, in a good way, when a game is on and beer is flowing. Favorite subs, which are huge, include The Downstairs, with salami, prosciutto, anchovies, and provolone, and The Beast Feast, which combines roast beef and pastrami with swiss and provolone cheeses. The knockwurst-and-pastrami Sailor sandwich is a signature, as well as The Dagwood, with its turkey, roast beef, and pastrami astride two kinds of cheeses.

The sandwiches still are made in "Peggy," the gas-powered broiler oven named after the original owner's wife. Peggy can accommodate only three at a time, so you might have to wait a while, but this is a comfy place to do just that.

Joe's Inn, 206 N. Shields Ave., Richmond, VA 23220; (804) 355-2282; joesinnrva.com; Eclectic; $$. It's hard to not make that hackneyed *Cheers* connection, but this really is a place where everyone knows your name. That's the gospel truth even if it's your first time at this 60-year-old breakfast, lunch, and dinner joint in the heart of Richmond's residential Fan District of turn-of-the-century homes and shaded streets. It's a little dark on the bar side of the business, and the music is a little loud, but regulars seated in wooden booths along 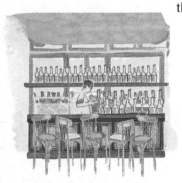 the wall enjoying enormous portions of the restaurant's legendary Spaghetti a la Joe (baked with provolone), forearm-sized subs or panfried chicken livers, don't seem to notice. A chalkboard menu proffers the ever-changing list of beer and a couple of hard ciders on tap, which they're pretty serious about here. A separate dining room offers dining without the bar vibe. But we like the bar. It's kinda messy. Kinda great.

Lemaire, 101 W. Franklin St., Richmond, VA 23220; (804) 649-4629; lemairerestaurant.com; Traditional Southern; $$$$. Coming to Richmond and bypassing The Jefferson Hotel would be like going to Paris and skipping the Eiffel Tower. The opulence—massive marble columns, fountains, a staircase that may or may not be the inspiration for the one that Scarlett O'Hara tumbled down—is a must-see. Better yet, make reservations for dinner at Lemaire, the hotel's award-winning main restaurant that combines a staunch Southern bent with an unwavering farm-to-fork philosophy. Chef Walter Bundy, a Richmond native, dreams up dishes such as Rooftop Honey-Glazed Pork Loin Chop, served with spoonbread, roasted apricots, "all day" turnip greens, and bourbon jus. Benne seed–crusted Loch Duart Scottish salmon gets its South on with sides of Carolina Gold rice, smoked Surry sausage, black-eyed pea hoppin' John, and mustard greens. Presentations are among the most stunning in the state. After dinner, take a moment to descend the lobby staircase, hang a sharp left at the foot of it to arrive at the alcove that houses artifacts from the hotel and restaurant's history. Then cross the lobby to the bar, and have a drink where Elvis drank.

Mama Zu, 501 S. Pine St., Richmond, VA 23220; (804) 788-4205; Italian/Seafood; $$–$$$. First know this: The mud-brown building with the battered screen door is not a crack house. Rather, it's one of Richmond's most celebrated restaurants, a status that's counter to almost every other element of the place: bowed walls, cement floor, notoriously surly seating host, no credit cards, no tablecloths, no reservations, no parking, no wine list, Sex Pistols playing on the jukebox. But take a look at that vast chalkboard menu behind the bar. A column of antipastos and pastas might include dandelion greens, sugar toads, and fried oysters. That abuts a column of Italian standards such as eggplant parmigiana, veal Marsala, and osso buco. The final column makes choosing even more difficult—lamb shank, chops, and sausage, duck breast, and in the springtime, shad roe, and in the summertime, cobia. A lamb shank arrived with a fist-sized ball of tender meat attached to the bone in a shallow pool of broth and cannelloni beans. Calamari Genovese—achingly tender rings and tentacles served over al dente pasta with ribbons of basil and a touch of lemon—is reason enough to venture here. The place is owned by Brad Wein and Ed Vasaio, who also own the more polished sister restaurant, Edo's Squid, just across town. Like the critics from *Saveur* magazine, who put the place on their top 100 picks in 2011, you'll likely leave not caring about the atmosphere. After all, it's the food that counts.

THE COOKBOOK THAT STARTED IT ALL

Mushrooms stewed with butter and red wine. Nasturtiums pickled with pepper and mace. Roast woodcocks. Sturgeon steaks. Sea kale. Spruce beer. And more.

Richmond residents and visitors fortunate enough to have a seat at "Queen Molly's" table in the early 1800s likely dined on these and other delicacies at her Cary Street boardinghouse. Queen Molly was the nickname of Mary Randolph, the most celebrated Richmond hostess of her day and author of *The Virginia House-Wife,* America's first truly regional cookbook.

Randolph opened a boardinghouse "for the accommodation of ladies and gentlemen" in 1808 after President Thomas Jefferson banished her husband from his government post and the couple's fortunes declined. Although Randolph's skilled slave cooks manned the kitchen, her cookbook makes it clear that she, too, possessed the knowledge of a skilled culinarian, coupled with the sensibility of a modern-day CEO.

Her mantra, "method is the soul of management," seasons most every recipe in the 240-page cookbook. First published in 1824 and written for the "young inexperienced housekeeper," girls who were still teens and thrust by marriage into the role of running a household, it met with near instant acclaim.

For turtle soup, she directs that the animal be killed "at night in the winter, and in the morning in summer." In baking cakes or puddings, she notes that "eggs injure everything unless they are made light (or beaten) before they are used." When making currant wine, she advises her charges to "gather full ripe currants on a dry day, pick them from the stalks and weigh them."

Randolph's writing assumes a tone that is firm, yet gentle, and a voice like Julia Child, so that you can imagine she's standing stove-side with the young, inexperienced mistress.

A full-color facsimile edition of *The Virginia House-Wife* was published in 2013. It provides fascinating reading, or for the more adventuresome cook, a challenge to step back in time. Oyster ice cream, anyone?

Mekong, 6004 W. Broad St., Henrico, VA 23230; (804) 288-8929; mekongisforbeerlovers.com; Beer Pub/Vietnamese; $$. It's the beer selection in this restaurant that causes some DC residents to fight horrendous traffic along Interstate 95 just for a visit. A large sign over the bar announces, BEER IS THE ANSWER, and the menu is wide with stouts, India Pale Ales and wheat ales. A fine selection of Belgian brews is available, and on some days more than half of the 17 or so drafts are Belgian, too. The beer list features more than a handful from Virginia, including some from Richmond's own Hardywood Park Craft Brewery. The food is Vietnamese and mostly fried. The *mon an choi* appetizer is a sampler platter with crispy and steamed spring rolls, shrimp toast, and shrimp with an onion and scallion filling. Lots of families and older customers dine throughout the day, though the clientele gets younger as the night wears on. The waitstaff proudly wears T-shirts proclaiming that Mekong was chosen as the top beer bar in America by the website CraftBeer .com. You'll want to grab a cold one and drink to that.

Millie's Diner, 2603 E. Main St., Richmond, VA 23223; (804) 643-5512; milliesdiner.com; on Facebook; American; $$$. A diner? Yes, there are vintage jukeboxes mounted on the wall of the booths that play real 45s. And there's a black-and-white checkered floor. Counter service, too. But expect much more than burgers and fries from this landmark eatery that has been open since 1989 and has earned accolades from *Bon Appétit, Southern Living,* and the *Los Angeles Times.* The menu changes every three weeks. In the fall, you might be offered an appetizer of Surryano Ham and Pear Salad with arugula, manchego, and pine nuts, for example. Like a proper diner, the main dish offerings are eclectic, ranging from expertly grilled steaks to fish stew to all manner of fowl. If you're in Richmond on a Sunday, find time to wait in line for a table for brunch where patrons partake of filling favorites including the General Lee, a pair of poached eggs, topped with sausage gravy on a homemade cheddar biscuit. No way y'all won't enjoy that.

Strawberry Street Cafe, 421 **Strawberry St., Richmond, VA** 23220; (804) 353-6860; **strawberrystreetcafe .com; Casual American; $$.** This restaurant in the city's Fan District is one of the few indepen- dent eateries that still feature a salad bar, but what's really unusual about this place is where some of the salads are found. Many of the fresh  vegetables, fruits, pasta, and other salads and house-made soups are located in an old-fashioned, claw-footed bathtub that once was the subject of a TV game show question on *Jeopardy!* The tub was owner Colin Eagles's idea for a cheap alternative to a real salad bar when he opened the cafe in 1976, but it has become local lore. It's also helped the restaurant reap top salad-bar honors in many local contests. The restaurant has a strong following among locals who crave such house specialties as the crab cakes, pasta jambalaya, chicken potpie, and spin- ach lasagna. Wine and beer are available, but what most folks come here for is located in an old bathroom fixture.

Specialty Stores, Markets & Producers

Addison Street Cafe, 116 S. **Addison St., Richmond, VA** 23220; (804) 728-2292; **lamplightercoffee.com.** This is the original cafe of three Richmond residents who got together in 2009 to open Lamplighter Roasting Co. Husband-and-wife team Zachary and Noelle Archibald and Jennifer Rawlings now have a separate location for their roasting operation, and it's there that Lamplighter coffee is created. Jennifer is the roastmaster behind the coffee, which is a favorite among some of the area's finest restaurants. The cafe on Addison is a full coffee bar, with a shabby chic atmosphere and a breakfast and lunch menu. When the weather's nice, you can sit outdoors, or take a seat in the small space inside. The cafe is a gathering spot for locals, and a large bulletin board is crammed full of flyers announcing local concerts, plays, and biking events. A biking theme runs through the place, and that's appropriate. Lamplighter brings its products to some homes through a bicycle delivery service.

Belmont Butchery, 15 N. Belmont Ave., Richmond, VA 23221; (804) 422-8519; belmontbutchery.com. Inspiration struck Tanya Cauthen one night while watching the Food Network, when she heard celebrity chef Alton Brown tell viewers to "ask their local butcher." A Swiss-trained chef who had run her own restaurant, Tanya realized that local restaurants had access to the best cuts of meat but that Richmond residents didn't. That led her to open this retro-style shop in 2006, and it's one of the coolest butcheries we've ever seen. Tanya, who wears one earring in the shape of a meat cleaver, often runs the register, so she can talk to every customer who comes through her doors. But you'll also find her behind the counter, especially on days when she and her crew are breaking down pieces of meat. She stocks products from as many local farms as she can, and the cases are filled with grass-fed beef. All steaks and chops are cut to order, by thickness, and blocks of wood show customers the different measurements. You can find beef, pork, lamb, and some exotics, as well as a line of charcuterie. "I believe in feeding Richmond well," Tanya says, "and I like to do that with lots of local stuff."

Bev's Homemade Ice Cream, 2911 W. Cary St., Richmond, VA 23221; (804) 204-2387; facebook.com/BevsHomemadeIceCream. A Richmond favorite for 15 years, Bev's dishes standards such as mint-chocolate chip and mango sorbet, but why even go there? Instead, lick on a scoop of dark chocolate-peanut butter or venture even further out of your ice cream comfort zone with a ginger variety, Mexi Cali Chocolate with a touch of heat, or pear sorbet. Not in the mood for ice cream? Try an egg cream, a rare treat in these parts. Or grab a home-made cookie. The immaculate shop has a Zen-mod vibe with Chinese paper lanterns and a palette of purple, olive green, and tangerine. Seating is offered both inside and out. Sometimes they do run out of the special flavors, but given their popularity, you have to expect that. Go early. Go often.

Bombolini Pasta, 1606 W. Main St., Richmond, VA 23220; (804) 213-0212; **bombolinipasta.com.** Lolita and John Kreckman launched this business in 2008, relying on her skills as a pasta maker at a local Italian restaurant and his background in culinary arts. Today, they have a store that is a pasta lover's dream. Fresh raviolis, fusillis, and shells might be seen in the refrigerated display case, and strands of spinach and tomato garlic fettuccine and basil linguine might be drying on racks. The pasta is made fresh daily, and the longer varieties, such as spaghettis, linguine, and lasagna, are cut to order. The pastas come in various flavors, and their website lets customers know the varieties of the week. They offer cooked pasta dishes you can eat at one of the three tables fashioned from wine barrels or take home. They also have a pungent line of vinegars crafted from Virginia wines, and John says it's OK to water them down a bit because he purposely creates them strong. He's a friendly guy who's quick to chat with strangers, offering cooking suggestions and cracking a joke or two. The couple's sense of humor is reflected in the store's name. "It's just a fun word to say," John explains. "Food's got to be fun."

Carytown Cupcakes, 3111 W. Cary St., Richmond, VA 23221; (804) 355-2253; carytown-cupcakes.com. The storefront looks as pretty as the cupcakes inside, with its pink paint job and apple-green door. The color scheme continues in the interior, but your eyes are focused on the glass case, where one side offers Classics, such as carrot, red velvet, and vanilla, and the other offers specialty treats such as berry flavors. Gluten-free cupcakes in a few flavors also are available. The cupcakes are light and moist, with buttercream and other frostings that will have you licking your fingers. Dawn and Albert Schick opened the boutique in 2009, when Dawn decided to give up teaching and instead educate the young and old alike about the world of cupcakes. You can taste samples at the checkout counter, and adults tend to hover there when they first come in. Kids, on the other hand, fixate on the actual cupcakes. You can watch them being made in the kitchen at the back of the store through three large windows, and it's a sweet way to pass the time.

Dixie Donuts, 2901 W. Cary St., Richmond, VA 23221; (804) 359-1119; facebook .com/DixieDonutsRVA. Even if we had all day to dream up doughnuts, we'd never dream up these. The ever-changing menu at this tiny takeout shop on the east end of Carytown's strip of eateries and eclectic stores never ceases to surprise. One day, it might be coconut lime verbena. On another, a B.E.F.T., a little bit of bacon and a candied over-easy "egg" atop a french toast doughnut. Or, how about the Virginian, a sweet potato doughnut with maple glaze and a sprinkle of pecans on top? Even the "mainstream" doughnuts here would put a chain to shame. Think raspberry and strawberry shortcake. The all-cake doughnut shop was rumored to be set to offer fried chicken, too. But during our visit, the only thing that was frying was doughnuts. That was more than enough.

El Rey Latino Market, 6006 W. Broad St., Richmond, VA 23230; (804) 658-2351. The signs in the windows of this cinderblock building offer a clue to the clientele; they're written in both Spanish and English. Inside is a locals' favorite for Latino products, though you can also shoot a game of pool at one of three tables near the door. The breads come from the family-owned La Sobrosita Bakery in nearby Chesterfield County, where you'll spot loaves with *tomillo* (thyme) and *romero* (rosemary) and the pink pinwheeled *rollo Mexicano*. The produce section includes plantains, mangos, cilantro, and a few peppers, and the dairy section offers Honduran-style sour cream and Salvadoran dairy spread. In the aisles, there's a large selection of beans—red, refried, Roman, black, navy—and a variety of rice. Silvery piñatas dangle from the ceiling, just waiting to be filled with goodies and then busted open.

Ellwood Thompson's Local Market, 4 N. Thompson St., Carytown, Richmond, VA 23221; (804) 359-7525; elwoodthompsons

.com. Earthy patchouli and fresh produce. That's the new-age aroma that greets shoppers at this independent, full-service, natural-food market in the Carytown section. It's a grocery store with a mission statement: "Every choice we make and every action we take will somehow, big or small, directly impact our community. From where we're sourcing our food to how much waste we produce, it all comes back around—full circle." Buy produce, bulk herbs (even dandelion leaf), local salami and other meats, seafood, fresh baked goods, seeds, nuts, pastas, and health and beauty aids. Get a growler of microbrew, or an elixir from the juice bar, where baristas jam fresh celery, kale, and fruits into juicers. Grab a bite from the deli—specialties include vegetarian and vegan dishes, gluten-free meals, low-sodium options, natural meat, poultry and seafood selections, made to order sandwiches, wraps, soup, and sushi. There's a seating area at the front of the store where you can dine with the like-minded. Check the schedule for the community room events. Recently, Virginia farmer Joel Salatin, whose bellwether **Poly-face Farm** (p. 226) is featured in *The Omnivore's Dilemma*, delivered a talk titled "Forgiveness Farming." Elwood Thompson's walks the walk.

For the Love of Chocolate, 3136 W. Cary St., Richmond, VA 23221; (804) 359-5645; lovchoc.com.

It's cliché, but it's also the truth: When you enter this shop in the heart of Carytown, you feel like you're a kid in a candy store. Only a few of the goodies, some cookies and other treats, are freshly made, but it's still a treat to be surrounded by so much sweetness. Bulk candies in old-fashioned jars line one wall, and the choices seem endless: dark ginger bitters, margarita cordials, dark chocolate marzipan. Near the back are bulk candies that will take you back to your childhood: bite-sized Bit-O-Honeys, Bazooka bubble gum and Atomic Fireballs. Chocolate from around the globe, in bars and nuggets, fills the center, and flags of the represented nations hang from the ceiling. Near the checkout counter are display cases brimming with more than 25 kinds of truffles and other creations. You keep noticing the smiles of customers as they wander from aisle to aisle in this beloved place, where betrothed couples have been known to get their engagement photos taken. Some sugar-free options are available, but this place is really all about the sugar.

Gelati Celesti, 8906-A W. Broad St., Richmond, VA 23294; (804) 346-0038; gelatiicecream.com. The scent of freshly made waffle cones greets you as you enter this ice cream shop on Broad Street. It's run by Peter Edmonds, who started the business in 1984 with his father, John. A chalkboard lists the 23 house flavors and 12 daily specials, and one in particular makes you inquire. The Just Ask flavor is a white chocolate ice cream with Oreo bits and peanut butter. It's popular, but not as popular as the Chocolate Decadence, an intensely flavored variety with the consistency of fudge. You can opt for a cone or a cup, which comes in four sizes. Don't let the toddler size fool you; so many scoops are jammed into the container that it's definitely made for an adult. For the kids, there's a huge chalkboard on the wall that lets them work off some of their sugar high. This shop is near the back of the West Tower Shopping Center and can be difficult to find—just look for the large Gold's Gym sign from the street and you'll see the much smaller shopping center sign below. **Additional location:** 3004 Stony Point Rd., Richmond, VA 23235; (804) 320-0000.

GlobeHopper Coffeehouse and Lounge, 2100 E. Main St., Richmond, VA 23223; (804) 523-8083; globehoppercoffee.com. The brownies here are "cosmic"—really, just check out the handwritten sign next to the cash register—and they provide a jolt of chocolate that pairs nicely with the caffeine you've come in for. There's a laid-back vibe in this funky corner shop that makes you want to sip slowly. Grab one of the stuffed olive-green chairs or the church bench with the inviting red cushion and pillows. The coffee is smooth and the espresso rich, and both can be ordered iced or hot. You can get breakfast—offerings such as oatmeal and an English muffin with cheese and egg—or sandwiches and salads. The Masala Bowl is hearty, with curried chicken mixed with romaine lettuce and crunchy noodles. You can use the free Wi-Fi with a laptop or tablet, or go the old-fashioned route and read one of the free newspapers or books available to customers. Or settle in with Scrabble or another board game from the back of the shop. When you're through, deposit your dirty dishes under the chalkboard sign that reads SISTERHOOD OF THE TRAVELING DIRTY DISHES.

Jean-Jacques Bakery & Cafe, 3138 W. Cary St., Richmond, VA 23221; (804) 355-0666; richmondfrenchbakery.com. Belgium-born Jozef Bindas stands behind the counter of this French bakery and does his best to convince customers that his baked goods aren't that bad for the waistline. "They're European calories," he says, his English spoken with a heavy French accent, "so they're good for you. Really." He's exaggerating, of course, but it's hard to deny how good everything looks. Jozef, a master baker who graduated from the International Culinary Institute in Brussels, has been at the helm of this Carytown shop since 1983. French specialties such as baguettes and sourdough rounds, as well as loaves of multigrain, white, and wheat line the shelves behind the counter. A display case is filled with European pastries such as napoleons, éclairs, and *allumettes*. Locals rave about the lunch options, which are more eclectic than the baked goods. Try the gumbo, paninis, or chicken salad mixed in with the *croque monsieur* and the vol-au-vent.

Libbie Market, 400 Libbie Ave., Richmond, VA 23226; (804) 285-6414; libbiemarket.com. To say the service here is friendly doesn't do it justice. Here's an example: You're at the back of the store, trying unsuccessfully to find a ginger beer among the chilled shelves of brews. An employee offers to help, and not succeeding, enlists an assistant manager, who then calls in a beer expert who works here.

This neighborhood market has earned its reputation as a place where customers come first. The deli is a big draw, with prepared foods such as pasta dishes, sweet potatoes topped with currants and pine nuts, and artichoke salad. A butcher is on staff, and meat offerings include T-bones, rib eyes, Boston butts, and plump racks of veal. The seafood counter tempts visitors with cod, shrimp, swordfish, and even soft-shell blue crabs. The center of the store is where you'll find the kinds of things you expect any grocery to carry, from condiments to paper products. The wine selection is large, with most of it from the usual places. But there's a healthy sampling of Virginia varietals, including bottles from Chatham Vineyards in Machipongo and Cooper Vineyards in Louisa. The bakery has cupcakes, tiramisu, and cookies made on the spot, and there are a few tables by the checkout counters where you can enjoy your purchases from the deli or bakery.

Montana Gold Bread Co., 3543 W. Cary St., Richmond, VA 23221; (804) 359-7700; montanagoldbread.com. This bakery, near the western edge of Carytown, is known for its bread. The most popular kinds are the cinnamon raisin, a sweet bread that works well on a breakfast table or as a dinner dessert, and the challah, the braided loaves that get special places on Jewish tables at holidays and the Sabbath. A Blue Ridge Mountain Herb is another local favorite, and on Wednesday the store offers a baker's choice that one week might be tomato basil and the next jalapeño corn bread. In the morning, customers can watch as dough is kneaded behind the counter before being baked. Depending on the day, wire racks near the door might hold

garlic knots, pound cakes, and pumpkin bread. There's white, wheat, and sunflower every day, and a selection of jams and preserves if you're looking for something to put on the yeasty goodness.

Sweet Dreams Are Made of Yogurt

The concept was simple: Launch a frozen yogurt place that would allow customers to help themselves and provide so many toppings that they couldn't possibly put them all in one dish. The timing was difficult: It was 2009, and the national economy was still fighting its way back from one of the worst recessions ever. But Derek Ya relied on his faith and opened the first **sweetFrog** yogurt store in the Short Pump suburb of Richmond. Today, it's become a national chain, with more than 250 locations, most of them east of the Mississippi River. Pink-and-lime-green decor is standard, as is a wall of frozen yogurt–dispensing machines that allow customers to pick among various flavors. Customers then move to the counter, where employees add the toppings, and that's where the decisions become hard. There are fruits, shaved chocolate, nuts, mini peanut butter and chocolate chips, coconut, M&Ms, gummy bears, Nerds, and that's just the beginning. Derek prides himself that the stores try to be good neighbors, working with local organizations on various fund-raisers. That's part of the chain's mission, and the name reflects that. "Frog" stands for "Fully Rely On God." You can visit the store where it all began at *11638 W. Broad St., Richmond, VA 23233; (804) 874-8440; sweetfrogyogurt.com.*

Proper Pie Co., 2505 E. Broad St., Ste. 100, Richmond, VA 23223; (804) 343-7437; facebook.com/ProperPieCo. New Zealand meets Virginia at this shop, which offers the savory pies of the South Pacific island nation and the sweet ones of the South. Arrive early, because a line usually forms before this place opens, and sometimes it stretches down the block. Once inside, look down at the floor, where you'll see these words in Maori, one of New Zealand's official languages, "Haere Mai." The phrase means "welcome," and it's easy to feel that way as the staff tells you about the day's offerings. The

small savory treats range from a combination of chicken and *kumara,* a type of New Zealand sweet potato, to a lamb, chickpea, and spinach curry creation. The savory versions, sized for individual servings, are almost 3 inches high, with a golden brown crust that sometimes is topped with poppy seeds. The list of sweet pies is long and includes strawberry rhubarb and lemon meringue. A pear and almond pie tastes like an almond-flavored cake with a caramelized pear topping. The shop opened in 2011 and has been so popular that there's a limit on the number of pies each customer can buy. Most folks take them to go, but there are a few tables and some stools if you want to dig in on the spot. Wash it down with a bottle of Coca-Cola from Mexico that's sweetened with real sugar.

Sweet Spot, West Broad Village, 2228 Old Brick Rd., Glen Allen, VA 23060; (804) 360-7768. This candy store in the West Broad Village section of the city is a favorite place for kids' birthday parties. And for good reason. The walls are lined with sweet stuff, including more than 200 containers of bulk candies and chocolates. The jelly bean section seems endless, and you also can find gumballs, licorice, and gummy candies in the shape of fried eggs, rattlesnakes, and the more common bears. You can wash it down with more than 70 kinds of soda. There are jawbreakers bigger than golf balls, and large swirled suckers that last hours. The walls feature words that sum up the inventory: sparkly, yummy, fizzy, gooey. At the center is a communal table with 10 stools, where you can partake of some of your goodies or, if you're in the mood, play a game of Candy Land. After a visit, let the little ones work off some steam at the Children's Museum of Richmond, located a few doors away.

Wise Choice Convenience Store, 1751 Ashland Rd., Rockville, VA 23146; (804) 749-3335. Out front, it looks like a Citgo station,

Three Sisters, One Delicious Snack

Growing up, the Spilman sisters loved to visit their grandmother, Louise Wilmer Spilman, who owned a downtown Richmond women's clothing store. She was a great cook, and the girls especially enjoyed her cheese straws, a cheese-flavored pastry that's perfect for a snack, with soups, or almost anytime when you're south of the Mason-Dixon Line. These days, the three sisters—Isabel Bates and Peggy Crowley of Richmond and Alice Frankovitch of Weirton, WV—are carrying on two Southern traditions. They've taken their grandmother's recipe—and sharing recipes is what we do down here—and turned it into a business that promotes cheese straws—and though there's a debate about where the original ones came from, there's no doubt that the South is where you'll find the best ones today. "We started small, making our cheese straws just like our grandmother did," Peggy says. "Business grew, and our uncle, an engineer, streamlined the process. We even brought in our mother to help with packaging." Packaged under the **Three Sisters** brand, the siblings' cheese straws are a buttery and spicy treat packed with a strong cheddar punch. They sell savory cheddar and spicy jalapeño versions in stores in Virginia, as well as in North Carolina, Pennsylvania, and West Virginia, and on their website at threesisters3.com. Grandma Louise would be so proud.

but you'd be crazy to come here just for gas. And, well, that would be darn near impossible because at the pumps, a good 20 yards away from the front door, the aroma of Southern fried comfort food takes hold of you. Even with your car windows rolled up. Inside the station, behind a glass-fronted warming table, sits a spread of crunchy, slightly salty fried chicken, fried gizzards and livers, fried whiting all curled up and crispy, and fried pork chop sandwiches that get snapped up by early-bird construction workers. Squares of just-baked corn bread make the perfect side, and why not grab some of that homemade apple or peach cobbler for dessert? Everyone leaves with a little square box of goodness. If you don't have a Southern granny, get a box full of fried things and pretend that you were thusly blessed.

Yellow Umbrella Fresh Seafood, 5600 Patterson Ave., Ste. E, Richmond, VA 23226; (804) 282-9591; on Facebook. It's hard to believe that this market began as a one-man operation in 1980. Then, George Whitby would sell crabs and oysters from his car, marking his location with a yellow patio umbrella. The business is now in the hands of his son, David Whitby, but the name has stuck. The market, far more than a place to buy seafood, moved to its current location in early 2013. Some local fresh produce is available, and charcuterie meats such as *foie gras* mousse and Serrano ham fill a refrigerated case. Cuts of beef, pork, poultry, and lamb are for sale, as well as fresh vegetable, beef, veal, and chicken stocks. Customers can opt for prepared foods, such as crab quiche and shepherd's pie, or key lime and lemon chess pie, from the 4+20 Bake Shop in nearby Maidens. A big draw continues to be the fish counter, where on any given day you might find blue crabs, grouper, mussels, oysters, or red snapper. Near the front of the shop is a selection of artisanal cheeses and wines.

Winery & Breweries

Blue Bee Cider, 212 W. 6th St., Richmond, VA 23224; (804) 231-0280; bluebeecider.com. The city's only urban winery produces fermented cider—two semisweet varieties and a dessert option.

Hardywood Park Craft Brewery, 2408 Ownby Ln., Richmond, VA 23220; (804) 420-2420; hardywood.com.

Legend Brewing Co., 321 W. 7th St., Richmond, VA 23224; (804) 232-3446; legendbrewing.com.

Farmers' Markets

Lakeside Farmers' Market, 6110 Lakeside Ave., Richmond, VA 23228; (804) 262-6593. Wed from dawn to dusk, Sat from 8 a.m. to noon, Apr through Nov; Sat from 9 a.m. to noon, Jan through Mar.

Midlothian Mines Farmers' Market, intersection of N. Woolridge Road and Coalfield Road, Midlothian, VA 23114. Sat from 2 to 5 p.m., May through early Dec.

17th Street Farmers' Market, 100 N. 17th St., Richmond, VA 23219; (804) 646-0477. Sat and Sun from 8:30 a.m. to 4 p.m., late Apr through early Nov.

South of the James Market, Forest Hill Park, New Kent Avenue and 42nd Street, Richmond VA 23225. Sat from 8 a.m. to noon, May through early Dec.

West End Farmers' Market, 12450 Gayton Rd., Richmond, VA 23238; (804) 364-8213. Sat from 8 a.m. to noon, late Apr through early Nov.

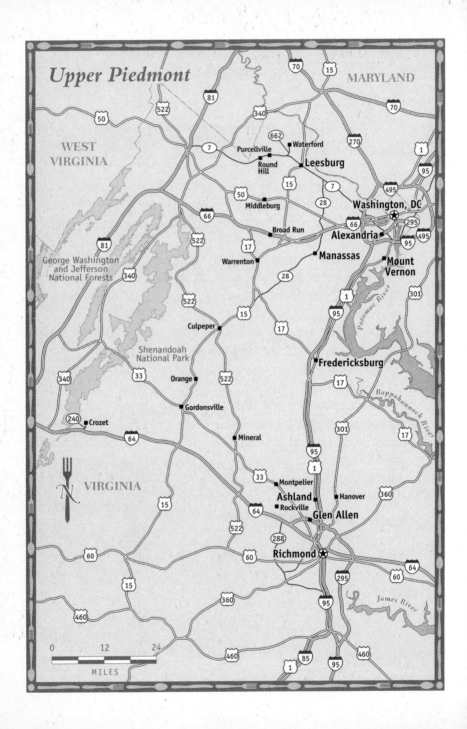

Upper Piedmont

Upper Piedmont

Put the top down and relax. This is blue-highway Virginia, where traffic tie-ups are rare. The tree-lined, winding lanes of the Upper Piedmont give way to fertile farms known for their year-round beef, early summer tomatoes, and fall apples—all part of the bounty of raw materials put to use by adventurous chefs. The lush orchards found here are home to a number of award-winning wines, and farm stands beckon from the roadside. There's also history to savor. Here, you'll find the homes of four of the nation's first five presidents—George Washington, Thomas Jefferson, James Monroe, and James Madison. As you work up an appetite, enjoy the local delights, hopping from chic restaurants to wine tastings, bakeries to diners, coffee shops to country stores.

Foodie Faves

Bistro Bethem, 309 William St., Fredericksburg, VA 22401; (540) 371-9554; bistrobethem.com; Seafood/Steaks; $$–$$$. This restaurant, located in the heart of Fredericksburg's historic downtown, is a wine lover's paradise. Honored multiple times by *Wine Spectator* magazine for its extensive offerings, the bistro's reds come from the West Coast, Chile, France, and Spain and the whites hail from California, France, Italy, and around the globe. The high ceiling gives the dining room a spacious feel, and the long pine bar is a showcase. The menu,

What's Cooking? It Could Be You

You begin as strangers, just a group of eight or so people who are taking a class at the **Glenfiddich Farm Cookery School** (*17642 Canby Rd., Leesburg, VA 20175; 703-771-3056; glen farmcookery.com*) outside of Leesburg. By the time the four-course meal you've prepared is done, you sit down with your classmates, now newfound friends, and share the fruits—and proteins and vegetables—of your labor. Overseeing it all is Olwen Woodier, a trained chef and cookbook author whose calm demeanor and culinary expertise keeps it all running smoothly. A jambalaya that won't thicken? Olwen and her assistants are there, adding this and that until—presto!—the right consistency is reached. An inexperienced salad crew unsure how to plate their creation? Olwen is there, too, offering suggestions to make sure the dish looks as good as it tastes. Classes are offered every other Wednesday and occasionally on Saturday, beginning at 10:30 a.m. The cuisine changes monthly—sometimes it's Cajun, other times French or comfort foods, still other times Italian. Students can bring wine, but bottles aren't opened until the food is made and the feasting begins. It all takes place at a 170-year-old dairy farm, and it's a delicious way to learn your way around the kitchen or to become comfortable cooking different dishes.

which changes often, offers new takes on Southern cuisine. A shrimp-and-scallop entree uses pork belly and grits, and a beef dish offers local meats prepared in two ways. The mac-and-cheese appetizer replaces the pasta with gnocchi and is served with a three-cheese or red sauce. You can get lunch and dinner, along with a Sunday brunch, and any time's a good one for a glass of vino.

Claire's at the Depot, 65 S. 3rd St., Warrenton, VA 20186; (540) 351-1616; clairesrestaurant.com; Seafood/Steaks; $$–$$$. A former railroad depot dating to 1852 is the setting for this restaurant, opened in 2005 by former schoolteacher Claire Lamborne. The building has the curved windows and wooden floors that harken back to its bygone days, but the menu is thoroughly modern. Lunch and dinner are served, as well as Sunday brunch. The she-crab soup is spicy and filled with large lumps of blue crabmeat. On summer days, you might find a refreshing chilled cucumber soup as a daily special. The salads are exquisite; in one, ginger-glazed salmon sits over baby greens and saffron pearl couscous and is brought to life by tropical fruits and a house-made balsamic vinaigrette. If the weather is nice, eat on the patio out back. If it's crowded, grab a seat at the generous-sized bar, where you can watch TV or make new friends. See the recipe for **Claire's Southern Shrimp & Grits** on p. 249.

Elmwood at Sparks, 124 W. Main St., Orange, VA 22960; (540) 672-0060; elmwoodcatering.com; New American; $$$$. Elmwood at Sparks is "the restaurant that chicken salad built," says Chef-Owner Randy Cooper. Not that it's lowbrow. It's located, after all, in the county that was home to President James Madison and his wife, Dolley. Elmwood is the sort of place that makes its own mayonnaise and seeds the cucumbers. The expansive open kitchen, with a rack of polished copper pots dangling from above, forms the backdrop. The menu, which leans toward local, local, local, changes weekly, and it's dependent on what's being harvested nearby. Might be pecan-dusted "Rag Mountain" trout, pulled from an ice-cold bubbling spring just up the road. Might be honey- and thyme-fried sweetbreads, served with local arugula. A triple blackboard dishes the daily specials, and it's always chicken salad day—dual scoops of finely chopped chicken in a modicum of house-made mayonnaise with candied pecans atop fresh greens dressed with vinaigrette. A house builder, for sure.

Foti's Restaurant, 219 E. Davis St., Culpeper, VA 22701; (540) 829-8400; fotisrestaurant.com; New American; $$$. This storefront establishment, with a tin ceiling, wood plank floor, and exposed brick walls, has been gaining accolades from elite critics since it opened in 2005. Owners Frank and Sue Maragos honed their chops 25 miles up the road at the Inn at Little Washington, which has earned five stars from *Forbes* for 22 years running. Frank rose to the rank of executive sous chef, Sue to senior server. Their rarefied background is evident in Foti's service and menus, which cleave to the seasons. But the vibe at their place is decidedly relaxed, the fine-dining prices far more egalitarian, and the menu inventive and sometimes even whimsical. Leg of lamb is braised with cinnamon and tomato and served over cardamom-scented jasmine rice and a side of garlicky sauteed vegetables, with a bright note of tzatziki. The chocolate brûlée dessert comes with a bacon spoon. Around town, you might hear Foti's referred to as the "poor man's Inn at Little Washington." Rest assured, there's nothing poor about it.

Iron Horse Restaurant, 100 S. Railroad Ave., Ashland, VA 23005; (804) 752-6410; ironhorserestaurant.com; New American; $$–$$$. It's called the Iron Horse, and it's located on Railroad Avenue, so there's no surprise when three trains go by while you're dining in this early 1900s structure. Originally a department store, the building takes you back in time, with the black-and-white floor tiles, ceiling fans, and low platforms near the front that once held window displays for passersby. More than 50 trains pass each 24 hours, and it's cool to watch them while you're munching on fried green tomatoes, made with nearby Hanover tomatoes, or a cheese plate that offers an entire roasted garlic bulb. The menu is long on steaks and seafood, but the brined pork loin is a treat. It's stuffed with andouille sausage, blue cheese, and pecans and served with a blueberry gastrique. Bread pudding, a Southern favorite, is the side, though this one is made with

HEAVENLY CHEESE

You start to wonder whether you've made a wrong turn along the winding, country roads outside of Crozet and then you spot the massive brick structure in the foothills of the Blue Ridge Mountains. Keep going, and you'll soon reach **Our Lady of the Angels Monastery** (*3365 Monastery Dr., Crozet, VA 22932; 434-823-1452; olamonastery.org*), where nuns from the Cistercian, or Trappist, order produce 2-pound wheels of Gouda cheese that have helped make them self-supporting since coming to this part of Virginia in 1987. The cheese, made by cooking cultured milk until the whey separates from the curd, is produced on the property, which had been set up for Gouda-making by a previous owner. Monastery Country Cheese is legendary, made from curds shipped from Wisconsin, brined, and sealed in red wax. You can get it at some stores in the commonwealth or by ordering online, but it's an experience to pull into one of the few visitor parking spaces outside the monastery and head inside and down a hall. In a small room, one of the nuns will make the transactions personally. And the cheese itself? Heavenly.

mushrooms. It's common to hear live music coming from the bar on weekends and, of course, the rumble of trains anytime.

Restaurant Pomme, 115 S. Main St., Gordonsville, VA 22942; (540) 832-0130; restaurant-pomme.com; French; $$$$. The Main Street in Gordonsville, population about 1,500, pretty much contains all the bustle of this central Virginia hamlet, once home to a Colonial tavern that served the likes of Thomas Jefferson, James Madison, and the Marquis de Lafayette. Today, the main thoroughfare is home to a couple of antiques shops, a haberdashery, a garden shop, a blacksmith and, most notably, Restaurant Pomme. Here, Parisian-born Chef-Owner

Gerard Gasparini—formerly of the Palace de Lucerne in Switzerland and New York City's Rainbow Room—prepares classic French dishes such as *salade Montrachet,* a goat cheese purse with apples, walnuts, and bacon over mixed greens, and *canard aux ceries,* a duck breast with cherry sauce. The *filet de sole St. Germain,* prepared meunière-style with a whisper of a crunch on the outside, ethereally tender within, is a destination dish. Everything is artfully plated on china, and the dining-room decor achieves the relaxed feel of a slightly refined farmhouse kitchen with a fireplace, bay window, hardwood floors, and brick archways separating seating areas. Service is perfect, but not at all stuffy. If it's not too busy, the chef will stop by to make sure your experience was exceptional.

Landmarks

City Tavern, 9405 Main St., Manassas, VA 20110; (703) 330-0076; citytaverngrille.com; American; $$. Stop at the tavern any time, and it feels like old-home week. This one is a locals' favorite, and you can tell because the diners and staff all call each other by name. The tavern is a homey place where framed *Life* magazines and old photos line the walls. The menu is extensive, ranging from appetizers such as fried zucchini sticks and nachos to entrees such as filet mignon and chicken piccata. Lunch and dinner are served daily, and brunch is available on Sunday. A disc jockey often is on hand, providing tunes for dancing, and sometimes there's an open-mic night for poetry. Folks rightfully rave about the fries, perfectly crispy yet tender inside, and some diners have been known to say that they could have made an entire meal of them.

Crozet Pizza, 5794 Three Notch'd Rd., Crozet, VA 22932; (434) 823-2132; crozetpizza.net; Pizza; $$–$$$. It's been called the best pizza around, maybe in the state, and a trip to this quaint building in

Give Me Liberty . . . and Lunch

Long before Patrick Henry fanned the flames of the Revolutionary War by uttering those famous words—"Give me liberty, or give me death"—the Colonial statesman lived for a bit at Hanover Tavern, owned by his first wife's father, where he sometimes entertained guests with his fiddle.

Hanover Tavern, located at a rural juncture northeast of Richmond, dates back to 1733. It's a rare example of a Colonial-era tavern, which was often the community and business hub of the fledgling nation. George Washington slept here, and so did the British Lord Cornwallis. Later, in 1836, P.T. Barnum had an argument with the innkeeper here.

Today, you can't stay at the tavern, but you can partake of a traditional Southern lunch on the upstairs porch and Sunday brunch or dinner in the rustic dining room. You can even take in a live professional show in the 50-seat Barksdale Theatre in the basement of the inn.

The inn's Southern-centric menus feature fried green tomatoes, plain or in a BLT, fried oysters, hanger steak cooked on cast iron (and updated with a drizzle of chimichurri), and shrimp and grits made with Byrd's Mill grits from nearby Ashland, topped with a saffron cream sauce. But if you order that, you'll miss out on the buttermilk fried chicken served with white pepper country gravy and a flaky biscuit. Decisions, decisions. Then, follow your dinner with a serving of Virginia Repertory Theatre in the nation's first dinner theater. **Hanover Tavern,** *Hanover Courthouse Rd., Va. Route 301, Hanover, VA 23069; (804) 537-5050; Traditional Southern; $$. (Theater tickets are purchased separately from Virginia Repertory Theatre, 804-282-2620; va-rep.org.)*

the tiny town of Crozet is an experience. But don't drop in without a reservation. Otherwise, it's tough to get a seat in the two-room joint, where locals and loyals crowd into the well-worn booths. There's a wood stove and walls of business cards left by satisfied customers. On the chalkboard, you'll see only pizza, the dish that put this place on the map after Bob and Karen Crum opened the doors in 1977. For 27 years, Bob handmade each pizza, before turning the business over to his daughter and her husband, Colleen and Mike Alexander. The pies come in three sizes but endless variations. You can order one of the specialties or create your own. And if you can't find a seat, you can always opt for takeout. Either way, you'll know why people travel for miles just for a bite.

Lake Anna Smokehouse & Grill, 131 Mineral Ave., at the corner of US 522 and VA Route 208, Mineral, VA 23117; (540) 894-0500; lakeannasmokehouse.com; Barbecue; $. Who can resist checking out this barbecue joint at the red light in Mineral? There's no smoker outside, no wheelbarrow, no shovel. But the aroma, the aroma. That's what made us stop. Inside we found Pitmistress Sue Robbins, who had just taken 10 pounds of pork butts out of the smoker. "Gosh, this smell makes us want to stay," we said to no one in particular while scanning the menu of ribs, chicken, barbecue, baked beans and such. "That's what happened to me," said a guy in an apron, an assistant to the pitmistress, famous for her secret dry rub and sweet hot barbecue sauce. Her joint is just a few miles from Lake Anna State Park, formerly known as Gold Hill, home to an honest-to-goodness gold mine. We think Miss Sue has a gold mine here. You?

Blackstone Coffee Co., **1113 Jefferson Davis Hwy., Fredericksburg, VA 22401; (540) 479-1355; blackstonecoffee.com.** This coffee shop, tucked in a shopping mall across from the University of Mary Washington, serves up its own roasted brew in espressos, lattes and macchiatos, as well as iced and chilled drinks. The pale mustard walls, with accents of chocolate brown and brick red, provide a cheery atmosphere. Customers sit at wooden tables or in comfy, stuffed chairs—chatting, reading or taking advantage of the free Wi-Fi, while indie rock plays in the background. For breakfast, there's a vegetarian quiche and bagel options. Sandwiches include chicken salad and turkey and the vegetarian Don Corleone—the sandwich you can't refuse—with tomato, mozzarella, lettuce, pesto, and a balsamic glaze. A sign on a bookshelf, however, sums up the main reason this place has a steady stream of patrons: I DRINK COFFEE FOR YOUR PROTECTION.

Carl's Frozen Custard, **2200 Princess Anne St., Fredericksburg, VA 22401; (540) 373-1776.** This roadside ice-cream stand, also known as Carl's Ice Cream, has been a fixture in Fredericksburg since Carl Sponseller started the business in 1947. Now run by three descendants, the shop keeps it simple. The menu has only three flavors of ice cream—vanilla, chocolate, and strawberry—but the taste—rich, dense and creamy—keeps the crowds coming back. You'll often see a long line waiting to get to the outdoor walk-up window to place an order, but an efficient staff keeps things moving, so you never have to wait long. A few concrete benches out front give you a place to down your treats. The shop, with its Art Moderne façade, is on the National Register of Historic Places, but it's the soft-serve that's the real treasure.

GEORGE WASHINGTON'S WHISKEY BUSINESS

Every first-grader knows that George Washington chopped down a cherry tree, never told a lie, and was the first president. But did you know he also made whiskey? Lots and lots of whiskey. They don't teach that in elementary school. Today, the president's distillery and gristmill have been reconstructed and are open to the public. Here's a little quiz for the road:

1. Washington oversaw thousands of acres of farmland at and around Mount Vernon, his beloved family home on the Potomac River near Washington, DC. Always seeking ways to make his vast operation more profitable, he was one of the first Virginia planters to ditch tobacco, a labor-intensive crop that depleted the soil, in favor of:
   A. Peanuts
   B. Grains

2. Washington operated a commercial, water-powered gristmill on his Dogue Run Farm. He was the only founding father to:
   A. Own a bakery
   B. Own a distillery

3. In Colonial times, candidates for public office often offered voters a drink at the polls. When Washington made a run for the Virginia House of Burgesses in 1755, he did not follow that custom. In that election, he:
   A. Won
   B. Lost

4. Washington served beer, rum punch, wine, strong cider, and brandy to voters during his 1758 bid for a Burgess seat. In that election, he:
   A. Lost
   B. Won

5. Later, in 1777, as commander of the Continental Army, Washington—who believed in drinking in moderation—worried in writing about his troops. "When they are marching in hot or Cold weather, in Camp in Wet, on fatigue or in Working Parties," Washington said it was "essential" that troops have "moderate supplies" of:
    A. Coffee
    B. Spirits

6. In 1789, Washington became the nation's first president. By then, sugar and molasses, products of the British West Indies essential in making rum, were hard to come by and had the taint of political incorrectness. Next to his mill, Washington built a distillery, one of 3,500 in Virginia. At its peak, Washington's distillery was:
    A. An average-sized operation
    B. The largest in the country

7. Washington's distillery was lost over time. After being rediscovered by archaeologists, it was reconstructed. With the reopening of the distillery in 2007, you could say that Virginia is:
    A. For lovers
    B. The "gateway" to the American Whiskey Trail, a series of distilleries in Virginia, Tennessee, Pennsylvania, and New York that explore the cultural heritage and history of spirits in America

Answers: B is the correct choice for all of the questions.

George Washington's Distillery & Gristmill, *on Va. Route 235, 3 miles south of Mount Vernon at 5514 Mount Vernon Memorial Hwy., Alexandria, VA 22309; (703) 780-2000; mountvernon.org.*

1st AVE Bakery, 11294 Russell Rd., Purcellville, VA 20132; (540) 668-9089; 1stavebakery.com. Want the best pies in the state? The best brownies? The best cakes and cookies? You've come to the right place, but you don't have to take our word for it. The master baker behind this boutique bakery, Violet LaBrecque, and her husband, Bob, have won more than 100 first-place ribbons and more than 30 best-of-the-best honors from the State Fair of Virginia in almost every baked-goods category. The LaBrecques bowed out of the amateur state competition after they opened their shop in 2008. Their pies are legendary, as much for their robust flavor as their intricate designs. Consider the lattice-topped cherry or peach varieties, or the three-layer **Peanut Supreme Pie** that has been designated the state pie of Virginia (see recipe on p. 257). "It's all about the flavor, and it's all about the presentation," Bob says. *Good Housekeeping* magazine has named Violet one of the top pie bakers in the country, and it's easy to see why when you visit this shop.

Greenwood Gourmet Grocer, 6701 Rockfish Gap Tpke., Crozet, VA 22932; (540) 456-6431; greenwoodgourmet.com. This small-town market has a big-city feel, with gourmet cheeses, local produce, meats, sandwiches, wine, and more in a maze of aisles where you keep finding additional surprises. There's a coffee station with freshly made baked goods, as well as a few kitchen supplies. The breads come from Goodwin Creek Farm & Bakery in nearby Afton. The meat section is small, but you might discover goat rib chops or rabbit or quail.

Asparagus, Asian peas, and other local produce are offered, and wines and beers from Virginia and beyond line several shelves. The deli produces sandwiches such as the Landrance, with prosciutto, mozzarella, roasted tomatoes, arugula, and garlic vinaigrette on a baguette, and the Araucana, house-made egg salad with Virginia bacon and sliced local tomatoes. "We've been biking for a while and eating at gas stations," said a motorcyclist who stopped with a friend, "and this is so much nicer." We couldn't have said it better.

Red Truck Bakery & Market, 22 Waterloo St. at Courthouse Square, Warrenton, VA 20186; (540) 347-2224; redtruckbakery.com. Brian Nowes left his high-powered career as an art director for national publications to open this bakery, which quickly has become beloved near and far. He began by selling baked goods out of a red farm truck purchased from fashion designer Tommy Hilfiger's Connecticut farm, but soon found a permanent home in a renovated gas station. You're in luck if you find the savory ham-and-cheese scones—made only a couple of days a week—because they sell out quickly. But the temptations are many—breads, cookies, croissants, cupcakes, and other treats. There's a double-chocolate cake flavored with local hooch, and a bourbon variety made with root beer and cherries. You can snack at the communal farm table in what used to be a garage bay and, on your way out, grab a sugar cookie shaped like a truck and decorated in red icing. Then stop and admire the real thing—the namesake 1954 Ford F-100 that sits in the parking lot.

Stanley's Store, 14242 Mountain Rd., Glen Allen, VA 23059; (804) 752-7789; on Facebook. Here, at the corner of US 33 and Va. Route 623 outside of Richmond, is a gem of a store, proof that gas stations, or retrofitted gas stations such as this one, are well worth a look-see. Inside Stanley's Store, circa 1944, is an eye-popping menu that ranges from meaty crab cakes to state fair corn dogs, from grass-fed beef burgers to pulled pork barbecue. Despite being more than 100 miles from the coast, Chef-Owner David Ruggiero even keeps a crock of crab bisque heated up behind the counter and dares you to find any better. There are all manner of breakfast foods, sandwiches, chili cheese, and slaw dogs. And all the side salads and desserts—think coconut cake and massive chocolate chip cookies—are homemade. Grab a cold bottle of co-cola from the old-school case for the full old-school vibe.

Wineries & Breweries

Battlefield Brewing Co. and The Pub, 4187 Plank Rd., Fredericksburg, VA 22407; (540) 785-2164; brewpubfredericksburg .com.

Blue & Gray Brewing Co. and Lee's Retreat Brewpub, 3300 Dill Smith Dr., Fredericksburg, VA 22408; (540) 538-2379; blueandgraybrewingco.com.

Bogati Bodega, 35246 Harry Byrd Hwy., Round Hill, VA 20142; (540) 338-1144; bogatibodega.com.

Boxwood Estate Winery, 2042 Burrland Rd., Middleburg, VA 20117; (540) 687-8778; boxwoodwinery.com.

Breaux Vineyards, 36888 Breaux Vineyards Ln., Purcellville, VA 20132; (540) 668-6299; breauxvineyards.com.

On the Vine

The fertile grounds of the northern Piedmont are home to more than 150 wineries, producing whites such as Chardonnay, Pinot Grigio, Riesling, and Sauvignon Blanc; reds such as Cabernet Franc, Malbec, and Merlot; and several fruity varieties.

Cana Vineyards and Winery of Middleburg, 38600 John Mosby Hwy., Middleburg, VA 20117; (703) 348-2458; canavineyards .com.

Chrysalis Vineyards, 23876 Champe Ford Rd., Middleburg, VA 20117; (540) 687 8222; chrysaliswine.com.

Corcoran Brewing Co., 14635 Corky's Farm Ln., Waterford, VA 20197; (540) 882-9073; on Facebook.

868 Estate Vineyards, 14001 Harpers Ferry Rd., Purcellville, VA 20132; (540) 668-7008; 868estatevineyards.com.

Granite Heights Winery, 8141 Opal Rd., Warrenton, VA 20186; (540) 349-5185; graniteheightsorchard.com.

Midnight Brewery, 2410 Granite Ridge Rd., Rockville, VA 23146; (804) 356-9379; facebook.com/ midnightbrewery.

Pearmund Cellars, 6190 Georgetown Rd., Broad Run, VA 20137; (540) 347-3475; pearmundcellars.com.

Starr Hill Brewery, 5391 Three Notch'd Rd., Crozet, VA 22932; (434) 823-5671; starrhill.com.

Tarara Winery, 13648 Tarara Ln., Leesburg, VA 20176; (703) 771-7100; tarara.com.

City of Manassas Farmers' Market, 9431 West St., Manassas, VA 20110; (703) 361-6599. Thurs and Sat from 7:30 a.m. to 1 p.m., Apr through Nov, and Sat from 10 a.m. to 1 p.m., Dec through Mar.

Culpeper Downtown Farmers' Market, corner of E. Davis and Commerce Streets, Culpeper, VA 22701; (540) 825-4416. Sat from 7:30 a.m. to noon, late Apr through late Nov.

Fredericksburg Farmers' Market, Hurkamp Park on Prince Edward St., Fredericksburg, VA 22401; (540) 847-2287. Mon through Sat from 7 a.m. to 2 p.m., June through Sept.

Leesburg Farmers' Market, Virginia Village Shopping Center, 20 Catoctin Circle at Fairfax Street, Leesburg, VA 20175; (703) 737-8387. Sat from 8 a.m. to noon, May through Oct.

Warrenton's Farmer's Market, corner of 5th and Lee Streets, Warrenton, VA 20188; (540) 347-6267. Sat from 7 a.m. to noon, Apr through Nov.

Charlottesville

The "farm-to-fork" movement is no stranger to this charming college town nestled in the foothills of the Blue Ridge Mountains. In fact, you could say it began here, with Thomas Jefferson. The third president was a connoisseur of the finer things in life, and he used his nearby Monticello estate as a testing ground for seeds and plants of all kinds. That spirit continues today in the area's fertile farm fields and pastures that provide apples, beef, eggs, grapes, pumpkins, and more to the vibrant restaurant scene. Jefferson's influence is evident there, too. He founded the University of Virginia in 1819, and it drives the local economy and means that, among the city's more than 200 restaurants, you'll find college hangouts where food can be had on the cheap and upscale eateries where the menus are creative and more costly. The choices reflect the school's diversity—Asian, Chinese, French, South African, Spanish, and, of course, good old Southern goodness.

Foodie Faves

Bang!, 213 2nd St. SW, Charlottesville, VA 22902; (434) 984-2264; bangrestaurant.net; Asian Fusion Tapas; $. On weekends, it can be difficult to get a seat inside this tapas bar just a few blocks from the city's pedestrian mall. If you do, you'll understand the restaurant's name when you take a bite of the sesame tuna with wasabi cream—bang! Or

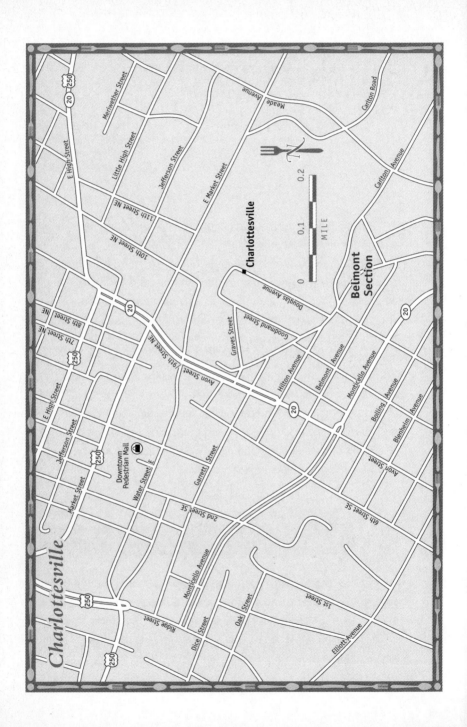

the cilantro wontons with chile sauce—bang! The menu includes more than 15 vegetarian offerings and even more choices for carnivores. Portions are generous, so it's easy to share with friends. On Wednesday, a reduced-price menu cuts down on your bill. You can dine inside on the first or second floors or on the patio out front, where at night you can gaze at the white lights entwined in the small trees. There's a small bar in the back, but be careful. It's dark, and there's one step down. The martini list is lengthy, and the temptations make choices difficult. Sin City, a wallop of berry vodka, pomegranate liqueur, and blackberry puree, is the most popular. For the guys, there's Mr. Big, a cosmo made with white cranberry juice that won't make you look as though you're sipping a girlie cocktail.

Citizen Burger Bar, 212 E. Main St., Charlottesville, VA 22902; (434) 979-9944; citizenburgerbar.com; Gourmet Burgers; $$. Opened in 2012, this chic restaurant cooks burgers to order, serves them on buns made down the road at Albemarle Baking Co., and, when cheese is requested, often uses a Virginia variety made at Mountainview Farm in Fairfield. The eatery is located in the town's pedestrian mall and offers indoor and outdoor seating. Inside, the friendly but upscale atmosphere is punctuated by an exposed brick wall, dark-wood tabletops, a sleek bar, and TV screens where you can watch sports. The burgers, made with grass-fed beef from nearby Timbercreek Farm, are what bring customers back. They're mile-high, and the meat is juicy. You can choose your own toppings, or opt for a burger from the menu. The namesake Citizen Burger comes with swiss cheese, black onion, and garlic aioli. The sweet potato fries are hard to put down, and the drinks menu has 93 beers and hard ciders, as well as wines and cocktails. It's all part of owner Anderson McClure's vision of what this place should offer: good eats, cold drinks, and common ground.

BABY, THESE CUPCAKES ARE GOOD

It's not unusual to see pregnant women—we're talking seriously pregnant, days-overdue, desperate women—making their way into the cupcake shop in the white painted-brick storefront off Charlottesville's downtown pedestrian mall. They're after one thing at **Cappellino's Crazy Cakes** (*103 3rd St. NE, Charlottesville, VA 22902; 434-293-2964; cappellinoscrazycakes .com*)—the Lemondrop, a cupcake that might be the sweetest way known to women to induce labor naturally. Close to 200 have given birth after eating the baked good, and those are just the ones that owner Dotty Cappellino knows about. Dotty, who opened the bakery with her brother, Frank, credits the birthing success to the fresh lemon juice and lemon zest she puts into each creation. The cupcake is topped with a lemon hard candy, and Dotty says it's important to eat that, too. In fact, she recommends two of the Lemondrops to ensure that the baby gets

moving. If you're not pregnant, it's fun to head to the store and check out the board that is updated with each new birth. And there's a wealth of other cupcake flavors to choose from. Oh, and dads? They can join in, too, but Dotty says they shouldn't share the Lemondrop with their wives. They need to get their own.

Fellini's #9, 200 Market St., Charlottesville, VA 22902; (434) 979-4279; Italian; $$–$$$. The original Fellini's had been closed for 10 years when Jacie Dunkle came to town to visit a friend in the hospital. Dunkle bought the place, reopened it, and added the number to the name, a twist on the title of Italian director Federico Fellini's ninth film, 8½. The restaurant is located in a rustic old house built in the mid-1800s, with distressed-pine floors whose wood was recovered from old buildings and barns. A few Fellini movie posters adorn the walls, along with original works by local artists. Upstairs is an old-fashioned speak-easy, and you'll need a password to get in, just as in the days of Prohibition. The password changes nightly, but it's written on the door, so you don't have to worry about being left out. At the eatery, the fare is Italian, with lots of pasta and marinara dishes. The real fun comes on Sunday morning, when the make-your-own Bloody Mary bar opens. It's a perfect, hair-of-the-dog pick-me-up. You start with a basic vodka and tomato-flavored drink, then doctor it up your way. You'll find a bunch of sauces, including A-1, barbecue, Tabasco, Worcestershire, and more than a handful of hot ones. Then it's fruit-and-veggie time, with choices that include carrots, lemons, limes, olives, and pickles. Then it's time for brunch, unless, of course, you'd rather drink yours.

Glass Haus, 313 2nd St. SE, Charlottesville, VA 22902; (434) 244-8439; New American; $$$$. This industrial-chic restaurant in the city's warehouse district is a spacious place, where upstairs seating rings an atrium on three sides, yet each table feels intimate. A large mural of grazing cows offers a hint to the cuisine, which is an ode to locally sourced food. The man behind the meals is Executive Chef Ian Boden, a 2013 James Beard Foundation semifinalist for the mid-Atlantic's top chef award. On his inventive menu, which changes often, you'll discover words like "fiddleheads" and "zaatar." You might find halibut, poached to perfection, with a red pea ragout, ramps, and pistachios, or braised rabbit served over pappardelle pasta with a dandelion green pesto. It's hard to go wrong, and the waitstaff suggests that it's best to "pick your plate, not your protein"—meaning that guests should take into account the side dishes and sauces when ordering. Dinner is served Tues through Sat, and there's a bar menu on Fri and Sat. The restaurant opened in 2011 and has quickly become a foodie favorite. One tip: Bring a cell phone or small flashlight; the romantic atmosphere is dark, and you'll want to make sure you can read all of Boden's menu options.

MAS Tapas, 501 Monticello Rd., Charlottesville, VA 22902; (434) 979-0990; mastapas.com; Tapas; $–$$. This tapas bar in the up-and-coming Belmont neighborhood has an industrial look, with exposed brick walls and ductwork and a concrete floor. But there's nothing harsh about the vibe. It's a hopping place, particularly on Friday and Saturday nights, and it's a favorite of locals and college students. When the weather's nice, the patio area out front is full, as is the large bar area near the entrance. The dining room is at the back, in a lower level, and customers can feel the temperature drop slightly as they descend a few steps to it. The restaurant's moniker is a play on the first name of Chef-Owner Tomas Rahal, who showcases local ingredients in his small plates. The brussels sprouts and parsnips have a sweet, caramelized taste that contrasts nicely with the garlic and pine nuts. The *gambas al' parilla* is a treat, with grilled jumbo shrimp enhanced by garlic aioli and gray salt. The *medulla,* with its beef marrow and truffles, is rich and buttery. Fun to consume are the dates roasted in applewood-smoked bacon. Finish with the chocolate torte—a true one, no flour here—flavored by dark bittersweet Guanaja chocolate.

Peter Chang's China Grill, 2162 Barracks Rd., Charlottesville, VA 22903; (434) 244-9818; peterchang-charlottesville.com; Chinese; $–$$. When the Scallion Bubble Pancakes arrive at your table, you're not sure whether to laugh, marvel, or dig in. The wafer-thin pancakes are fried, causing them to bubble up into three-dimensional spheres the size of cantaloupes. You can't imagine how you'll wolf them down, but the waitress suggests using your fingers to tear them into small bites and dipping the pieces in the accompanying curry sauce. It's good advice. The restaurant is the one of three in Virginia opened by Chinese-born chef Peter Chang, who specializes in Szechwan cuisine. The restaurant's interior is a mixture of colors—seafoam green, black, and white—and textures—slick gray tile, exposed brick—that somehow meld together. The menu does much of the same, mixing dishes such as garlic beef, steamed pork soup buns, and dry-fried eggplant (akin to french fries, with a golden outer crust encasing a creamy inside) into a culinary adventure. You'll find so many twists on Chinese food that you won't be sure where to begin. **Additional locations:** 1203 Richmond Rd., Williamsburg, VA 23185, (757) 345-5829, peterchangrestaurant.com (see p. 123); 11424 W. Broad St., Glen Allen, VA 23060, (804) 364-1688, peterchangrva.com; 1771 Carl D. Silver Pkwy., Fredericksburg, VA 22401, (540) 786-8988, peterchangschinese.com; and 3364 Princess Anne Road, Suite 505, Virginia Beach, VA 23456, (757) 468-2222.

The Shebeen, 247 **Ridge-McIntire Rd., Charlottesville, VA 22903; (434) 296-3185; South African; $$.** This pub bursts with personality, with wooden beams in the high ceiling, terra cotta walls and a weathered wood floor. A large smoker out front, which is fired up two or three times a week, hints at the deep flavors you'll find in the meat. The menu is South African, and one dish sizzles with a spicy piri-piri sauce and the next refreshes with cucumber-mint yogurt. Those unfamiliar with the cuisine might start with the Samosas, spiced ground beef and lamb encased in triangular fried pastry shells. You can eat them plain, but the mango chutney sauce, with its earthy curry undertones, adds the right amount of sweetness. The Zambezi satay is a twist on a traditional Malaysian dish, with pieces of skewered chicken that get their kick from ground peanuts and ginger. The Brinjal fries will make you rethink the whole idea that such dishes must be potato-based. Here, eggplant strips are encrusted with panko and deep-fried until they're crunchy on the outside and tender on the inside. The cocktail menu offers creative concoctions, like the light Ginger Square, with splashes of bitters, ginger beer, and a zing of citrus from lime juice.

Landmarks

Blue Moon Diner, 512 **W. Main St., Charlottesville, VA 22903; (434) 980-6666; on Facebook; Casual American; $.** Take one step into this old-fashioned diner, plop down on one of the swiveling barstools, and you'll feel as if you've gone back to the 1950s. This small eatery, a favorite of students from the University of Virginia, serves updated, simple food for breakfast, lunch, and dinner. Sunday brunch is popular, and customers often have to wait in line to get served. On other days, one of the favorites is the huevos-bluemoonos, where the house salsa adds spice to eggs and hash browns. A smoky breakfast sandwich uses goat cheese and capers to complement smoked salmon. Burgers and fries are a staple, but an artisanal bacon also is offered. For libations, five beers are on tap, including a St. George India Pale Ale and a bourbon barrel stout. Scrabble boards rest in the windowsills, unless customers have already grabbed them for an afternoon of wordplay. It might not be fine dining, but it's a fine time.

Bodo's Bagels, 1418 Emmet St., Charlottesville, VA 22903; (434) 977-9598; bodosbagels.com; Bagel Sandwiches; $. The doorknobs on most of these locations are a giveaway; they're large wooden O's that resemble the breadstuffs these places are known for. Even some transplants from New York City, where the bar is high, are known to offer praise for these bagels. An institution for more than 20 years, Bodo's, as it's known around here, serves sandwiches, soups, and salads, but it's the bagels most folks come for. Customers order at the counter, and the line can get long, especially in the morning, but it moves quickly. Use your waiting time to study the extensive menu. You can choose premade selections or get creative and make your own. The normal toppings are available—cheese, lettuce, lox, mayo, and mustard—but so are more unusual choices, such as a Kalamata olive spread, feta cheese, and pepper spread. You also can get chicken and tuna salads and such. Wolf down your selections in the bare-bones dining area or take them to go. **Additional locations:** 505 Preston Ave., Charlottesville, VA 22903; (434) 293-5224; 1609 University Ave., Charlottesville, VA 22903; (434) 293-6021.

C&O Restaurant, 515 E. Water St., Charlottesville, VA 22902; (434) 971-7044; Seafood/Steaks; $$$$. The name comes from the Chesapeake & Ohio Railroad, and you can get a taste of the area's railroad history—as well as some good food—at this old standby, which opened in 1976. The formal dining room is upstairs, surrounded by windows that overlook a rail yard. During the Depression, the room was a bunkhouse for railroad workers. The bar, its walls covered in old barn wood, is on the main floor, where guests can dine more casually. A patio offers outdoor seating. The restaurant has won acclaim from *Bon Appétit* and *Food & Wine* magazines, and one of its more popular dishes is the steak chinoise. Inspired by the a delicately flavored oyster soup once served here, the dish ramps up a flank steak with garlic, ginger, tamari sauce, and a cream sauce. It's a zesty biteful that keeps you intrigued. C&O's is a comfortable place to settle in for the ride.

l'etoile, 817 W. Main St., Charlottesville, VA 22903; (434) 979-7957; letoilerestaurant.com; French; $$$$. Chef-Owner Mark Gresge showcases local ingredients in a menu that offers French food with a Southern twist. Start with the shrimp and grits, an appetizer where the smokiness of the bacon marries nicely with the Gulf shrimp and ground-corn grits, or a soup such as the nutty butternut squash or the zesty gazpacho. The duck is done right—a crisp skin covering the dark juiciness inside. Sunday brings brunch; on other days, only dinner is served. The waiters are gracious and attentive, and they're quick to point out the freshness of the ingredients, joking—or maybe they're not—that the fowl on your plate was running around this morning. It's a romantic spot, with exposed brick and work by local artists on the walls. A few outdoor tables let you eat alfresco. The restaurant dates back to 1993, when it opened as The Tea Room. The new name means "the star," and the eatery is a perennial favorite of locals hankering for a touch of Paris.

Michie Tavern, 683 Thomas Jefferson Pkwy., Charlottesville, VA 22902; (434) 977-1234; michietavern.com; Traditional Southern; **$$.** You'll get a taste of old Virginia at this historic landmark, where the servers wear period costumes and the menu, or should we say "bill of fare," is Southern comfort food. The tavern was originally opened circa 1784 by William Michie on a well-traveled stagecoach route and was moved to its current location in 1927. A buffet-style lunch in the restaurant, called The Ordinary, is served daily, and it's best to get there when it opens—11:15 a.m. April through October and 15 minutes later during the other months—because tour buses arrive shortly thereafter and lines can grow long. Fried chicken, baked chicken, and pulled pork are featured, along with various sides and desserts. Servers bring you seconds—or thirds. A tour lets you visit the oldest part of the tavern, and you can browse afterward at the gift shop, metalsmith, and general and clothing stores. Raise a glass of apple cider to Thomas Jefferson, then head up the road a half-mile to visit his Monticello estate.

Specialty Stores, Markets & Producers

Albemarle Baking Co., 418 W. Main St., Charlottesville, VA 22903; (434) 293-6456; albemarlebakingco.com. The breads here are baked over a hearth, and locals love 'em, whether it's a thick-crusted baguette, an even smaller baguette called a *baton,* the light ciabatta or the perfect-for-sandwich focaccia. Behind the counter, the loaves are stacked in cubbyholes, which you might find empty if you arrive too late in the day. Even if that happens, there's much to look at. A window lets you watch a baker put the finishing touches on a chocolate cake or other creations. In the display cases, oversized cinnamon rolls get higher as they spiral toward the center. The Princess cakes, which layer

Score a Peck of Doughnuts

Henry Chiles, a third-generation fruit grower, was in California a few years ago when he first bit into the peach of his dreams. The mild, creamy sweetness of the doughnut peach impressed him.

The fruit—flat, with deep dimples on bottom and top—resembles a doughnut. It has reddish skin streaked with yellow, a rumor of fuzz and flesh the color of sunshine. Chiles marveled that it felt nearly as firm as an unripe pear and yet it burst with juice like a citrus.

Back at his family orchard near Charlottesville, he uprooted thousands of gnarled peach trees and planted the doughnut variety in their place.

The Chiles' family's operation is consolidated under the Crown Orchard brand and actually contains seven orchards—1,000 acres of apples and 500 acres of stone fruit spread across 15 miles of the Virginia Piedmont countryside. Summer is the season for doughnut peaches. Pick up a peck at the family's **Carters Mountain Orchard** (*1435 Carters Mountain Trail, Charlottesville, VA 22902; 434-977-1833; cartermountainorchard.com*), located within sight of Thomas Jefferson's Monticello. It's a steep drive up the hill to the fruit stand, but there's a tower up there that you can climb for free, and on some days they say you can see all the way to Richmond.

Bavarian cream and vanilla sponge cake and are topped with marzipan, look inviting. Then there are the cookies, croissants, French *macarons,* scones, sticky buns, and tarts. The intricately decorated petits fours are mouthful-sized bites of sweetness. "They're perfect for special events," a customer offers. "Or, if it's the afternoon, or the morning or . . ."

Chandler's Bakery, 202 Albemarle Square, Charlottesville, VA 22901; (434) 975-2253; chandlersbakery.com. The lace curtains and black-and-white-tiled floor provide a homey feel to this bakery in the Albemarle Square shopping center. The store, opened in 1995 by owner Carolyn Chandler Mucherino, consistently wins honors as the area's top bakery. It can be a bit overwhelming when you first walk in; there's simply so much goodness to take in. Multiple cases show off normal bakery fare such as bonbons, brownies, cookies, pies, and scones. Ice cream cakes are displayed in another case, and more sweets rotate in yet another one. Try one of the more popular items, a "radio" bar—a chocolate cake with buttercream filling that has been dipped in melted fudge. Or a "mooch" bar, a chocolate or yellow cake with buttercream and fudge filling that also has been dipped in melted fudge. Ask about the mini cheesecakes, and you'll learn that they, too, have been dipped in melted fudge. You start to get the feeling that everything has been finished that way, but a worker who admits to loving chocolate sets you straight. "Just the real, real good stuff," she says.

Food of All Nations, 2121 Ivy Rd., Charlottesville, VA 22903; (434) 293-7998; foodsofallnations.com. This grocery has been bringing foods from around the world to Charlottesville for more than 50 years. It's a place to pick up hard-to-find ingredients and items such as *foie gras,* prosciutto, organic split green peas—even 10 to 15 kinds of cigars. Some foodstuffs, such as lentils and quinoa, can be purchased in bulk. The specialty oils aisle is extensive, and shoppers can find products from Africa, Asia, Greece, and Indonesia. Virginia specialties, such as country hams and the sweetest-tasting honey around, are for sale, as are a large selection of jellies and relishes. You'll also find everyday items like toilet paper and canned foods, but there's a nice selection of fresh produce, cheese, meats, and seafood, and a butcher and fishmonger can help with special cuts.

Gearhearts Fine Chocolates, 416 W. Main St., Ste. C, Charlottesville, VA 22903; (434) 972-9100; gearhartschocolates.com. You think you've mistakenly stepped into a jewelry store when you enter this chocolate shop. A glass display case sits at one end of the shop, and two neatly dressed women hover behind it. A few exquisitely packaged boxes rest on a table to one side. Then it hits you: The chocolates made here, which have won acclaim from *Southern Living* and *Chocolatier* magazines, are truly gems. The candies are made by hand in small batches, using top-quality cacao from prized beans in Venezuela. The chocolates are decorated with intricate patterns, and the rich taste is equally complex. Sixteen flavors are offered, including the Taj, a bittersweet chocolate ganache that gets its exotic flavor from candied ginger and cardamom, and the Apricot Brandy, a milk-chocolate ganache that relies on cognac-soaked dried apricots for its liqueur-laced fruitiness. The most popular is the Maya, another candy with a bittersweet ganache base, though this one is set apart with hints of cinnamon, ancho chile, and orange. If you want to try them all, there's a sampler pack.

Great Harvest Bread Co., 1701 Allied Ln., Charlottesville, VA 22903; (434) 202-7813; greatharvestcville.com. The ovens are fired early, around 3:30 a.m., in this yellow-painted brick storefront in McIntire Plaza. That ensures that the racks will be filled and that the store will be bursting with a glorious aroma when the first customers arrive. A chalkboard above the counter offers the baking schedule for the week and a list of available sweets. Another board details a recently added line of sandwiches, including vegetarian options, for lunch. The two most popular breads—the whole wheat Dakota, topped with pumpkin, sesame, and sunflower seeds, and honey wheat—are made each day. The other kinds—maybe cheddar garlic, challah, or potato sourdough—rotate. Some breads, especially those that work well on sandwiches, come in traditional loaf shapes as well as more free-form rounds. The friendly staff, looking surprisingly trim for workers surrounded by so many carbs, answer questions freely and encourage customers to try the large samples.

Shenandoah Joe Coffee Roasters and Espresso Bar, 945 Preston Ave., Charlottesville, VA 22903; (434) 295-4563; shenandoahjoe.com. As you pull into the parking lot of this simple brick building, the aroma somehow wafts into your car, even with the windows rolled up. It's your first whiff of the roasted coffee that locals swear by. The atmosphere inside is laid-back; you'd never know this place was full of so much caffeine. Customers hang out at leisure in the lounge area, and workers casually point out the scones, pumpkin muffins, and other homemade goodies in the display cases. The beans are roasted on the spot, and you can watch it happen in this open-air space. The walls of the roasting area are filled with decorated burlap bags that once held bulk coffee beans from Africa, Indonesia, South America, and other spots around the globe. More than 25 varieties are available, and a large blackboard details the choices. The java is the real thing—deep, bold, and rich—so get a cup to drink and a pound or two to go. It'll come in handy on Sunday, when this place is closed and you're hankering for a cup.

The Spice Diva, 410 W. Main St., Charlottesville, VA 22903; (434) 218-3482; thespicediva.com. You'll often find the Spice Diva herself, Phyllis Hunter, behind the counter inside the small purple building that houses her store. She opened the shop in 2011, and more than 250 spices and 25 specialty teas line the shelves. The aroma is at once exotic and tangy, but Phyllis offers an even more close-up sensory experience. "You're absolutely welcome to smell," she says, before removing the lid from a jar and letting you inhale. Some of the items are the usual suspects—basil, oregano, and such—but there are unusual ones like *ras el hanout,* an earthy blend of Moroccan flavors that means "top of the shop." The spices come in bulk, so you can buy as much or as little as you want. Phyllis is a cook, and one of her prouder moments was providing the spices for a dinner prepared locally by Alice Waters, the California chef credited with helping launch the locavore movement. Phyllis is quick to share stories of her own culinary successes and blunders, telling a shopper that lavender is lovely paired with rack of lamb. "But," she advises, "don't use too much. I almost learned that the hard way."

The Virginia Shop, Barracks Road Shopping Center, 1047-B Emmet St., Charlottesville, VA 22903; (434) 977-0080. You can save yourself a lot of miles with a visit to this store smack dab in the center of a shopping center. No need to drive to Surry; you can get Surryano ham from Surry Farms. Don't bother traveling to Berryville; you can pick up honey from Bark Farm. Forget the trip to Ashland; you'll find mixes for grits—both yellow and white—from Byrd Mill Co. And that's just the beginning. You'll find the state's well-known items, such as peanuts—in cans, in boxes, in bags—and wine—from the nearby While Vineyards and Glass House Winery and many others. But you'll also discover the exquisite espresso, blueberry, and other chocolates from Gearharts and jugs of apple cider from Albemarle Ciderworks. With all the travel time you'll save, you'll have more hours to savor the best foods the commonwealth has to offer.

Wineries & Breweries

Blenheim Vineyards, 31 Blenheim Farm, Charlottesville, VA 22902; (434) 293-5366; blenheimvineyards.com.

The Grape Escape

Touring the 250-plus wineries in Virginia would take weeks, but Charlottesville is a great place to use as a base to visit some of the 30 spots on the state's premier **Monticello Wine Trail.** They're all located within a stone's throw or two from Thomas Jefferson's Colonial home, and in many ways the third president could be considered the grandfather of the Virginia wine industry.

Jefferson always dreamed of having vineyards at his estate, and he tried several times to grow grapes but found little success. Luckily, others have met better fates, and the commonwealth is now the sixth-largest wine-producing state in the union.

The Monticello Wine Trail takes visitors to a series of boutique wineries located on a web of state and US highways in the rolling foothills of the Blue Ridge Mountains.

To take in the entire trail, get a brochure online at monticello winetrail.com or at the Convention and Visitors Bureau at 610 E. Main St. in Charlottesville.

Here's a sampling of what the trail has to offer:

Afton Mountain Vineyards, *234 Vineyard Ln., Afton, VA 22920; (540) 456-8667; aftonmountainvineyards.com.* Dating back to the 1970s, this vineyard makes Chardonnay, Cabernet Sauvignon, and Cabernet Franc, as well as a sparkling wine and a fruity Gewürztraminer. The tasting room is cozy, and two large patios overlook the mountains and a pond. Tastings are offered on all days but Tuesday and a few major holidays.

Barboursville Vineyards, *17655 Winery Rd., Barboursville, VA 22923; (540) 832-3824; barboursvillewine.com.* Established in 1976, this vineyard has more than 100 acres devoted to growing grapes. There's a lot to see: a large tasting room, a gift shop with accessories and books about wines, a restaurant, and an inn. Tastings are offered daily. Visitors can camp out at outside tables or on the lawns to enjoy more than 15 of the award-winning varieties.

Glass House Winery, *5898 Free Union Road, Free Union, VA 22940; (434) 975-0094; glasshousewinery.com.* There's a tropical flair here, with its plant-filled, glass-encased conservatory where you can sip wine while nibbling on handmade chocolates. A deck offers a stunning view of the orchards and mountains. Wines include Pinot Gris, Viognier, and the locally named C-Villian, a blend of Chambourcin, Cabernet Franc, and Merlot grapes. Wine tastings are available Thurs through Sun, and a bed-and-breakfast provides lodging.

Horton Vineyards, *6399 Spotswood Trail, Gordonsville, VA 22942; (540) 832-7440; hvwine.com.* The first grapes were harvested in 1991 at this vineyard, where tastings occur daily in a faux medieval chateau that boasts a turret. Popular varieties are the Horton Norton, based on a native Virginia grape; Viognier; and Norton Port.

Jefferson Vineyards, *1353 Thomas Jefferson Pkwy., Charlottesville, VA 22902; (434) 977-3042; jeffersonvineyards.com.* This is where it all started, and the majority of this vineyard's grapes are grown on sites that Thomas Jefferson selected in 1774. Tastings are available daily except Thanksgiving and Christmas. Available are more than a handful of varieties, including Pinot Gris, Petit Verdot, and Viognier. It's a great stop after touring the former president's home at Monticello.

Keswick Vineyards, *1575 Keswick Winery Dr., Keswick, VA 22947; keswickvineyards.com.* This vineyard's 2007 Cabernet Sauvignon won the state's top wine award, the Governor's Cup. More than 10 varieties are produced here, a former plantation that was used as a Confederate campsite during the Civil War. The tasting room on the 400-acre estate is small, but the patio looks out on ponds, where swans often can be seen.

Mountfair Vineyards, *4875 Fox Mountain Rd., Crozet, VA 22932; (434) 823-7605; mountfair.com.* The inviting patio overlooks the mountains in this small winery that specializes in red Bordeaux-style blends. The patio also is the place where musicians often set up to entertain crowds. Visitors can taste wines Fri through Sun.

White Hall Vineyards, *5282 Sugar Ridge Rd., White Hall, VA 22987; whitehallvineyards.com.* Established in 1992 with 6 acres, this vineyard has grown to more than seven times that size and produces nearly a dozen varieties, including Chardonnay, Pinot Gris, and Gewürztraminer. Twice, White Hall wines have won the state's Governor's Cup. The vineyard has a tasting room and shaded picnic area, with views of the mountains. Tastings are offered Wed through Sun.

Champion Brewing Co., 324 6th St. SE, Charlottesville, VA 22902; (434) 295-2739; facebook.com/ChampionBrewingCompany.

First Colony Winery, 1650 Harris Creek Rd., Charlottesville, VA 22902; (434) 979-7105; firstcolonywinery.com.

South Street Brewery, 106 South St., Charlottesville, VA 22902; (434) 293-6550; southstreetbrewery.com.

Trump Winery, 3550 Blenheim Rd., Charlottesville, VA 22902; (434) 984-4855; trumpwinery.com.

Virginia Wineworks/Michael Shaps Wines, 1781 Harris Creek Way, Charlottesville, VA 22902; (434) 296-3438; virginiawineworks.com.

Farmers' Markets

Charlottesville City Market, corner of Water and South Streets, Charlottesville, VA 22902. Sat from 7 a.m. to noon, Apr through Oct, and Sat from 8 a.m. to 1 p.m., Nov and Dec.

Farmers in the Park, Meade Park on the corner of Chesapeake Street and Meade Avenue, Charlottesville, VA 22902. Wed from 3 to 7 p.m., May through Sept.

Forest Lakes Farmers' Market, 1650 Ashwood Blvd., Charlottesville, VA 22902. Tues from 4 to 7 p.m., Apr through Oct.

Central Virginia

In Central Virginia, cradled between the Tidewater low country and the soaring Blue Ridge Mountains, residents have been sustained by Southern specialties for centuries. Collards, pork belly, and slow-cooked stone-ground grits nourished the earliest settlers, brave folk who long before the American Revolution settled a wilderness where buffalo roamed and rattlesnakes ruled. Today, with the exception of Richmond and Charlottesville, where the vibrant food scenes merit chapters all their own, and a smattering of small cities, it's a largely rural region where every county seat has a courthouse, and maybe a restaurant. Or maybe not. No matter. There's plenty to chew on, from gourmet burgers to barbecue to frenched rack of lamb. While traveling from here to yonder, switch on the radio for an earful of country, or gospel—you are, after all, in the buckle of the Bible Belt. On Sunday, it's best to arrive for lunch at restaurants just before noon. That way, you'll "beat the Methodists," an age-old saying in these parts that refers to the tendency for Baptist sermons to run past the noon hour and Methodists' to end on time. Oh, and those endless rows of leafy, lush, silvery plants growing in fields in spring and summer? They're not for salads; they're for smoking. Tobacco, Virginia's original cash crop, is still grown in the region today.

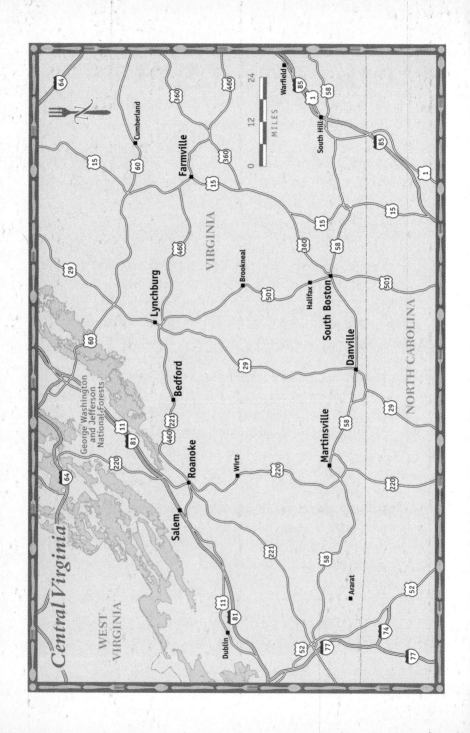

Blue Apron Restaurant & Red Rooster Bar, 210 E. Main St., Salem, VA 24153; (540) 375-0055; blueapronredrooster.com; French; $$–$$$. We've noted elsewhere in this guide that French restaurants seem to pop up in Virginia in the most unexpected places. This one's in Salem, next door to better-known, bigger-town Roanoke, and set in a renovated building that's more than 130 years old. The classic French brasserie has Scott Switzer at the helm, the chef-owner who earned his chops at the Culinary Institute of America. His menu changes every other month or so but might offer crisp rendered duck breast with a golden raisin and cherry *mostarda*, Vidalia onion soubise, and wild mushrooms, or herb-roasted chicken with green *charmoula*, couscous with white grapes and smoked almonds, and roasted garlic and lemon aioli. The ambience created by the exposed brick walls, gleaming wood floor, and fresh flowers and the unhurried pace adds to the European feel. The fact that most menu items are offered in small and large plates makes it a perfect spot for lingering over lunch or dinner, as the French like to do.

Checkered Pig, 1014 Liberty St., Martinsville, VA 24112; (276) 632-1161; checkeredpig.com; Barbecue; $. Zipping along US 58, aka the Jeb Stuart Highway, it's hard to tell exactly when you've crossed into NASCAR country, but by Danville, you've done it. It's the home to International Racing Hall of Famer Wendell O. Scott Sr., stock-car racing's first African-American driver and the first black winner of what is now called the Sprint Cup Series. The next town to the west, Martinsville, is home to the Martinsville Speedway, the only track that has hosted NASCAR Sprint Cup Series races every year since the division's inception in 1949. The Checkered Pig crew is pretty famous around here, too, for its award-winning barbecue, served in a pair of restaurants heavy in NASCAR decor, including the big, red hood of a racecar hanging on a

In a Stew, but a Tasty One

Brunswick stew. Them are fightin' words in south-central Virginia, where not too awfully long ago local men wielding oar-like paddles went to war because of them. Brunswick County historian Gay Neale has traced the origins of this iconic dish to around 1828, when a local doctor, his hunting buddies, and an African-American cook named "Uncle" Jimmy Matthews camped out on the Nottoway River. When the hunters had wandered into the woods, Uncle Jimmy shot squirrels, dressed them and made a stew of butter, onions, bread and seasonings. Eventually, the stew became a staple in the county. People took to making it in cast-iron wash pots out in the yard. Lima beans, okra, and potatoes were added. Squirrel gave way to chicken, or sometimes rabbit, ham, or lamb.

By 1958, a squabble had developed with Brunswick, Georgia. By the 1980s, "stew crews" from each state traveled to and fro for cook-offs. Finally, in February 1988, the Virginia General Assembly declared Brunswick County, Virginia "The Original Home of Brunswick Stew." Georgia followed suit shortly thereafter. In Virginia, historical markers went up on roadsides, and the commonwealth's

wall at the register in Martinsville. Make a pit stop here for the huge portions, including ribs with a smoke ring that attests to the skill of the pitmaster. The chopped pork is lean and smoky, and the brisket is as tender as a mother's love. Feeling like a hotshot? Try the "hot slaw," bound with hot sauce, not mayo. **Additional location:** 155 Crown Dr., Danville, VA 24540; (434) 793-7447.

Kahill's Restaurant, 1791 N. Mecklenburg Ave., South Hill, VA; (434) 447-6941; on Facebook; Seafood/Steaks; $$–$$$. When you're in South Hill, you're equidistant from Virginia Beach and the Blue Ridge Mountains. And so goes the menu at Kahill's, a food lover's oasis at the convergence of all the major thoroughfares in this spot in the southern

provenance is generally considered correct.
Today, Brunswick County stew crews and stew
masters guard their recipes, stirring immense
pots for 6 to 12 hours at a time for cook-offs
and hunt club and charity fund-raisers. When
the paddle stands up on its own, the stew is done.

Unless you happen upon a fund-raiser or the Taste of Brunswick Festival held on the second Saturday in October, the only eatery in the county consistently serving Brunswick stew is in Alberta,
a speck of a town a hop off of Interstate 85. Cheryl Johnson and her
husband, Chuck, a native stew master, are making their restaurant
and general store into the county's "stew quarters," resembling a
sports bar except decked out with stew-related memorabilia. They're
off to a good start with all sorts of items on display. The couple's
220-quart cast-iron pot on wheels, complete with two paddles,
greets guests at the door. Enjoy a bowlful at the store, or get some
frozen rock solid to go. **Alberta General Store,** *106 W. First Main
Ave., Alberta, VA 23821; (434) 949-7020; albertageneralstore.com.*

See Brunswick County historian Gay Neale's recipe for **Brunswick Stew** on p. 250.

part of the state. Kahill's will save you from fast-food depression with
dishes such as fried scallop salad with lightly grilled asparagus, feta,
and chopped bacon over fresh spinach. Or how about a frenched, pan-
seared rack of lamb? Seafood gets rapt attention here and is often on
the specials board. Check out the recipe in the back of the book for
Kahill's **Bacon-Wrapped Pecan Salmon** with honey vinaigrette (p. 253).
As we said, even in a town like South Hill, population 5,000, there's no
reason to resort to chain burgers and fries. But if you're in the mood
for them, Kahill's has house-made versions of both.

**Local Roots Restaurant, 1314 Grandin Rd., Roanoke, VA
24015; (540) 206-2610; localrootsrestaurant.com; New American;**

$$$–$$$$. It's not surprising that a restaurant named Local Roots champions the farmers and producers of central and southwest Virginia. It's the philosophy of owner Diane Elliott, who took over the place in 2009 from her son, Rives. She grew up in a household where Mom put home-cooked meals on the table each night and Dad stressed the importance of supporting local businesses. Her restaurant does the same. With its earth-toned color palette, pressed-tin ceiling, and ample shocks of natural wood, the restaurant is a sophisticated yet comfortable place to grab dinner or lunch in Roanoke's Grandin Village neighborhood. The menu, which changes often, can seem simple—only a handful of selections are available each night—but the flavors are complex. Appetizers might be scallops with a bourbon glaze and Benton's bacon from the Smoky Mountains of Tennessee or a collection of white beets in a butter sauce. Entrees might showcase chicken from the nearby Bramble Hollow Farm in Montvale or grass-fed lamb from Border Springs Farm in Patrick Springs. To drink, try a local craft beer and, while you're at it, take a look at the beer-tap handles on display above the bar.

Molasses Grill, 63 S. Main St., Halifax, VA 24558; (434) 476-6265; molassesgrill.com; Neo-Southern; **$$$.** In the vast expanse of central Virginia, towns are like islands surrounded by moats made of miles of rolling farmland. It's impossible to guess where gourmets gather. That's the case in Halifax. Across from the stately, pillared courthouse, circa 1777, on the single street that is all of downtown proper, the Molasses Grill has been pleasing refined palates since 2005. That's when Chef Steven Schopen, an English chap with experience in restaurants worldwide, and his wife, Karen, with more than 25 years in the restaurant and hospitality sector, opened their quaint place on Main Street. Inside, brick walls and burnished pine floors lend a sense of calm, but opening the menu causes the heart to skip a beat. Schopen gathers Southern staples—black-eyed peas, collards, grits, pork belly, sweet potatoes, and, of course, molasses—then fuses them with top-quality ingredients sourced locally whenever possible. He spins out dishes such as grilled pork tenderloin with a shellac of bourbon and molasses, and serves that with a side of mashed sweet potatoes, coconut black-eyed peas, and collards seasoned the old-school way with pork. Fried chicken is dredged in cornmeal, a Southern secret that adds crunch, and is served with pimiento mac and cheese. Sausage and breads are made in house, as are stunning desserts, such as the four-layer, rum-drunk coconut cake. It's a place to please the most discriminating city slicker, and well worth the 5-mile or so detour from the straightaway.

The Ploughcroft Tea Room, 1215 Commerce St., Lynchburg, VA 24504; (434) 832-7467; ploughcrofttearoom.com; British; $. Open the heavy front door of this historic downtown shop and step into a setting straight out of *Pride and Prejudice*. Tables are set properly with starched napkins, silver spoons, and bone china teapots. Tiered plates are filled with old country English fare such as cucumber-and-butter sandwiches or crumpets or scones with Devonshire cream. No matter the nibble, there's always an endless pot of tea. The tearoom's name comes from the English countryside home of the owner, Patricia Hutto. Days here start with lunch—Cambridge cottage pie or Balmoral bangers and mash, savory English sausages with gravy and mashed potatoes. The pace slows for afternoon tea, when lingering is proper. Before you go, check the Facebook page for the secret saying of the month. Whisper it to the waitress, and the tea is free. Sit up straight, dears, and long live the queen!

{RA} Bistro, 1344 Main St., Lynchburg, VA 24504; (434) 845-1601; rabistro.com; American/Gourmet Burgers; $–$$. Life's too short to eat boring burgers. Here, in this 75-year-old building in historic downtown Lynchburg, there's not a boring burger in the house. Char-grilled certified Angus beef provides the bedrock for some of the most outlandish—and oddly delicious—burgers in the state. The Bayou Burger is strafed with spicy bombs of flash-fried crawfish, knobs of andouille sausage, a sheet of melted provolone, and a smear of Creole remoulade—way messy but worth the work. The 'Merica Burger, for the indecisive, gets topped with mac and cheese, an all-beef hot dog, shreds of pork barbecue, and slaw. The funnel cake, which we heard locals rave about, is a cheeseburger rolled in funnel cake batter, flash-fried with a dusting of powdered sugar (just like at the fair), and served with a raspberry dipping sauce. There's also a crab cake–topped burger and, for the traditionalist, a classic burger. But what's the fun in that?

Shoemakers American Grill, 1312 Commerce St., Lynchburg, VA 24504; (434) 455-1510; shoemakersdining.com; Seafood/ Steaks; $$$$. Spot a cherry-red stiletto two stories tall and you've found this restaurant, recently honored as the best in the region. In Lynchburg, shoes and tobacco once ruled, and soaring brick warehouses for both hug the banks of the James River, which runs right past downtown. Shoemakers' stunning setting combines the bones of the old brick warehouse—think towering arched windows and exposed beam ceilings—with metropolitan sleek and chic—think starched alabaster linens, Sinatra, and a waitstaff clad in black. The menu follows suit with appetizers such as Scallops Casino served on the half shell, escargots, and garlic-lime shrimp. The Kona Filet, rubbed with coffee before being grilled to order, is a carnivore's dream. The whole—but head-less—crab-stuffed trout showcases the chef's respect for ingredients. Pure, unadorned blue crab is stuffed into the fish, which is roasted to perfection and served with a scattering of tomato chutney, a surprise pairing that makes this a destination dish. The dessert menu is no less inventive. Our pick: the New York cheesecake. Unlike so many places that import this dessert, Shoemakers makes it right here in Lynchburg, on a pecan graham cracker crust, thankyouverymuch.

Landmarks

Charley's Waterfront Cafe, 201 Mill St., Farmville, VA 23901; (434) 392-1566; charleyswaterfront.com; Eclectic; $$. People come to Farmville to get college educated and to get furniture. It's home to two colleges, one university, and Green Front, a furniture merchant housed in 12 soaring old tobacco warehouses stuffed with breakfronts, lamps, recliners, rugs, statuary, and more. For years, Charley's is where the shop-weary have come to refuel. The decor in this pre–Civil War tobacco warehouse is stuck in the '80s, with faux brass barstools and aging wood floors and banisters. But the menu is refreshingly contemporary. Specials might include a charcuterie plate or paella. The Tuscan Oriental Fusion Ahi Tuna Tacos, listed as an appetizer, make a satisfying light lunch, and the roasted red pepper and crab soup has been a hit since the place opened in 1994. And know this: there's a bona-fide pastry chef at work here. Carrot cake aficionados must save room for the four carrot-spice-and-cranberry layers mortared with just the right amount of smooth cream cheese icing. If it's a pretty day, request a seat on the deck, which is lined with flower-filled planters and overlooks the Appomattox River. When Union soldiers captured a bridge on this waterway, it led to Confederate General Robert E. Lee's surrender and the end of the Civil War.

Cumberland Restaurant, 1465 Anderson Hwy., US 60, Cumberland, VA 23040; (804) 492-4646; Traditional Southern; $.

Honestly, it's the cutest little old place, harkening back to the 1950s with cream-and-red tiled floors and a line of red-topped stools along the counter that runs the length of the restaurant. There, a waitress with a pad and pen takes your order, lickety-split. Here's where to try a couple of Southern standbys. The bologna burger pays homage to a lunch that many a child in our commonwealth has enjoyed and likely made for himself while knee-high to a tadpole. Bologna gets fried in a hot pan till it curls up, and then gets served on white bread with mayo. Here, the bologna is cut thick as a thumb and served on a bun. Afterward, a sweet tooth is assuaged with a slice of buttermilk pie, mostly sweet, just a tad tangy, and so darn good that we forgive the premade crust. But honestly, one of the most memorable treats is a tall glass of sweet tea—medium sweet and amber in color with a wafer of a lemon wedge hanging on the rim. Iced tea doesn't get any better than this.

Nottoway Restaurant, at the intersection of US 1 and Interstate 85, Warfield, VA 23889; (804) 478-7875; Southern; $$. OK. So there's Campbell's soup on the menu. Put that out of your mind. Instead, listen for that gurgling grease in the pan coming from the kitchen. We had just bitten into a panfried chicken thigh, piercing the skin (the rest of which properly remained intact) and sinking our teeth into seasoned meat that fairly fell from the bone. At that very moment, a fellow diner asked, "Did I just hear the angels sing?" We could only nod in the affirmative. This restaurant, with its way high-in-the-sky neon sign beckoning to in-the-know interstate travelers, is nearing its ninth decade serving old-style Southern fare in a rural stretch of Central Virginia. The walls are knotty pine, the decor plain and simple, and the motherly waitresses with just-so hair and spotless tennies deliver platters of fried chicken, the skin blistered by a turn in the pan, chicken-fried steak, ham rolls, and fried catfish. That's all accompanied by buttery, house-made yeast rolls, themselves worth a swerve off of the interstate. But don't rely on Google to get you here. Those directions are wrong, but after a few goose chases, we found it well worth the sleuthing.

The Regency Room, 110 Shenandoah Ave. NW, Roanoke, VA 24016; (540) 985-5900; hotelroanoke.com/dining; Southern-inspired French; $$$–$$$$. This restaurant is housed in the Hotel Roanoke, a grand structure originally constructed by the Norfolk and Western Railway in 1882 and renovated many times since. The structure now sports a Tudor look, and the Regency Room is the premier dining spot inside. Executive Chef Sandra Krebs has fashioned a French-inspired Southern menu where diners can feast on pork chops with a sweet-and-spicy honey glaze or shrimp and cheddar-and-chive grits. A recent renovation gave the dining room a new look, including a wall of French doors that add an additional touch of class to the establishment. The Sunday brunch is a tradition and a locals' favorite, with a spread of offerings that include mouthwatering pastries and an omelet station where you can gets yours made to order.

Specialty Stores, Markets & Producers

Cao Artisan Chocolates, 119 N. Bridge Rd., Bedford, VA 24523; (434) 485-1918; caoartisanchocolates.com. "Farm to fork" has become quite fashionable. At Cao, in the tiny town of Bedford, the mantra is "bean to bar." Burlap sacks bulging with the world's finest cacao beans lounge near the front door. A sharp, heady aroma permeates the small shop. Self-taught chocolatiers Mary and Carl Matice roast the beans using exacting specifications, stone-grind them, and turn them into chocolate using just a few organic ingredients. Then they turn out chocolate bars the way vintners turn out wine, each with complex and distinct flavors. Come in for a free tasting, expertly and unhurriedly led by Mary Matice. One bar evokes citrus and mango, with banana at the very tip of the tongue; another has toffee with a rosemary finish. There are truffles, barks, and bags of nibs, too.

Gross' Orchard Apple Valley, 6817 Wheats Valley Rd., Bedford County, VA 24523; (540) 586-2436; grossorchards.com. This is apple country, and this fifth-generation orchard in the foothills of the Blue Ridge has all you could want. From August through November, fresh-picked fruit is piled onto sloping wooden shelves out the front of the market, beckoning with beguiling names—Arkansas Black, Black Twig, Lodi, Rambo, Stayman, York, and more. Pick your own apples in season, or peaches from mid-June to early September. The Grosses also grow blackberries, cherries, grapes, and nectarines. Inside, market shelves stay stocked with the Gross family's jams, sorghum syrup, sourwood honey, fried apple pie, and such. Take a few minutes to wander across the street and dip your toe into the cool, mountain creek water. The Grosses don't mind a bit. They built picnic tables to share the view. Apple Blossom Festival takes place the second Saturday in April; the Harvest Festival takes place the third Saturday in October. It's open year-round but closed on Sun.

Homestead Creamery, 7254 Booker T. Washington Hwy., Wirtz, VA 24184; (540) 721-2045; on Facebook. In 2001, a pair of farmers in Franklin County opened this dairy and farm store as a way to secure the future of the farms that had been in their families for generations. The company went retro, adopted the motto "The Milkman Is Back," and began delivering glass-bottled milk to residents in surrounding counties. Travelers can buy a bottle at the farm store, or better yet, get a dip or two of the dairy's ice cream, rich, smooth wonderfulness made with their own milk, cream, and local eggs. How about a dip of chocolate-pecan, gingerbread, pumpkin, or strawberry cheesecake ice cream? The market also offers local eggs, jams, jellies, meats, produce, sammies, soups, and Virginia maple syrup. In town around the winter holidays? Don't dare leave without a bottle of Homestead's eggnog, a best-selling treat.

Levering Orchard, 163 Levering Ln., Ararat, VA 24053; Cherry Hotline: (276) 755-4837; leveringorchard.com. Early June is generally when the cherry trees become lush with ripe fruit at this orchard on the southeastern slope of the Blue Ridge Mountains that has been in the Levering family for more than a century. It's the South's largest cherry orchard, where 43 varieties of sweet and sour cherries are available for the picking. Peaches and nectarines also are available. If they can, the Leverings are glad to give tours and always welcome picnicking amid the stunning panoramic views. Ardent locavores will appreciate that the orchard sells only to local grocers and restaurateurs.

Night Sky Farm, 148 Robin Rd., Brookneal, VA 24528; (434) 426-4886; nightskyfarm.com. It looks pretty chaotic here in the cheese room, where a vat of frothy goat's-milk laundry soap heats up on the stove, dishes fill the sinks, and every inch of refrigerator space is a mosaic of jars and jars and jars of fresh goat's and cow's milk, solids risen to the top, ready to be pasteurized and turned into artisanal cheeses. But outside the cheese room window, cows named Annabelle and Emily seem serene in their pasture. Cheesemaker and dairy farmer Jennifer Downey learned the craft of cheesemaking in her native Vermont. Today, she makes cow's milk cheddar, goat cheese feta, ricotta, and slightly tangy, mild chèvre flavored with dill, Italian seasonings, and even figs. Mostly, she sells at regional farmers' markets, but if you call ahead in the early part of the week, you can make an appointment to meet here in the cheese room, where her motto is, "You have good milk; you have good cheese."

Mead, hard cider, craft beer and wine. Rural Nelson County, on the "sunrise side of the Blue Ridge," has got it all—seven wineries and three breweries along a 15-mile stretch of certified, eye-popping Virginia byway. Destinations range from fledgling, family-owned vineyards to award-winning craft breweries. Trail information can be found at nelson151.com or by calling the Nelson County Visitor's Center at (434) 263-7015. Along the **Nelson 151**, you'll find the following. And no, the vintners and brewmasters didn't plan that their places would make for a neat little tour. Thank Bacchus, the god of wine, for that.

Blue Mountain Brewery, *9519 Critzers Shop Rd., Afton, VA 22920; (540) 456-8020; bluemountainbrewery.com.* This farm brewery grows its own hops, crafts several lagers and ales, plus about 20 seasonal draft-only offerings each year. Tour the brewery, see the hops, and stay for lunch or dinner.

Cardinal Point Winery, *9423 Batesville Rd., Afton, VA 22920; (540) 456-8400; cardinalpointwinery.com.* This place, which advocates a "like what you like" approach to wine tastings, makes Chardonnay, rosé, and red and white blends.

Devils Backbone Brewery, *200 Mosbys Run, Roseland, VA 22967; (434) 361-1001; dbbrewingcompany.com.* This is an award-winning house that uses a traditional German-style brewing system and pours fresh from 12 taps in the pub area, which also serves lunch and dinner.

Flying Fox Vineyard, *27 Chapel Hollow Rd., Afton, VA 22920; (434) 361-1692; flyingfoxvineyard.com.* Flying Fox recently began bottling

Wade's Foods, 200 Broad St., US 11, Dublin, VA 24084; (540) 674-4042; wades-foods.com. OK, so it's a grocery store, yes. But Wade's Foods has been around since 1950, a full-service, locally owned grocery store for all those years. In addition to all of the usual groceries and health and beauty aids, there's the deli. We got a tip about it from a Richmond chef and Pulaski County native who went all nostalgic

Cabernet Franc, Petit Verdot, and Viognier. Warm by the fireplace in the winter and take in the mountain views on the patio in the summer months.

Hill Top Berry Farm & Winery, *2800 Berry Hill Rd., Nellysford, VA 22958; (434) 361-1266; hilltopberrywine.com.* This one specializes in wines made from apples, berries, peaches, and plums, but never grapes. It also offers handcrafted honey mead.

Pollak Vineyards, *330 Newtown Rd., Greenwood, VA 22943; (540) 456-8844; pollakvineyards.com.* This place offers Cabernet Franc, Cabernet Sauvignon, Merlot, Petit Verdot, Pinot Gris, Viognier, rosé, and red and white blends. Picnic on the veranda, patio, or on a blanket by the pond. When there's a chill, hang by the fire in the tasting room.

Veritas Vineyard, *151 Veritas Ln., Afton, VA 22920; (540) 456-8000; veritaswines.com.* This vineyard produces Chardonnay, Sauvignon Blanc, sparkling wine, Viognier, and red and white blends. After the tasting, enjoy a bite at a picnic table or in the shady forest.

Wild Wolf Brewing Company, *2461 Rockfish Valley Hwy., Nellysford, VA 22958; (434) 361-0088; wildwolfbeer.com.* Wild Wolf crafts blonde ale, brown ale, pale ale, pilsner, stout, and seasonal beers. The outdoor *biergarten* is shaded by elms, and the restaurant serves lunch and dinner with a locavore bent.

Wintergreen Winery, *462 Winery Ln., Nellysford, VA 22958; (434) 361-2519; wintergreenwinery.com.* Wintergreen offers Viognier, Chardonnay, Cabernet Franc, Merlot, red and white blends, and fruit wines.

talking about the chili dogs, the legendary fried chicken, and the potato wedges, coated in chicken breader and deep-fried. Or pick up a ham or turkey dinner to go and eat out in the gorgeous mountain countryside. **Other locations:** 510 Roanoke St., Christiansburg, VA 24073; (540) 382-4995; 405 First St., Radford, VA 24141; (540) 639-9233.

Bedford Farmers' Market, Washington and Center Streets, Bedford, VA 24523. Tues from 3 to 7 p.m. and Fri from 7 a.m. to 2 p.m., May through Oct.

Danville Farmers' Market, 629 Craghead St., Danville, VA 24541. Sat from 7:30 a.m. to noon, May through Oct, and Wed from 4 to 7 p.m., July and Aug.

Lynchburg Community Farmers' Market, 1219 Main St., Lynchburg, VA 24504. Wed from 11 a.m. to 2 p.m., May through Thanksgiving.

Martinsville Uptown Farmers Market, 65 W. Main St., Martinsville, VA 24112. Mon from 5 to 7 p.m., Wed from 7 to 11 a.m. and Sat from 8 to 11 a.m., May through Nov.

Roanoke Historic City Market, 213 Market St., Roanoke, VA 24011. Mon through Sat from 8 a.m. to 5 p.m. and Sun from 10 a.m. to 4 p.m., year-round.

South Boston Farmers' Market, 300 Broad St., South Boston, VA 24592. Mon through Fri from 10 a.m. until sold out and Sat from 8 a.m. until sold out, mid-April through third week in Dec.

Mountains & Shenandoah Valley

It's easy to eat close to the farm in this area of Virginia, bounded on the west by the Alleghenies and on the east by the Appalachians. In between is the Shenandoah Valley, where the rolling hills and forests and hot springs give way to family farms and tiny villages. Railroad tracks criss-cross the region, and today many of the best restaurants can be found near the lines or in buildings once used by them. The offerings range from pasture-fed beef to homegrown produce—raw products loved by local chefs, who present them in both new and old ways.

 Foodie Faves

The Depot Grille, 42 Middlebrook Ave., Staunton, VA 24401; (540) 885-7332; depotgrille.com; American; $$–$$$. It's the bar that first draws your attention in this restaurant in a former train station renovated in the late 1980s. The 40-foot-plus wooden Victorian structure is a fine place to grab lunch or dinner. The bar was salvaged from the Ten Eyck Hotel in Albany, NY, and is the centerpiece of this two-room eatery. Old photos grace the wall and old church pews provide seats in the main dining room. Lunch offerings include salads,

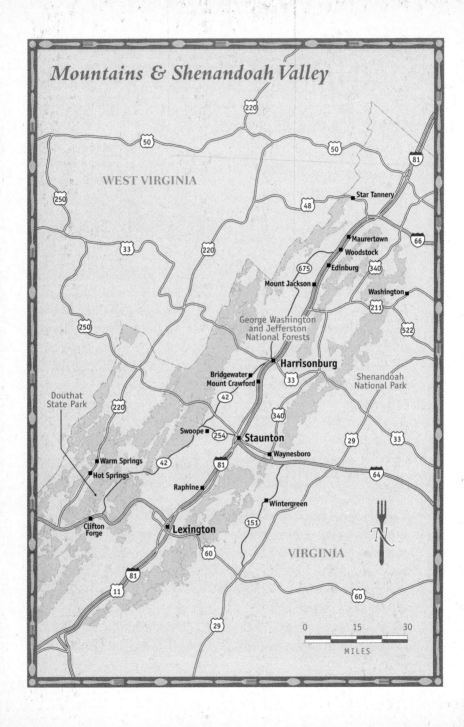

Mountains & Shenandoah Valley

WEST VIRGINIA

VIRGINIA

Star Tannery
Maurertown
Woodstock
Edinburg
Mount Jackson
Washington

George Washington
and Jefferston
National Forests

Harrisonburg

Bridgewater
Mount Crawford

Shenandoah
National Park

Swoope
Staunton
Waynesboro

Douthat
State Park

Warm Springs
Hot Springs

Raphine

Wintergreen

Clifton
Forge

Lexington

N

0   15   30

MILES

sandwiches, pastas, and burgers, and dinner adds chicken, seafood, and steak to the mix. The burgers, both beef and bison, are popular, and patrons also favor the ahi tuna, encrusted in sesame seeds and seared at the edges but pink in the middle. The tuna is available as an appetizer or as part of a salad.

Jack Mason's Tavern, 400 E. Ridgeway St., Clifton Forge, VA 24422; (540) 862-5624; jackmasonstavern.com; Casual American; $. You can leave a little piece of yourself at this pub, but it will cost you. The pillars of the bar are covered with $1 bills that customers have signed, often with a birth date or anniversary. The pub was opened in 2008 by Martha Mason, who named it after her grandfather, Jack Hiram Mason. It's located across from the train station in this railroad town, and there's a CSX train mural on the back wall of the main dining area. 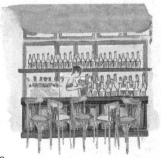 You'll often hear excitement coming from the adjoining game room, where customers play pool, video games, and pinball. The food is typical bar fare—burgers, sandwiches, soups, and wraps—and there's a wide selection of beers, wines, and spirits. The train theme continues on the menu, where the Chew-Choo Platter offers rings, wings, cheese sticks, and fries. For a less heavy option, order the fried green beans, lightly breaded and served with ranch dressing. The soups are house-made, and the potato-leek is hearty on a chilly afternoon. In an appropriate touch, water is brought to the table in mason jars.

Local Chop & Grill House, 56 W. Gay St., Harrisonburg, VA 22802; (540) 801-0505; localchops.com; Seafood/Steaks; $$$–$$$$. This restaurant is located next to railroad tracks in the century-old former City Produce Exchange building, which once housed ice-making

FOOD WITH A VIEW

Lake View Restaurant *(Douthat State Park, 14239 Douthat State Park Rd., Millboro, VA 24460; 540-862-8100; virginia.org; Casual American; $–$$)* has one of the most scenic views of any eatery in Virginia. The building overlooks Lake Douthat, the centerpiece of a state park that opened in 1936, and the restaurant features a glass-enclosed porch and an open-air deck that lets you enjoy the breathtaking sight that gives the restaurant its name. The lake sits amid the tree-covered Allegheny Mountains, and summer provides sights of boaters and swimmers and autumn offers foliage in brilliant reds, oranges, and yellows. The restaurant, like most structures in the park, was built by the Civilian Conservation Corps. Breakfast, lunch, and dinner are served. Lunch includes sandwiches and burgers, and rainbow trout, quail, fried chicken, and ribs are among the dinner specialties. The restaurant has reliable Wi-Fi, one of the few places in the park when you can easily access the outside world. When you're finished eating, walk off some of those calories with a relatively level hike around the lake.

facilities and cold storage for the egg and poultry industry. Inside, it's airy and warm, with lots of wood and brick. Executive Chef Ryan Zale, who has worked at the acclaimed Inn at Little Washington, celebrates the farm-to-table concept, with a menu that includes hand-cut steaks, locally grown produce, and organically raised poultry. Begin by selecting one of a dozen entree options, which include filet mignon, New York strip, scallops, and tofu steak. Then the fun begins. Three rubs are available, including the simple but deeply flavored house-smoked sea salt and a garden variety that features parsley, oregano, rosemary, sage, and lemon zest. You can opt for one of 14 sauces, such as mango barbecue (one of the sweet and tart options), chimichurri (savory), or horseradish and crème fraîche (hot and spicy). Dinner is offered Tues through Sat, and there's a popular brunch on Sun.

Zynodoa Restaurant, 115 E. Beverley St., Staunton, VA 24401; (540) 885-7775; zynodoa.com; Neo-Southern; $$$$. This restaurant is tucked into a historic building in the town of Staunton, but it's got a modern, urban feel inside. Chic wooden tables and cozy booths provide seating, though you'll be tempted to gather at the sleek bar, with its illuminated liquor supply and funky, low-backed barstools. The place is named after the ancient word for "Shenandoah," and that's appropriate for a restaurant that celebrates products grown in the Shenandoah Valley, as well as the nearby Piedmont region. Executive Chef James Harris once worked at the Inn at Little Washington, and he's brought the inn's penchant for details to his new place. The menu is Southern with a modern twist. The pan-seared scallops can be perched atop a ham-and-bean stew with a side of cornbread stuffing or served with a cranberry orange chutney, spicy beans, and caramelized brussels sprouts. The chicken cassoulet features poultry from the nearby **Polyface Farm** (p. 226) and andouille sausage from Nelson County's Rock Barn. Eggs, both chicken and duck, come from the farm of owners Susan and Jeff Goode, and the restaurant grows its own kale, okra, potatoes, squash, tomatoes, and other veggies, as well as an assortment of herbs. You can also drink local, too; many Virginia varietals dot the wine list. See Chef Harris's recipe for **Smoked Scallop, Arugula & Cucumber Salad** on p. 246.

The Inn at Little Washington, Middle and Main Streets, Washington, VA 22747; (540) 675-3800; theinnatlittlewashington .com; New American; $$$$. The late Craig Claiborne of the *New York Times* called this place "the most magnificent inn I've ever seen, in this country or Europe, where I had the most fantastic meal of my life." With good reason. You're pampered from the moment you walk into this 1895 inn. At the restaurant, you sit at one of 30 intimate tables, where romantic lighting comes from hanging lamps encased in silk shades. Four-course prix-fixe dinners—unless you want to opt for the 11-course offering—are offered nightly, and prices teeter at $200 a person. It's worth it to see what Executive Chef Patrick O'Connell has in store. He's a self-taught cook who uses local ingredients in marvelous ways. For starters, it might be *foie gras,* two ways, or a mac and cheese with country ham and truffles. Entrees might be veal shortbreads with a hint of curry and roasted plums or Chesapeake Bay rockfish encrusted in olives. The stable of servers seem to always know what you need before you do, and a drink or silverware or bread often appears as if out of thin air. An amazing experience.

John's Steakhouse, Charger Lane, Warm Springs, VA 24484; (540) 839-2333; johnssteakhouse.com; Seafood/Steaks; $$$$. If it feels like you've dropped into John and Gudie Retzlaff's house when you eat at this steak house, it's because, in a way, you have. Originally from Germany, the Retzlaffs offer Old World charm in this intimate setting decorated with the couple's plates and other tchotchkes from around the world. John does most of the cooking; Gudie often is the server, though sometimes it's the couple's daughter. The menu is primarily steak and seafood, including local Allegheny trout, although you can get a taste of the couple's homeland in dishes like knockwurst on sauerkraut, served with German potato salad, and wiener schnitzel

FOOD SPRINGS ETERNAL

The 104-degree waters that give Hot Springs its name have long brought travelers to area. In 1766, Thomas Bullitt built an inn at the site, and in the next century it began operating as The Homestead. Today, Bullitt probably wouldn't recognize the place. Now called **The Omni Homestead** (*7696 Sam Snead Hwy., Hot Springs, VA 24445; 540-839-1766; thehomestead .com*), it has almost 500 guest rooms. It's a massive and elegant structure that overlooks the town, and guests sleep on feather beds by night and enjoy golf courses or pools by day. The Homestead is known for its exquisite service and Southern charm and counts 22 US presidents among its most famed guests. On-site dining options are plenty. There's the main dining room, with its crisp white linens and baby grand piano, where fine dining is available and a dress code is enforced. There's Jefferson's Restaurant and Bar, a more casual option with small plates and beef raised at Milligan Creek Farms in nearby Lewisburg, WV. There's the cozy Martha's Market, a coffee and pastry shop, as well as two restaurants located at Homestead golf courses. And across the street is Sam Snead's Tavern, a pub that celebrates the local golf star. You can stay here a week without wanting to leave the grounds.

with red cabbage. Dinner is offered on all nights but Wednesday, and the only tricky part is getting here. The restaurant sits at the end of a steeply graded road that will test your vehicle's climbing power. But once you reach the parking lot, you're rewarded with a great view of the surrounding mountains.

The Purple Foot, 1035 W. Broad St., Waynesboro, VA 22980; (540) 942-9463; thepurplefootwaynesboro.com; Sandwiches; $. You'll be tempted to browse the extensive wine and gift shop that you first encounter, but that can come later. First, go straight to the back, where you can have lunch in the homey dining room or on the outdoor patio called The Garden of Eatin' with its fountain and lush plants. The restaurant, which opened in 1978, offers a lunch menu of crepes, quiches, salads, sandwiches, soups, and wraps, as well as fancy baked potatoes. The Reuben, with its corned beef and kraut on a grilled rye, is a local favorite. Ten other sandwiches can be ordered on as many bread options, or opt for one of the "dream" potatoes. The German Dream is topped with corned beef, sauerkraut, and swiss cheese. Bush's Nightmare—a nod to George H.W.'s dislike for a certain veggie—comes loaded with broccoli. When you're finished eating, take time to check out the wine selection in the shop, where you can also pick up cheese plates, T-shirts, wind chimes, and more.

Sam Snead's Tavern, 2849 Main St., Hot Springs, VA 24445; (540) 839-7666; samsneadstavern.com; Pub Fare; American; $$$–$$$$. This bar is a nice place to watch a game, grab an adventurous meal, or celebrate one of the country's greatest golfers. Sam "Slammin' Sammy" Snead grew up near here and began caddying at age 7 at The Homestead, where he honed the skills of his lifelong love. In his PGA career, he won 82 tournaments, and at the pub you can view photos of him as well as some of his memorabilia, including the golf balls he used to record 35 holes-in-one. The pub, originally purchased by Snead, is now part of the nearby Omni Homestead. The **Pimiento Cheese** features four local cheeses and peppadew chiles (see the recipe on p. 248), grilled squash, and honey-pepper bacon and is served, sandwich-style, on buns. Entrees, which change seasonally, might include duck braised in cider or aged sirloin steak. The brussels sprouts, drizzled with honey, are a sweet-tasting savory treat. End with the bread pudding made with cinnamon doughnuts and topped with a bananas Foster sauce. It's been a Homestead specialty for more than 70 years.

Waterwheel Restaurant, 124 Old Mill Rd., Warm Springs, VA 24484; (540) 839-2231; gristmillsquare.com; New American; $$–$$$. There's been a mill at this site since 1771, about the same time Thomas Jefferson was constructing Monticello farther east. The current one, built in 1900, now houses a restaurant, but the mill's past remains on display. The big wooden wheel on the side of the building once powered the flour and grain operation, and it gives this eatery its name. In 1972, the building was renovated and reopened as a restaurant by the McWilliams family. Wooden ceiling beams, worn hardwood floors and original hardware give the place character, and the staff provides charm. Fresh trout is the specialty, but the seared duck breast and grilled salmon over citrus risotto are flavorful options as well. If the dining room is full, consider eating in the intimate pub, named for Simon Kenton, a friend of Daniel Boone. It's small but cozy; when you need another drink, you can almost reach the bar from your seat at either of the two small tables. And if you're stuffed when you're through, see if a room is available. The restaurant is part of the adjoining Inn at Gristmill Square, which has guest rooms in a variety of 19th-century buildings.

Specialty Stores, Markets & Producers

All Things Virginia @ The Farmhouse, 125 N. Main St., Woodstock, VA 22664; (540) 459-9006; allthingsva.com. Enter this shop in downtown Woodstock, population 5,097, and it feels as though you've walked into an old-time country store, with its collection of handmade pottery, jams and jellies, and meats. The store is chock full of stuff—on shelves, on bookcases, on the floor—and celebrates all things Virginia, particularly products made in the Shenandoah Valley. Originally located in Harrisonburg, the store has found a new home in the building called The Farmhouse. The shop is run by Vicki Ruckman and her son, Mike Seal. Vicki's husband, Monty, owns a coffee-roasting business, and Cabin Creek Roasters java, as well as his artwork, is on sale. You'll find some of the best local craft beers, from stouts to ales, and you can fashion your own six-pack. There's also a variety of foods from the commonwealth, as well as work by local artists, kitchen items, and soaps and lotions.

Earth & Tea Cafe, 120 S. Main St., Harrisonburg, VA 22801; (540) 432-8280; earthandteacafe.com. There's an international flair in this tea room and cafe, and it starts with the exotic aromas that engulf you as soon as you walk through the door. The decor is Middle Eastern, with tapestries adorning the mustard-colored walls and paper lanterns providing a romantic glow. You can gather in love seats and comfy chairs or opt for a booth or table. Owner Aarom Millones opened the shop in 2006 after being inspired by tea rooms in larger cities. The menu features more than 40 teas, divided into blacks, greens, herbals, oolongs, and whites. Get a small pot for two, or linger for a while with a pot for four. The Masala Chai is one of the more popular varieties, and it's blended in the store. Millones, who moved to the States from Peru, has expanded the offerings to include salads, sandwiches, soups, tapas, and wraps, as well as breakfast items Mon through Sat and brunch on Sun.

Polyface, 43 Pure Meadows Ln., Swoope, VA 24479; (540) 885-3590; polyfacefarms.com. This 550-acre farm west of Staunton has been at the forefront of the nation's sustainable agriculture movement for more than three decades. It's been run by Joel Salatin, who inherited the mantle from his father, William, who bought the place in 1961 with his wife, Lucille. Joel is an evangelist, preaching the virtues of farming that is rooted in the symbiotic relationship between the sun and the earth and the plants and the animals. Joel and his family raise cattle, chickens, pigs, rabbits, and turkeys that he says are one step better than organic—safer, more nutritious, and more respectfully treated. Many of the area's finer restaurants are faithful customers. The farm's products are available at some stores in the region, and the farm itself has a shop that's open weekday mornings and Saturday. Shipping is out of the question; that goes against Joel's philosophy. He encourages out-of-town visitors to find local farms to patronize.

Wineries & Breweries

Blue Lab Brewing Co., 123 S. Randolph St., Lexington, VA 24450; (540) 458-0146; bluelabbrewing.com.

Blue Mountain Brewery and Restaurant, 9519 Critzer Shop Rd., Afton, VA 22920; (540) 456-8020; bluemountainbrewery.com.

Bluestone Vineyard, 4828 Spring Creek Rd., Bridgewater, VA 22812; (540) 828-0099; bluestonevineyard.com.

Bold Rock Cidery and Brew Pub, 1020 Rockfish Valley Hwy., Wintergreen, VA 22958; (434) 361-1030; boldrock.com.

Cave Ridge Vineyard, 1476 Conicville Rd., Mount Jackson, VA 22842; (540) 477-2585; caveridge.com.

Cedar Creek Winery, 7384 Zepp Rd., Star Tannery, VA 22654; (540) 436-8394; cedarcreekvineyard.com.

CrossKeys Vineyards, 6011 E. Timber Ridge Rd., Mount Crawford, VA 22841; (540) 234-0505; crosskeysvineyards.com.

The vineyards in this region provide a variety of wines, including reds such as Cabernet Franc and Merlot and whites such as Chardonnay, Sauvignon Blanc, and Riesling.

Devils Backbone Outpost Brewery, 50 Northwind Ln., Lexington, VA 24450; (540) 462-6200; dbbrewingcompany.com/theoutpost.aspx.

North Mountain Vineyard & Winery, 4374 Swartz Rd., Maurertown, VA 22644; (540) 436-9463; northmountainvineyard.com.

Ox Eye Vineyards, 44 Middlebrook Ave., Staunton, VA 24401; (540) 849-7926; oxeyevineyards.com.

Queen City Brewing, 834 Springhill Rd., Staunton, VA 24401; (540) 213-8014; queencitybrewing.com.

Rockbridge Vineyard, 35 Hill View Ln., Raphine, VA 24472; (540) 377-6204; rockbridgevineyard.com.

Shenandoah Vineyards, 3659 S. Ox Rd., Edinburg, VA 22824; (540) 984-8699; shentel.net/shenvine.

Three Brothers Brewing, 800 N. Main St., Harrisonburg, VA 22801; (540) 421-6599; threebrosbrew.com.

Wolf Gap Vineyard & Winery, 123 Stout Rd., Edinburg, VA 22824; (540) 984-3306; wolfgapvineyard.com.

 *Farmers' Markets*

Harrisonburg Downtown Farmers' Market, 228 S. Liberty St., Harrisonburg, VA 22801; (540) 476-3377. Tues and Sat from 7 a.m. to 1 p.m., Apr until late Nov.

Shenandoah Heritage Market, 121 Carpenter Ln., Harrisonburg, VA 22801; (540) 433-3929. Mon through Fri from 10 a.m. to 6 p.m., Sat from 9 a.m. to 6 p.m., year-round.

Staunton/Augusta Farmers' Market, 35 S. New St., Staunton, VA 24401; safarmersmarket.com. Wed from 7 a.m. to 1 p.m., Sat from 7 a.m. to noon, Apr through mid-Nov.

Waynesboro Farmers' Market, 215 W. Main St., Waynesboro, VA 22980; (540) 466-4679; waynesborofarmersmarket.org. Wed from 2:30 to 6 p.m., Sat from 8 a.m. to noon, Apr through Oct.

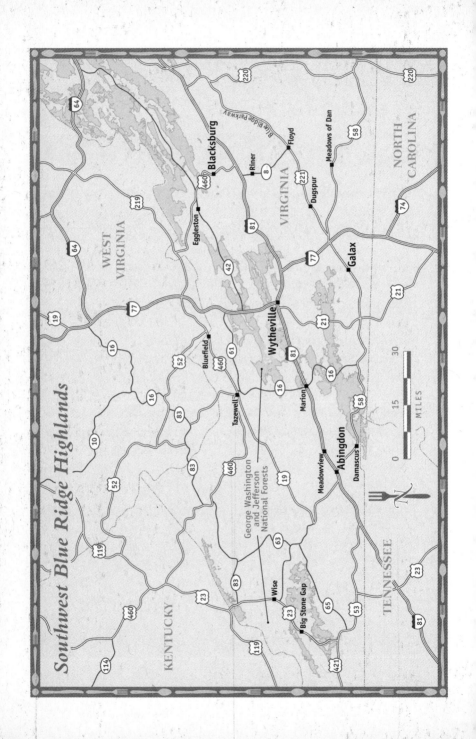

Southwest Blue Ridge Highlands

Southwest Blue Ridge Highlands

Virginia's westernmost region covers a triangle of peaks and valleys wedged like an axe between North Carolina, Tennessee, Kentucky, and West Virginia. Stand at the tip of the wedge, and you're standing west of Cleveland, Ohio. Astonishing in its breadth and depth, it's home to trout streams and tobacco fields, cattle farms and coal mines, blue-grass greats, grazing buffalo, and a mountain-ringed bowl called "God's Thumbprint." It's mostly rural, the kind of place where main highways can feel like back roads snaking as they do up and down mountain ranges. Towns are just as likely to have a quilting shop and fiddle store as a church. Mom-and-pop restaurants dish standard-issue comfort food, but at a hit-and-miss pace. So it's best to plan your next meal. Like the rest of the state, there's a smoking barbecue rig at every turn, and the vinegar-pepper style popular in the east gives way to more complex saucing. But the region also boasts restaurants that have embraced the farm-to-fork movement, a moonshiner, and fine-dining destinations that have earned national acclaim. With a bit of planning, your meals can be as memorable as the magnificent mountain landscape.

Buffalo and More, 4040 Riner Rd., Riner, VA 24149; (540) 381-9764; buffaloandmore.com; Buffalo; $. You must question your status as a committed foodie if this 4-mile detour off Interstate 81 seems like too far to go for a restaurant that serves everything buffalo. And talk about locavores. Chef-Owner Connie Hale and her partner, Carla George, actually raise the buffalo in pastures about 15 miles from the restaurant. On the day of our visit, the herd was 56 strong, with a few calves on the way. Buffalo meat is much leaner than beef, and Connie and Carla make it into buffalo-chili nachos, buffalo burgers, buffalo barbecue, buffalo Philly cheesesteak, buffalo brisket, buffalo hot dog—you get the idea. Get some to go from the freezer case, where rib eyes, roasts, short ribs, and, ahem, mountain oysters are sold by the pound. But if you want buffalo tongue, well, good luck with that. The wait list runs long. Assuage your defeat with a slice of sweet. Connie's mom, Reba, makes the desserts. If she's had a notion to bake chocolate chess pie, here's where to experience that particular delight.

The Galax Smokehouse, 101 N. Main St., Galax, VA 24333; (276) 236-1000; thegalaxsmokehouse.com; Barbecue; $$. Find this big ol' barbecue joint just a few doors down from the fiddle store in Galax, the "World Capital of Old Time Mountain Music." A line of stools at the old-time soda fountain, an open kitchen, and plush pigs swinging from the ceiling set the stage for the area's best barbecue. Order some hickory-smoked pulled pork or mesquite-smoked brisket or applewood-smoked chicken and your waitress/guide will walk you through a critical element of the meal: the four squeeze bottles of sauce standing sentry at each table. There's the molasses-based; the "Mountain" sauce, vinegar-based and sweet and tangy; "Tennessee Sweet," which is tomato-based with brown sugar; and the "House," a tomato-based, black pepper sauce. The best plan: As soon as your Styrofoam platter heaped with vittles hits the table, put a squirt on a forkful till you find your match. But don't get any on your slightly lumpy, smoked mashed potato heap, the side dish of choice. The spuds are sprinkled with a little bit of secret spice and are not to be messed with.

Harvest Table, 13180 Meadowview Sq., Meadowview, VA 24361; (276) 944-5142; meadowviewfarmersguild.com; Eclectic; $$. *Animal, Vegetable, Miracle: A Year of Food Life,* published in 2007, is best-selling author Barbara Kingsolver's account of tossing in the Tucson towel and moving with her family to a farm in southwestern Virginia to become locavores for a year. Harvest Table is the family's restaurant, and you can't help but feel a little healthier just walking in the door. Every item on the seasonal menu is made from ingredients procured from local or regional producers and purveyors. What matters most here is carbon footprint, community, sustainability, and, of course, flavor. After carefully sourcing everything from rabbit to radishes, they don't muck it up by dunking it in a deep-fat fryer or drowning it in gravy. Natural flavors shine. The trout for the simple, memorable trout cake and red pepper sauce appetizer comes from a third-generation family farm across the border in North Carolina. Produce is likely to come from the restaurant's own farm. Locavore restaurants are a challenge to keep going, and this one has earned honors. If you're a fan of Kingsolver, or the locavore way, it's a bucket-list destination.

The Palisades Restaurant, 168 Village St., Eggleston, VA 24086; (540) 626-2828; thepalisadesrestaurant.com; American; $$. This little restaurant in a tiny town near the New River in a retrofitted general store recently earned a sweep in *Virginia Living* magazine's best-of edition, including southwest Virginia's best overall restaurant, best Sunday brunch, and honors in the vegetarian and dessert categories. A succinct menu offers a stacked Cobb salad that comes with tender braised chicken, pancetta, tomato, buttermilk blue cheese, and avocado. All the beef, pork, and trout come from local purveyors and get a decidedly gourmet spin. The trout arrives grilled with a hint of tarragon; the pork chop with a curry puree and rhubarb chutney. Steaks are hand-cut. A flight of pizzas includes the standards, plus unusual versions such as the restaurant's namesake, topped with grilled tenderloin, Gorgonzola, and mozzarella and another with ground lamb, arugula, and yogurt sauce. On Sunday, the belt-loosening buffet offers tough choices: meat and meatless frittatas, local sausage, sweet potato biscuits, local grilled beef tenderloin. And here's a nice touch: the grits of the day.

Rain, 283 E. Main St., Abingdon, VA 24210; (276)-739-2331; rain abingdon.com; Seafood/Steaks; $$$. This sleek eatery on the eastern edge of the historic district dishes inventive dishes with traditional Southern touches. Butternut squash soup gets updated with coconut milk, spicy peanuts, cilantro, and chile oil. The New York strip gets a good soaking in whiskey. Lunch and dinner are served, and reservations are recommended.

Landmarks

Chateau Morrisette, 287 Winery Rd. SW, Floyd County, VA 24091; (540) 593-2865; thedogs.com; Neo-Southern; $$. Yes, sir, that's right. It's a winery, more than 30 years old and one of the state's best-known, easily recognized by the iconic black dog on cobalt blue bottles. And, yes, sir, there's also a chateau of sorts up here in the Blue Ridge, and it houses a restaurant that treats Southern staples with a bit of whimsy that is so tempting that it's hard to read past the appetizer offerings. Consider for a moment what they've done with collards: blanched them and swapped out the nori from sushi, rolling those collards tight with sweet sushi rice and a trio of fillings. One variety of sushi features blueberries, mashed sweet potatoes, and walnuts with soy-molasses; Another has stewed black-eyed peas, bacon, mirepoix, and tomato with Tabasco-red pepper coulis. Yet another has pickled beets and green tomatoes with crème fraîche. The Southern Sushi Sampler appetizer is served as artfully as any sushi master's. Another appetizer: the apple rabbit galette, fresh rabbit stewed with apples and bacon, then baked in a house-made pastry and served with a cheddar wedge. On the entree side, shrimp and grits come atop smoked Gouda grits, and the salmon comes topped with a Southern Comfort citrus sauce. Well worth the winding trip up the mountainside.

Gillie's, 153 College Ave., Blacksburg, VA 24060; (540) 961-2703; gilliesrestaurant.net; Seafood/Vegetarian; $$. When you're up this way, there's no escaping the fact that you're in Virginia Tech Hokie country. This corner breakfast–lunch–happy hour–and–dinner restaurant abutting campus has been serving, soothing, and slaking Hokie thirsts for 40 years. The man behind the bar noted that the banana walnut french toast and the signature 122 Special—a full, standard breakfast—are the elixirs of choice for the morning-after set. But there's so much more. While the restaurant is vegetarian and pescatarian—meaning it also serves seafood—there's a lot more than hummus coming out of the kitchen. An Asian eggplant appetizer combines sauteed eggplant strips seasoned with tamari and tossed with red peppers, asparagus, and cashews. The quinoa-chickpea burger is topped with feta and served on a chickpea bun with tahini-lemon dressing. Basin Street shrimp gets tossed with sun-dried tomatoes, a Cajun-Alfredo sauce and served over penne. Many dishes can be made vegan upon request.

ABINGDON—FINE DINING IN APPALACHIA

Even if you're speeding along Interstate 81, white knuckling the wheel as tractor-trailers blow by doing 80 or so. Even if you're hell-bent on crossing the border into Tennessee or Carolina. Even if you're not quite ready to eat, make a detour to dine in historic downtown Abingdon, an epicurean oasis in the heart of Appalachia. Here, most every building and abode along shaded brick sidewalks date back to the 1700 or 1800s. The town itself is named for first lady Martha Washington's English home, Abingdon Parish. The township centerpiece is the famed Martha Washington Hotel & Spa, which served as a Civil War hospital and then a women's college until 1932. Across the street from the inn is the historic Barter Theater, started during the Great Depression, where farmers could "trade ham for Hamlet." Ernest Borgnine and Gregory Peck have starred here, and George Bernard Shaw, a vegetarian, traded rights to his plays for spinach, not ham. It remains one of the finest playhouses in Virginia. Stroll the few blocks farther into downtown proper, and you'll also find a charming tearoom, a gourmet shop, an olive oil tasting room, and a few fine-dining options. Yes, there is gold in these hills.

Mabry Mill Restaurant, 266 Mabry Mill SE, Meadows of Dan, VA 24120; (276) 952-2947; mabrymillrestaurant.com; Traditional Southern; $. When traveling by car in Virginia, the Blue Ridge Parkway is like a gulp of fresh, mountain air. No trucks, no tolls, no billboards, no stoplights. It's hardly a dining destination, but suddenly, at an ear-popping altitude of 2,913 feet—think 290 stories up—Mabry Mill appears around a bend, a perfect match between menu and setting. Tourists migrate here each summer and fall for a stack of buckwheat, cornmeal, and sweet potato pancakes and freshly made biscuits doused with country gravy. For lunch, there's homemade pot roast and chicken potpie. Service is as sweet as the tea, and the mountain accents even sweeter. The dining room porch, rife with windows, is right nice. But we recommend getting everything to go, heading for the parkway's next scenic overlook and taking a meal with a mountain vista backdrop that goes on for miles. Open May through Oct.

Sisters at the Martha, at The Martha Washington Inn, 150 W. Main St., Abingdon, VA 24210; (276) 628-3161, themartha.com; Seafood/Steaks; $$$$. First, know this. You needn't be a guest of the inn nor be wearing a frock or sport coat to partake of its dining delights. Anyone can settle into a wide, white wicker chair on the expansive front porch overlooking manicured grounds, complete with fountain, and order a libation and even an appetizer. This is one of the state's finest settings for a 5 o'clock refreshment. Then, repair to the Sisters at the Martha, the inn's main dining room, for lamb osso buco or lobster-stuffed trout. Dinner only; reservations recommended.

The Tavern Restaurant, 222 E. Main St., Abingdon, VA 24210; (276) 628-1118; abingdontavern.com; German/Seafood/ Steaks; $$$$. The oldest building in Abingdon dates back to 1779. The sturdy plastered structure that was originally a Colonial-era stagecoach stop now houses The Tavern Restaurant. The place retains the rustic feel of that era with low log-beam ceilings, a fireplace, and sloping wood-planked floors. For the past 20 years, under the management of Max Hermann, it has proffered a modern menu studded with steaks (such as the Palermo-style filet mignon stuffed with shrimp, bacon, ricotta, and herbed cream cheese), duck, lamb, seafood (including achingly tender scallops pan seared and topped with basil cream sauce), plus the occasional German dish. Dinner only; reservations recommended.

The Floyd Country Store, 206 S. Locust St., Floyd, VA 24091; (540) 745-4563; floydcountrystore.com. Need to rest your dogs a bit? The sign right outside this century-old general store says LOITERING ALLOWED. Perched high in the Blue Ridge Mountains where the sweet breezes blow through tiny downtown, Floyd—or the "Republic of Floyd," as some call it—is an Appalachian outpost where country music, artistry, and rugged individualism converge. Wander around the store to the twang of banjo and bluegrass music to find barrels of penny candy, local and national country and gospel CDs, soaps, vegetable peelers, suspenders, and more. The chalkboard lunch counter menu is deceptively simple—sandwiches served on fresh-baked sourdough and locally sourced everything. The spot is a highlight of Virginia's Heritage Music Trail, and frequently local, regional, and sometimes national acts take the stage at the back of the store for music jams. The famed Friday Nite Jamboree is considered one of the nation's best places to hear live bluegrass, gospel, and country music. No drinking, no smoking, no cussin', no spittin'—just like at Granny's.

Foggy Ridge Cider, 1328 Pineview Rd., Dugspur, VA 24325; (276) 398-2337; foggyridgecider.com. The apples here aren't all pretty, and that's just as it should be, according to cider maker Diane Flynt, founder of the oldest of a new wave of Virginia cider houses. That's because it's the tannins and taste that matter, just as they always have. Back in Colonial times, most everyone made hard cider and bragged that theirs was best. But then hard cider fell out of favor. The water became drinkable, Prohibition came and went, and it seemed a dying craft when in 2005 Foggy Ridge offered its first bottles of the tart, faintly sparkling brew. They immediately sold out and have continued to do so every year since. Visitors are welcome from April through

December, although you might have to round up the staff via the walkie-talkie on the cider house door.

Mojoe's Trailside Coffeehouse, 331 Douglas Dr., Damascus, VA 24236; (276) 475-5505; mojoestrailsidecoffee.com. In Damascus, a stream of thirsty, hungry bicyclists and backpackers flow into town from the mountains, where four scenic hiking and biking trails converge, including the Virginia Creeper Trail and the Appalachian Trail. A smattering of mom-and-pop places service the flow, but Mojoe's is different. It offers cold-brewed iced chai lattes and frappes rather than milk shakes, and stacks of fresh blueberry pancakes and bagel sandwiches instead of burgers. With bistro tables and easy chairs, the vibe is more metro than mountain. But the baked goods are homemade and the barista skilled and friendly. On our visit, a pan of banana–chocolate chip whole-wheat muffins had just come out of the little oven behind the bar.

Vintage Cellar, 1338 S. Main St., Blacksburg, VA 24060; (540) 953-2675; vintagecellar.com. Say you've secured some local trout or a big, claret-colored, grass-fed T-bone for dinner. What to drink? Proprietor Keith Roberts and his expert staff at the Vintage Cellar have been advising Blacksburg-area oenophiles and occasional wine drinkers for the past 20 years. Recommendations take into consideration the type of event, the food, and, most kindly, the budget, all with an easygoing smile. The Cellar stocks hundreds of wines and beers from around the world, plus ciders, meads, and stouts, lagers, and other brews. Kegs and keg equipment, too. (This is a college town, after all. Go Hokies!) It's the region's best locally owned wine and beer depot.

Virginia Sweetwater Distillery, 760 Walkers Creek Rd., **Marion, VA 24354; (276) 378-0867; virginianwhiskeys.com.** No doubt about it, moonshining is a time-honored tradition in these hills, and in 2013 southwestern Virginia's first legal moonshine dripped out of the still and into bottles destined for Virginia's state-controlled liquor stores. Scott "Mash" Schumaker is the master moonshiner here, and he uses a corn whiskey recipe that he says has been handed down through generations. Call ahead to arrange a tour or to partake in a 4-hour-long, hands-on experiential run through the still house, complete with a moonshiners manual, a meal, and a shot glass to go.

Farmers' Markets

Abingdon Farmers' Market, corner of Remsburg and Cummings Streets, Abingdon, VA 24212. Tues from 3 to 6 p.m. and Sat from 7 a.m. to noon, third week in Apr through Nov.

Big Stone Gap Farmers' Market, 460 Shawnee Ave., Big Stone Gap, VA 24219. Sat from 8 a.m. to noon, May through Oct.

Blacksburg Farmers Market, northeast corner of Roanoke and Draper Streets, Blacksburg, VA 24063. Wed from 2 to 7 p.m. and Sat from 8 a.m. to 2 p.m., Apr through Oct; Wed from 2 to 6 p.m. and Sat from 9 a.m. to 2 p.m., Nov and Dec; Sat from 10 a.m. to 2 p.m., Jan through Mar.

Bluefield Farmers' Market, Walnut St., Bluefield, VA 24605. Sat from 8 a.m. to noon, May through Oct.

Four-Ways Farmers' Market, Hayes Drug Store Parking Lot on Va. Route 61, Tazewell, VA 24651. Sat from 8 a.m. to noon, June through Oct.

Wise Farmers' Market, 309 E. Main St., Wise, VA 24293. Thurs from 4 to 7 p.m., June through Sept.

Wytheville Farmers' Market, 355 E. Main St., Wytheville, VA 24382. Sat from 9 a.m. to 1 p.m., May through Oct.

Recipes

Oysters Lynnhaven on the Half Shell

There's a perfect marriage between the saltiness of the oysters and the sweetness of the pickled apples that makes these bivalves such a treat at Terrapin Restaurant in Virginia Beach. They're the work of a master, Executive Chef Rodney Einhorn, who lets the Virginia oysters shine and adds only a few complementary ingredients.

Makes: 2 appetizer-sized servings

1 cup piping hot tap water
½ cup Champagne vinegar
6 tablespoons sugar
2 teaspoons kosher salt
1 firm apple, peeled and cored

12 Pleasure House oysters (or other oysters with sweet meat but overall brininess)
Freshly ground black Tellicherry pepper

In a medium bowl, combine water, vinegar, sugar, and salt until sugar and salt are dissolved.

Cut apple into ¼-inch-thick slices, then ¼-inch strips and finally ¼-inch dice. Place the diced apples in a mason jar and pour the hot pickling liquid over them. Cool to room temperature, then refrigerate. Apples will be ready after 2 hours.

Meanwhile, prepare the oysters. Scrub them under cold water with a stiff brush to remove the dirt, then shuck them. Detach the meat from the shell, being careful not to disturb the liquid, or "oyster liquor."

Place shucked oysters on a bed of ice. Top each with a sprinkling of the pickled apples and black pepper. (You can make up to 5 dozen oysters with each batch of the pickled apples.)

Courtesy of Executive Chef Rodney Einhorn of Terrapin Restaurant in Virginia Beach (p. 87)

Smoked Scallop, Arugula & Cucumber Salad

This recipe looks complex, but the creator, Chef James Harris, says it's time-consuming but simple. It's also worth the effort.

Makes 4 appetizer-sized servings

- **4 large grapefruits**
- **8 cups water, divided**
- **2 cups sugar**
- **1 (750-milliliter) bottle Viognier (recommended: Michael Shaps)**
- **8 large (or U-10) scallops, a little under a pound**
- **Salt and black pepper, to taste**
- **2 English cucumbers, peeled, seeded, and cut into 2-inch pieces**
- **1 pint high-quality white wine vinegar**
- **1 shallot, finely diced**
- **1 egg**
- **2 cups light olive oil or grape-seed oil, plus a little more for caramelizing scallops**
- **4 ounces baby arugula, cleaned and picked**

Peel grapefruits with a peeler and remove the pith from the peels to avoid any unwanted bitterness. Slice peels into 2- to 3-inch-long pieces and cover with 2 cups of water in heavy pot. Bring to a boil on the stovetop and drain. Repeat process two more times. This removes any bitterness in the peels. The fourth time, add sugar to water and simmer for 1 hour. Set aside.

Meanwhile, juice three of the grapefruits, combine juice with wine in a heavy pot, and reduce on medium heat until you have about 3 ounces of liquid by volume. Set aside and cool to room temperature.

While that is cooking, peel and segment the remaining grapefruit, slicing between the white segment lines so that only fruit segments remain (no white pith.)

Prepare smoker. (See note.) Season scallops with salt and ground black pepper and place in smoker. Smoke for 3 minutes. Do not cook all the way through; there will be a second cooking to caramelize. Remove scallops from smoker and place in refrigerator.

Cut each cucumber piece into ⅛-inch-thick slices. In a bowl, cover cucumber slices with vinegar and shallots, and season with salt and pepper.

In a blender, put Viognier grapefruit reduction and egg together, and blend thoroughly. Drizzle in oil until emulsion is thick enough to coat the back of a spoon. Season with salt and pepper. Reserve for plating.

At this point, everything can be set aside until you are ready to serve. When that time comes, heat a cast-iron skillet over medium-high heat. Add a light coat of oil and sear scallops on both sides, adjusting heat as necessary. Scallops should have a rich caramel color. Do not overcook.

To plate, spread dressing on the bottom of each plate. In a large bowl, mix arugula and candied grapefruit zest, toss in a small amount of oil to coat leaves. Drizzle some of the syrup (made during the grapefruit zesting process) on leaves as well. Divide cucumbers onto each plate, divide arugula onto each plate, and divide grapefruit segments onto each plate. Divide scallops onto each plate. Open another bottle of wine and enjoy.

Note: If you don't have access to a smoker then grilling will impart almost the same flavor.

Courtesy of Chef James Harris of Zynodoa Restaurant in Staunton (p. 221)

Sam Snead's Tavern Pimiento Cheese

Pimiento cheese is a true Southern staple. Eat it as a dip with bread or crackers, or use it as the basis for a mouthwatering sandwich. Or, if the version is as luscious as this one, gobble it straight from the bowl.

Makes 4 servings

- ½ cup cream cheese
- ¼ cup aged cheddar, shredded
- ⅛ cup Sonoma Dry Jack cheese, shredded
- ⅛ cup Boursin herb cheese
- 2 tablespoons roasted red pepper, finely diced
- 1 tablespoon peppadew chile, finely diced
- 1 tablespoon chopped fresh parsley
- Smoked Maldon salt, to taste
- Freshly ground black pepper, to taste

Combine cream cheese, other cheeses, red pepper, peppadew, and parsley in a mixing bowl and mix well. Season with salt and pepper. Serve at room temperature.

Courtesy of Sam Snead's Tavern in Hot Springs (p. 224)

Claire's Southern Shrimp & Grits

"Grits are a staple in every Southern household," says Claire Lamborne, owner of Claire's at the Depot in Warrenton.

Serves 4

- 1 andouille sausage, diced
- 3 cups milk
- 1 cup water
- ½ teaspoon salt
- ½ teaspoon black pepper
- 1 cup stone-ground yellow grits
- Tabasco sauce, to taste
- 1 cup shredded smoked Gouda cheese
- 1 red bell pepper, diced
- 1 yellow bell pepper, diced
- 1 yellow onion, diced
- 2 tablespoons oil (equal parts olive and vegetable oils), divided
- 1 tablespoon chopped garlic
- 1 quart chicken stock
- 1 pint heavy cream
- 1 pound (about 24) shrimp, peeled and deveined (use 21/25 count)
- 1–2 scallions, tips removed and chopped

Cook sausage in skillet over medium-low heat to remove fat. Remove from stovetop and set aside.

Prepare the grits by combining milk, water, salt, and pepper in a large pot or dutch oven. Bring liquid to a boil, then gradually add grits until mixture is smooth and returns to a boil. Reduce heat to medium-low and simmer until grits are thick and tender, about 15 to 20 minutes, stirring often to avoid burning the bottom. Remove grits from heat, and stir in Tabasco sauce and cheese.

Saute peppers and onion in 1 tablespoon oil over medium-high heat until soft. Add garlic and cook 2–3 minutes. Add chicken stock and cream, and bring to a boil. Reduce heat and slow boil for 5–10 minutes, until thick. Add diced sausage and remove from heat. Saute shrimp in 1 tablespoon oil just until pink.

To serve, place a fourth of the grits on a plate or in a shallow bowl. Top with a fourth of the shrimp (about six each) and a fourth of the sauce.

Courtesy of Claire's at the Depot in Warrenton (p. 169)

Brunswick Stew

People in Virginia have waged war over this stew, which was originally made with squirrel. Here's an updated version. And take note, when Brunswick County stew masters cook up vast cast-iron vats of the stuff, they know it's done when the paddle used as a utensil stands up in it.

Makes 3½ quarts or about 8 entree-sized servings

1 whole (3-pound) broiler or fryer chicken

2 stalks celery, cut into 1-inch pieces

1 small onion, quartered

7 cups water, divided

2 (10-ounce) packages frozen baby lima beans

2 (10-ounce) packages frozen white kernel corn

1 cup onion, chopped

2 (28-ounce) cans whole tomatoes, undrained and chopped

1 (8-ounce) can whole tomatoes, undrained and chopped

3 medium boiling potatoes, peeled and diced

2 tablespoons butter or margarine

1 tablespoon salt

1 to 1½ teaspoons black pepper

½ to 1 teaspoon red pepper

10 saltine crackers, crumbled

Combine chicken, celery, onion, and 5 cups of water in a large dutch oven or stock pot; bring to a boil over medium-high heat. Cover, reduce heat, and simmer for 1 hour. Remove chicken, and remove and discard celery and onion, reserving broth in dutch oven. Cool chicken; remove skin and bones, and coarsely chop meat.

Add chopped chicken, lima beans, corn, chopped onions, tomatoes, potatoes, butter, salt, pepper, and red pepper to broth. Bring to a boil, then reduce heat and simmer uncovered, about 4½ hours, stirring often.

Add remaining 2 cups of water as needed. Add cracker crumbs and cook an additional 15 minutes.

From Gay Neale, historian of Brunswick County, Virginia (see sidebar, pp. 204–205)

Winnie Lee's Fried Chicken

Sydney Meers, chef-owner and head gardener at Stove, the Restaurant, in Portsmouth, learned to cook chicken in his native Mississippi in his Grandma Winnie Lee's cast-iron pan. Here, he shares the recipe for pitch-perfect bird.

Serves 4

For the brine:

1½ gallons cool water
1 cup salt
5 dried bay leaves, crushed

1 sprig fresh rosemary
1 (3- to 4-pound) whole
    chicken, cut into 8 pieces

For the fry:

3 cups all-purpose flour
1 cup stone-ground cornmeal
    (yellow or white)

Sea salt and freshly ground
    pepper (no prejudices
    here, either black or white
    is fine)
Lard or bacon drippings

To brine the chicken, combine the water, salt, bay leaves and rosemary in a large bowl, and stir until the salt is dissolved. Pat the chicken dry. Place the chicken pieces in the brine and refrigerate for at least 30 minutes but for no more than an hour.

To fry the chicken, sift the flour and cornmeal together in a shallow bowl. Season with salt and pepper to taste.

Remove the chicken pieces from the brine, flicking off any specks of herbs that cling to the skin. Dredge each chicken piece in the flour mixture, flipping and flouring the meat until it's completely coated.

Over medium-high heat, heat enough lard or bacon drippings to form a ½-inch pool at the bottom of a large cast-iron skillet until the lard bubbles and the sound it *makes shifts from a sizzle to a gurgle. If you want a more foolproof indicator, it's ready when you drop a pinch of flour in the oil and it hisses.*

Using tongs, place the chicken, skin-side up, into the skillet, being careful to handle only the big ends of the bones. You may need to work in batches and adjust the heat slightly so the chicken doesn't brown too quickly. Fry the chicken for 8 to 10 minutes on each side, until all the pieces are a shimmering golden brown.

Remove chicken from the pan and let the pieces rest a spell on paper towels before diving in.

Courtesy of Chef Sydney Meers, owner of Stove, the Restaurant, in Portsmouth (p. 85)

Bacon-Wrapped Pecan Salmon

Here's a great seafood dish worth stopping for when in Central Virginia—the bacon and pecans give it an updated Southern slant.

Serves 1

For the honey-Dijon vinaigrette:

3 tablespoons red wine vinegar

½ teaspoon Dijon mustard

3 tablespoons honey

6 tablespoons roasted garlic oil

Splash of fresh lime juice

Salt and black pepper, to taste

For the butterscotch cream sauce:

¾ cup heavy cream

1 shot butterscotch schnapps

1 tablespoon cold butter

For the salmon:

1 (8-ounce) salmon fillet

½ tablespoon candied pecans, crushed

1 slice raw bacon

To make the vinaigrette: *Whisk all ingredients together until emulsified.*

To make the butterscotch cream sauce: *Heat heavy cream in a saucepan over medium heat until warmed. Add butterscotch schnapps; reduce heat to low. Add butter. Stir until the butter is melted and the mixture is smooth.*

Rub salmon with vinaigrette. Press crushed pecans into salmon. Wrap with one slice of bacon. Pan sear over high heat until browned, about 2 minutes. Finish off in the oven on low broil, about 8 to 10 minutes.

To serve: *Swirl some of the butterscotch cream sauce on the plate, add jasmine rice, and place the salmon atop the rice.*

Courtesy of Kahill's Restaurant in South Hill (p. 204)

Country Ham

S. Wallace Edwards & Sons supplies some of the nation's best restaurants and gourmet shops with pork cured in the heart of Tidewater ham country. You don't have to cook a properly cured country ham, but if you prefer to, here's how third-generation curemaster Sam Edwards III does it.

Makes 1 ham

1 cured country ham
1 quart water

For the glaze:
About 2 cups light brown sugar
Whole cloves (optional)

Heat oven to 325°F.

Scrub the ham with stiff-bristled brush under cold, running water.

Place ham in roasting pan, fat-side up, add water, and cover tightly with aluminum foil. Bake for 4 to 5 hours, or until the internal temperature reaches 150 degrees. Remove ham from oven, remove foil, and let ham rest for 20 minutes to cool slightly, which will make it easier to handle. Remove ham from pan, and place on a large cutting board. Trim all excess skin, leaving ¼ inch of fat.

Raise oven temperature to 425°F. Score fat all over ham in a ½-inch diamond pattern, ¼-inch deep. Rub ham with brown sugar, patting a ¼-inch coating of sugar on the fat sides. Stud with whole cloves and return uncovered ham to the oven for 12 to 17 minutes, until brown sugar forms a nice glaze.

Remove ham from oven and place on a large cutting board, glazed-side up. Starting at the small, or hock, end and using a sharp knife, make the first cut down to the bone. Make the second cut at a 45-degree angle, cutting a small "notch" out of the ham. Continue slicing paper thin at a 45-degree angle to the bone. Country ham is best enjoyed when sliced as thin as possible.

Courtesy of Sam Edwards III, president and curemaster of S. Wallace Edwards & Sons in Surry (see sidebar, p. 102)

Potato Chip—Encrusted Crab Cakes

Chips may seem too humble to pair with the sweet, succulent meat of a Chesapeake Bay blue crab, but we fairly fainted the first time we bit into one of these.

Serves 4

- 4 eggs, divided
- 2 tablespoons mayonnaise
- 1 tablespoon hot sauce
- 2 cups fresh bread crumbs
- 3 green onions, chopped (green parts only)
- 2 teaspoons Old Bay seasoning
- 1 pound freshly picked jumbo lump crabmeat
- 1 cup all-purpose flour
- 4 cups lightly crushed potato chips
- 2 cups vegetable oil

In a medium-sized bowl, combine 1 egg, mayonnaise, hot sauce, bread crumbs, green onions, and Old Bay seasoning, and let flavors marry for 10 minutes.

Gently fold in crabmeat, being careful not to break up the lumps.

Form crab cakes, and let cakes rest in refrigerator for 30 minutes to set.

Set up a standard breading station: one container with flour, one with 3 beaten eggs, one with crushed potato chips. Dredge each crab cake, first in flour, then egg, then in potato chips.

In a large frying pan, heat vegetable oil over medium-high heat. When the oil is hot, place crab cakes in pan and fry until the bottom of each is golden brown. Turn over and continue frying until the top side is golden brown and the crab cakes are cooked through.

Courtesy of Chef Maurice Wilson of Suffolk, owner of Chef Mo on the Go, personal chef and catering services

Collard Salsa

The southern standard—boiled in a pot with a hit of ham—gets sparked up in this recipe from Laura Parker, owner of the Dancing Tomato in Virginia Beach. It can be kicked up as much as you like.

Serves about 6

- 5 slices thick-cut bacon, diced
- 1 medium onion, diced
- 1 colorful bell pepper, diced (red looks best)
- 2 garlic cloves, peeled and minced
- ½ teaspoon red pepper flakes
- 1 pound fresh collards, washed, stemmed, and chopped (see note)
- 3 tablespoons water
- Salt and black pepper, to taste
- 3 tablespoons cider vinegar
- Vinegar-based hot sauce such as Texas Pete or Crystal, to taste

In a large skillet over medium-high heat, sauté bacon until some fat is rendered. Add onion and pepper, stirring until onion is translucent and pepper softened. Stir in garlic and pepper flakes.

Add chopped collards and water. Combine, stirring, until collards are well mixed with other ingredients. Season with salt and pepper. Toss mixture, adding a bit more water if ingredients seem dry. You want collards to steam and sauté until they're tender but not mushy. This will take about 10 minutes.

When collards are tender and have darkened in color, add vinegar and hot sauce—1 teaspoon is a good place to start. Taste, and add more salt or hot sauce, if desired.

Tip: Serve salsa warm or at room temperature with sturdy corn chips, such as Fritos Scoops.

Note: This recipe can be made with frozen collards. Most frozen brands seem to contain more stems than leaves, so it might take a bit longer to get stems tender. Frozen collards also require more aggressive seasoning. The best way to get the perfect dish is to taste, taste, taste.

From Laura Parker, owner of the Dancing Tomato, Virginia Beach (p. 44)

Peanut Supreme Pie

This pie, from Violet LaBrecque of Purcellville, is recognized as the State Pie of Virginia. Four times it was awarded best-of-show honors at the State Fair of Virginia. Violet and her husband, Bob, now run a boutique bakery.

Makes one 9-inch pie

1 (9-inch) pie crust

For peanut fudge layer:

½ cup salted Virginia peanuts, finely chopped

½ cup creamy peanut butter

½ cup confectioners' sugar

½ cup half-and-half

For filling:

1 (14-ounce) can sweetened condensed milk

½ cup creamy peanut butter

1 cup milk

1 (4.6-ounce) package vanilla instant pudding mix

For topping:

¾ cup salted Virginia peanuts, finely chopped

Heat oven to 400°F.

Press unbaked pie crust into a 9-inch pie plate. Fold edge under; flute as desired.

For the peanut fudge layer, combine peanuts, peanut butter, sugar, and half-and-half in a medium bowl. Stir or whisk until well blended. Pour into pie shell. Bake about 20 to 25 minutes, or until crust is golden brown (reduce baking time about 10 minutes if using a convection oven). Cool completely.

For filling, combine condensed milk and peanut butter in a large bowl. Beat on low speed of electric mixer until well blended. Add milk slowly. Add pudding mix, and increase mixer speed to medium. Beat 2 minutes. Pour over the cooled peanut fudge layer in the pie shell.

For topping, sprinkle peanuts over filling. Refrigerate for one hour or more.

Courtesy of Violet LaBrecque of 1st AVE Bakery in Purcellville (p. 178)

Blue Talon Cocktail

After a turn through Colonial Williamsburg, contemplate the wisdom of the founding fathers over this tall, chilly libation from the Blue Talon Bistro in Williamsburg.

Makes 1 cocktail

1¼ ounces Tito's vodka
½ ounce Galliano
2 ounces orange juice
2 ounces tangerine juice

1 ounce passion fruit puree
½ ounce grenadine liqueur
2 slices of orange
1 lime wedge

In a cocktail shaker, combine vodka, Galliano, orange juice, tangerine juice, fruit puree, and grenadine. Shake vigorously.

Serve over ice in a hurricane glass with the fruit inside the glass, not on the rim or on a toothpick.

Courtesy of Blue Talon Bistro in Williamsburg (p. 119)

Appendices

Appendix A:
Eateries by
Cuisine

Coded for Corresponding Regional Chapters:
- **(CV)** Central Virginia
- **(CL)** Charlottesville
- **(ES)** Eastern Shore
- **(M)** Mountains and Shenandoah Valley
- **(UP)** Upper Piedmont
- **(RD)** Richmond
- **(SW)** Southwest Blue Ridge Highlands
- **(TW)** Tidewater
- **(WB)** Williamsburg

American

Shields Tavern, (WB), 127
Sunset Grille, (ES), 19
Stanley's Store, (UP), 179
Strawberry Street Cafe, (RD), 152
Tammy & Johnny's, (ES), 19

Chinese
Peter Chang, (WB), 123
Peter Chang's China Grill, (CL), 188

Colombian
El Desorden, (TW), 46

Cuban
Kuba Kuba, (RD), 143

Eclectic
Captain Groovy's Grill & Raw Bar,
    (TW), 38
Charley's Waterfront Cafe, (CV), 209
Harvest Table, (SW), 233
Joe's Inn, (RD), 148
99 Main Restaurant, (TW), 57
Six Little Bar Bistro, (TW), 63

Ethiopian
Addis Ethiopian Restaurant,
    (RD), 136

European
Cafe Europa, (TW), 71
Monastery, The, (TW), 81
Sonoma Wine Bar & Bistro, (TW), 67

French
Blue Apron Restaurant & Red
    Rooster Bar, (CV), 203
Blue Talon Bistro, (WB), 119, 258
Cafe Europa, (TW), 71
Can Can Brasserie, (RD), 139
l'etoile, (CL), 191
Le Yaca, (WB), 124
Pearl French Bistro, (TW), 59
Regency Room, The, at Hotel
    Roanoke, (CV), 211
Restaurant Pomme, (UP), 171
SeaSide Restaurant, (TW), 63

German
Bier Garden, The (TW), 33
Tavern Restaurant, The (SW), 237

Gourmet Burgers
Burger Bach, (RD), 137
Citizen Burger Bar, (CL), 185
{RA} Bistro, (CV), 207

Greek
Stella's, (RD), 147

Italian
Aldo's Ristorante, (TW), 70
Anzio Turkish Italian Cuisine
    (TW), 32
Cafe Europa, (TW), 71
Coppola's Deli, (RD), 140
Edo's Squid, (RD), 140

Fellini's #9, (CL), 186
Il Giardino Ristorante, (TW), 77
Little Italy Ristorante, (ES), 17
Mama Zu, (RD), 149
Mannino's Italian Bistro, (TW), 55
Olivia's in the Village, (TW), 58

Jamaican
Island Krave, (TW), 51
Jammin' Jerk BBQ, (TW), 51

Japanese
Kyushu Japanese Restaurant,
(TW), 80

Jewish Delicatessen
Route 58 Delicatessen, The,
(TW), 62

Laotian
Som Bao Cafe, (TW), 66

Mediterranean
Aziza's On Main, (RD), 137
Croc's 19th Street Bistro, (TW), 74
Leila's Mediterranean Kitchen, Deli
& Grocery, (TW), 54

Mexican
Baja Restaurant, (TW), 70
Jessy's Taqueria, (TW), 53
Luna Maya, (TW), 55

Middle Eastern
Anzio Turkish Italian Cuisine,
(TW), 32
Croc's 19th Street Bistro, (TW), 74

Neo-Southern
Cellars Restaurant, (TW), 72
Charles City Tavern, (TW), 72
Chateau Morrisette, (SW), 234
Handsome Biscuit, (TW), 49
Hanover Tavern, (UP), 173
Harper's Table, (TW), 50
Inn at Montross, The, (TW), 78
Julep's New Southern Cuisine,
(RD), 142
King's Arms Tavern, (WB), 127
Mallard's on the Wharf, (ES), 22
Merroir, (TW), 57
Molasses Grill, (CV), 206
Pasture, (RD), 144
Roosevelt, The, (RD), 145
Stove, the Restaurant, (TW),
85, 251
Traditions, (WM), 128
Vintage Kitchen, (TW), 89
Vintage Tavern, (TW), 90
Zynodoa Restaurant, (M), 221, 246

New American
Circa 1918 Kitchen + Bar, (TW), 39
Elmwood at Sparks, (UP), 169
Foti's Restaurant, (UP), 170
Glass Haus, (CL), 187

Merroir, (TW), 57
Olivia's in the Village, (TW), 58
Passion, The Restaurant, (TW), 58
Rain, (SW), 234
Rappahannock, (RD), 144
Shoemakers American Grill,
  (CV), 208
Sisters at the Martha, (SW), 237
Small's Smokehouse and Oyster Bar,
  (TW), 64
Steinhilber's, (TW), 84
Sting-Ray's Restaurant, (ES), 22
Stove, the Restaurant, (TW), 85, 251
Surf Rider Restaurant, (TW), 86
Swan Terrace, (TW), 67
Tavern Restaurant, The (SW), 237
Terrapin Restaurant, (TW), 87, 245
Tides Inn, The (TW), 88
Todd Jurich's Bistro, (TW), 88
Zöes, (TW), 91

South African
Shebeen, The, (CL), 189

Steaks
AJ's on the Creek, (ES), 19
Bill's Prime Seafood & Steaks,
  (ES), 20
Bistro Bethem, (UP), 167
Braise, (TW), 34
Byrd & Baldwin Bros. Steakhouse,
  (TW), 35
Chesapeake Grill, (ES), 15

Claire's at the Depot, (UP), 169, 249
C&O Restaurant, (CL), 191
Dudley's Bistro, (WB), 120
Eat, An American Bistro, (TW), 45
Fat Canary, (WM), 121
Fin Seafood, (TW), 47
John's Steakhouse, (M), 222
Kahill's Restaurant, (CV), 204, 253
Local Chop & Grill House, (M), 219
Olivia's in the Village, (TW), 58
Opus 9, (WB), 123
Passion, The Restaurant, (TW), 58
Rain, (SW), 234
River Stone Chophouse, (TW), 61
Shoemakers American Grill,
  (CV), 208
Sisters at the Martha, (SW), 237
Steinhilber's, (TW), 84
Swan Terrace, (TW), 67
Tavern Restaurant, The (SW), 237
Terrapin Restaurant, (TW), 87, 245
Todd Jurich's Bistro, (TW), 88
Zöes, (TW), 91

Tapas/Meze/Small Plates
Bang!, (CL), 183
MAS Tapas, (CL), 188
Stella's, (RD), 147
Trilogy Bistro, (TW), 69

Thai
SeaSide Restaurant, (TW), 63
Som Bao Cafe, (TW), 66

Traditional Southern

Big's Place, (ES), 14
Cotton Southern Bistro, (ES), 42
Cul's Courthouse Grille, (TW), 43
Cumberland Restaurant, (CV), 209
Hanover Tavern, (UP), 173
Lemaire, (RD), 148
Mabry Mill Restaurant, (SW), 236
Martin's Soul Food. (TW), 56
Michie Tavern, (CL), 192
Old Chickahominy House, (WM), 124
Smithfield Inn, The, (TW), 83
Sting-Ray's Restaurant, (ES), 22
Surrey House Restaurant, (TW), 87

Tides Inn, The, (TW), 88
Virginia Diner, (TW), 91

Turkish

Anzio Turkish Italian Cuisine,
   (TW), 32

Vegetarian-Friendly

Gillie's, (SW), 235

Vietnamese

Mekong, (RD), 151
Pho 79, (TW), 60
Saigon Village Restaurant, (ES), 18

Appendix B: Dishes, Specialty Stores & Producers

Coded for Corresponding Regional Chapters:
- **(CV)** Central Virginia
- **(CL)** Charlottesville
- **(ES)** Eastern Shore
- **(M)** Mountains and Shenandoah Valley
- **(UP)** Upper Piedmont
- **(RD)** Richmond
- **(SW)** Southwest Blue Ridge Highlands
- **(TW)** Tidewater
- **(WB)** Williamsburg

Bakery

Albemarle Baking Co., (CL), 192

Becca's Cakes and More, (ES), 23

Chandler's Bakery, (CL), 194

Heritage Amish Bake Shoppe, (TW), 101

Jane's Sweet Potato Biscuits, (TW), 103

Red Ribbon BakeShop, (TW), 106

Bakery/Cafe

Artisan's Bakery & Cafe, (TW), 94

Bergey's Breadbasket, (TW), 95

Carrot Tree Kitchens, (WB), 129

1st AVE Bakery, (UP), 178, 257

Floyd Country Store, The, (SW), 238

French Bakery & Delicatessen, (TW), 99

Jean-Jacques Bakery & Cafe, (RD), 159

Appendix C: Food & Drink Event Monthly List

January

Chocolate Festival, Norman

February

Bacchus Wine & Food Festival, Newport News

Gray Ghost Irresistible Chocolates and Cabernet, Amissville

Ravishing Red Days of Winter, Linden

SoVA Winter Wine Festival, Chatham

Taste of Hampton Roads, Norfolk

Virginia Wine Expo, Richmond

March

Chocolate Lovers Festival, Fairfax

Highland Maple Festival, Monterey

Virginia Chocolate Festival, Norfolk

April

Beaverdam Wine Festival, Beaverdam

Blacksburg Fork and Cork, Blacksburg

Bull and Oyster Festival, Buena Vista

Gnarly Hops & Barley Fest, Culpeper

Great Grapes Wine Festival, Reston

Rockin' Brews & BBQs, Smith Mountain Lake

Ruritan Club Shad Planking, Wakefield

RVA French Food Festival, Henrico

She-Crab Soup Classic, Virginia Beach

Shenandoah Apple Blossom Festival & Wine Fest, Winchester

Smithfield Wine & Brew Fest, Smithfield

Thomas Jefferson Craft Beer Tasting, Forest

Virginia Fly Fishing and Wine Festival, Waynesboro

White Top Mountain Maple Syrup Festival, Grayson County

May

BBQ Jamboree, Fredericksburg

Bluegrass, Barbecue & Brew Festival, Red Hill

Cape Charles Crabby Blues Festival, Cape Charles

Community School Strawberry Festival, Roanoke

Delaplane Strawberry Festival, Sky Meadows State Park

Eastern Shore Seafood Festival, Chincoteague

Gordonsville Famous Fried Chicken Festival, Gordonsville

Hogtown BBQ, Fredericksburg

Of Ale and History Microbrew and Imported Beer Tasting Festival, Middletown

Pungo Strawberry Festival, Virginia Beach

Rassawek Spring Jubilee Heritage and Wine Festival, Goochland

Sensible Seafood Fest, Virginia Beach

Shenandoah Valley Beer & Wine Festival, Massanutten

Shrine Seafood Festival, Richmond

Strawberry Festival, Roanoke

Town Point Wine Festival, Norfolk

Uncork the Cure Wine Festival, Daleville

ValleyFest—Shenandoah Valley Beer & Wine Festival, Massanutten

Virginia State Championship Chili Cook-off, Roanoke

Virginia Wine & Craft Festival, Front Royal

Whitetop Mountain Ramp Festival, Whitetop

Wine Festival at Monticello, Charlottesville

June

Ashland Strawberry Faire, Ashland

Bayou Boogaloo and Cajun Food Festival, Norfolk

Bluegrass, Barbecue & Brew Festival, Red Hill

Virginia Pork Festival, Emporia

July

BBQ Bash & Blackberry Bonanza, Bluemont

Hanover Tomato Festival, Hanover

Pork, Peanut and Pine Festival, Surry

August

Carytown Watermelon Festival, Richmond

Crab Pickin' at the Point, Norfolk

Dog Days Peach Festival, Bluemont

Taste of the Mountains Main Street Festival, Madison

Virginia State Peach Festival, Stuart

September

Apple Harvest & Apple Butter Festival, Lovingston

Cider Festival, Bluemont

Labor Day Wine & Cheese Pairing, Glen Allen

State Fair of Virginia, Doswell

Stratford Hall Wine and Oyster Festival, Stratford

Virginia Peanut Festival, Emporia

October

Apple Day & Craft Fair: A Celebration of Appalachian Heritage, Milboro

AT&T Town Point Virginia Wine Festival, Norfolk

Bluegrass, Barbecue & Brew Festival, Brookneal

Chincoteague Island Oyster Festival, Chincoteague

Harvest Festival, Cape Charles

Powhatan Festival of the Grape, Powhatan

Suffolk Peanut Festival, Suffolk

Taste of Brunswick Festival, A, Alberta

Virginia Wine and Garlic Festival, Amherst

November

Food and Feasts of Colonial Virginia, Williamsburg and Jamestown

Reedville Oyster Roast, Reedville

Urbanna Oyster Festival, Urbanna

December

Holiday Open House at Ingleside Vineyards, Oak Grove

Chocolate Festival, Norman

Index